On the Good Life

SUNY series in Ancient Greek Philosophy

Anthony Preus, editor

ON THE GOOD LIFE
Thinking through the Intermediaries in Plato's *Philebus*

Cristina Ionescu

Published by State University of New York Press, Albany

© 2019 State University of New York

All rights reserved

No part of this book may be used or reproduced in any manner whatsoever without written permission. No part of this book may be stored in a retrieval system or transmitted in any form or by any means including electronic, electrostatic, magnetic tape, mechanical, photocopying, recording, or otherwise without the prior permission in writing of the publisher.

For information, contact State University of New York Press, Albany, NY
www.sunypress.edu

Library of Congress Cataloging-in-Publication Data

Names: Ionescu, Cristina, 1977– author.
Title: On the good life : thinking through the intermediaries in Plato's Philebus / Cristina Ionescu.
Description: Albany : State University of New York, 2019. | Includes bibliographical references and index.
Identifiers: LCCN 2018036279 | ISBN 9781438475073 (hardcover : alk. paper) | ISBN 9781438475066 | ISBN 9781438475080 (ebook)
Subjects: LCSH: Plato. Philebus.
Classification: LCC B381 .I56 2019 | DDC 171/.4—dc23
LC record available at https://lccn.loc.gov/2018036279

10 9 8 7 6 5 4 3 2 1

To my mother,
who gracefully danced all the steps in between

The gods, as I said, have left us this legacy of how to search, and learn, and teach one another. But nowadays the clever ones among us make a one, haphazardly, and a many, faster or slower than they should; they go immediately from the one to the unlimited and omit the intermediaries, while it is exactly these that make all the difference as to whether we are engaged with one another in dialectical or only in eristic discourse.

—*Philebus* 16e3–17a5

Contents

Acknowledgments		ix
Introduction		xiii
I.	The Unity of the *Philebus:* Metaphysical Assumptions of the Good Human Life	1
II.	The Placement of Pleasure and Knowledge in the Fourfold Articulation of Reality	31
III.	Hybrid Varieties of Pleasure: True Mixed Pleasures and False Pure Pleasures	57
IV.	The Nature of Pleasure: Absolute Standards of Replenishment and Due Measure	75
V.	Pleasures of Learning and the Role of Due Measure in Experiencing Them	93
VI.	Plato's Conception of Pleasure Confronting Three Aristotelian Critiques	121
Appendix. The *Philebus's* Implicit Response to the *Aporiai* of Participation from the *Parmenides*		145
Notes		157
Bibliography		179
Index		187

Acknowledgments

This is a book about what it means to live a good life by aiming at the right combination of pleasure and knowledge, about the importance of the intermediary steps between given circumstances and the ideal result aimed for, about the significance of thorough reasoning through relevant distinctions, about due measure in words as well as in deeds, about listening, learning, and teaching, and certainly about Plato's *Philebus*, which sparked and sustained my interest in thinking along these lines over the last ten years.

In a world whose predilection is for an all-or-nothing mindset, and in which the divide between polarized alternatives has become the norm, it is timely to pause and reflect on the importance of mediation. This book is an invitation to recuperate the joy for figuring out not how to proceed absolutely, but rather how best to proceed *in the very next step*. It might at first seem paradoxical that one would turn to Plato to learn about mediation, when Plato's name has typically been associated with lofty ideals, and the most frequent criticism coming even from the quarters of expert scholars is that his approach is too idealistic and lacks interest in the concrete circumstances of our lives. Part of my intention here is to challenge the received view of a Plato detached from the concerns of our day to day life and from the weaknesses and vulnerabilities that make up the laced and layered texture of our lives. In the *Philebus*, perhaps even more than in other texts, Plato teaches us about the value of the immediately given, about the proper appreciation of the fleeting beauty of a simple musical tone, about the transient, yet meaningful, pleasures we take in our emotional life, about how laughing at what we find ridiculous reveals our ethical stance, while comedy and self-irony can become instruments for moral instruction, and about so much else.

I am profoundly indebted to a number of scholars and friends who have offered me tremendous support by engaging with my work over the years. The intellectual stimulation received by discussing with them numerous ideas that find their home in the pages of this book would not mean to me as much as it does, had it not been constantly joined by their steady and dedicated emotional support and encouragement. I wish to thank especially Kenneth Dorter, George Harvey, Zena Hitz, Marina McCoy, Mitchell Miller, Dana Miller, and Rachel Singpurwalla, who have been most keenly part of this experience. George Harvey's perceptive critical eye, his insight into things Platonic, and generous willingness to engage with my work have been the source of abundant pleasures of learning and joys of discovery at my end. He continues to inspire me. Mitchell Miller's nuanced suggestions and inexhaustible energy in offering hundreds of comments on earlier drafts of portions of this work have been of tremendous help. Kenneth Dorter remains my mentor in mediations both in the life of the mind and way beyond that.

I am grateful to the amazing graduate students I have had throughout the years at The Catholic University of America, who with their eager appetite for philosophical conversations have helped me refine my understanding of the *Philebus* and kept my interest for this dialogue alive. I learned so much from them! I thank especially Kevin Kambo and Nick Gerrard, who helped with proofreading and editing while preparing the manuscript for publication. I am very thankful for the leisure provided by a sabbatical semester in the spring of 2017, which helped a great deal toward making this project come together.

I am grateful for the help and support offered by the editors and staff at SUNY Press, who have made the process of this publication run very smoothly.

I am especially thankful to John Garner for engaging in detail with my work, as he went way beyond the call of duty as reviewer of my manuscript and generously offered his comments, in shared enthusiasm for Plato's *Philebus*. His comments are starting points for conversations that I look forward to continue over years to come.

The wonderful and supportive staff members working at the Library of Congress in the Hispanic Reading Room, which had become my work space during the Spring Semester of 2017, deserve my gratitude.

There are many more people who deserve my heartfelt thanks—family, friends, teachers, and students. Without them my own modest reflections on the good life would not have gotten a life of their own in the pages of this book and would have missed a great deal of experiential support that enabled them in the first place. You know who you are.

My siblings and their wonderful families provided steady support and living inspiration throughout this journey. I would not miss the joy of thanking them and mentioning their names in any book I write, so here they go: Diana, Lucian, Kyla, Aidan, Radu, Ioana, Tea, and Vlad. Above all, the memory of my mother, to whom this book is dedicated, remains for me the guiding light in life.

The first four chapters are based on articles that have appeared in print before and are here reprinted in revised version with permission from the editors. "The Unity of the *Philebus:* Metaphysical Assumptions of the Good Human Life," *Ancient Philosophy* 27 (2007): 55–75; "Plato's Understanding of Pleasure in the *Philebus*: Absolute Standards of Repletion and the Mean," *Journal of Philosophical Research* 33 (2008): 1–18; "Hybrid Varieties of Pleasure and the Complex Case of the Pleasures of Learning in Plato's *Philebus*," *Dialogue* 47 (2008): 1–23; "The Place of Pleasure and Knowledge in the Fourfold Articulation of Reality in Plato's *Philebus*," pp. 1–32 in *The Proceedings of the Boston Area Colloquium in Ancient Philosophy*, vol. XXX (2015). I thank the respective editors and publishers for the permission to reprint those materials here.

Introduction

The *Philebus* is, arguably, the most intriguing and complex of Plato's dialogues. Within a most economical space of merely fifty-something Stephanus pages, it suggests the contours of a good human life mapped onto a cosmic background with clear metaphysical articulations. The text moves within a couple of pages from talking about the concrete sensation of itching to the most abstract speculations about the Good, while never missing the layers that are in between. The text provides a theoretical framework within which even the most concrete feeling of ridicule or the laughter that we experience when watching comedy on stage or in life can be mapped onto the broadest metaphysical view of reality. This framework is not advanced dogmatically, but rather explored with playful dialectical openness, envisioning the possibility of subsequent refinements.

The dialogue begins in the middle of a conversation about the good life, at the very moment when we are witnessing a switch between Socrates's interlocutors. Up to this point Philebus has been championing the absolute hedonistic position that pleasure is the good for all creatures, while Socrates has been arguing that knowledge, understanding, memory, opinion, and whatever else goes with them are in fact *better than pleasure* for those who can have them. At the outset of the dialogue, Protarchus takes over from Philebus the task of defending his hedonistic position, while Philebus retreats in self-assured arrogant silence once he declares with unshakable and dogmatic confidence that, as far as he is concerned, his thesis always wins no matter what (12a). From this point on, the conversation between Socrates and Protarchus develops in strikingly constructive fashion, for Protarchus, unlike Philebus, is open to being challenged and to learning. Soon enough Plato's Socrates and Protarchus realize that, neither pleasure as such, nor knowledge all by itself, is the good and self-sufficient element of a good human life, but rather some combination of them is. The focus of the investigation is first on whether pleasure or knowledge is closer to the good for us, humans, and then, once the answer to this question is found, the focus is on exploring the right way to combine various kinds of pleasure with types of knowledge in a good human life. Note, however, that, from the very beginning Socrates has been defending only the more modest view that knowledge is *better* than pleasure, not that it is the absolute good, which is what Philebus has been claiming about pleasure. Hence, Socrates ends up defending throughout the dialogue, consistently, one and the same view, the superiority of knowledge over pleasure and the necessity to have a good combination of both as ingredients of a good human life.

The investigation is deepened and amplified when Socrates attempts to persuade Protarchus that there are several types of pleasures and, correspondingly, several types of knowledge, and, moreover, that sometimes we are mistaken in assessing the experience of pleasure that we have, confusing false pleasures with true ones. While for the absolute hedonist Philebus pleasure is all of one sort, reducible to some unreflective sensation of the moment, and absolutely good, Socrates provides a complex and nuanced account of pleasures, whereby there are distinct types thereof, some better than others, some intrinsically mixed with pains and others free of such admixtures, some more prone to be false than their truer counterparts, and all of them relying to a greater or lesser degree on our judgments and beliefs.

The major tools used to discern and arrange these types hierarchically are the dialectical method of collection and division and the fourfold articulation of reality in terms of Limit, the Unlimited, Mixture, the Cause of Mixture. These two pillars of the investigation, the dialectical method and the fourfold articulation of reality, will be essential in discerning the nature of pleasure, the possibility of various sorts of false pleasures, the hierarchical order of pleasures and of various types of knowledge. They constitute the metaphysical and epistemological scaffold without which the conversation would have dissolved in groundless speculations. Far from shifting Socrates's attention completely away from the immediate concerns of everyday life to some purely abstract speculations, the availability of this metaphysical and epistemological "arsenal" allows him to give more careful attention and detailed phenomenological description to the most concrete feelings and circumstances.

To put it simply, the method of collection and division is a strategy of reasoning which, while frequently used in any field of art (16c), is elevated in the hands of a dialectician to such an extent as to enable an account of things in terms of the ultimate principles of reality. What basically enables the elevation of this method in the philosopher's hands is the fact that he applies it within a horizon of assumptions consciously made about the structure of reality and with the ultimate aim of uncovering ever more clearly the actual structure of reality. In other words, we start off by identifying subdivisions within a unity and by collecting a plurality within corresponding units at first within a horizon of tentative presuppositions about reality, and then proceed with the aim of simultaneously discerning all the intermediaries between the one and the many and clarifying our understanding of that metaphysical horizon. In the *Philebus*, Limit, the Unlimited, the Mixture of these two, and the Cause of their mixture are the pillars of this ultimate metaphysical structure. Together they provide an understanding of reality that combines measure and determination, on the one hand, with indefiniteness and indetermination, on the other. The emerging worldview allows various degrees of happiness and accomplishment in our human lives, ranging from those bordering the level experienced by irrational animals to those bearing the highest resemblance to the divine. Whatever the object of the dialectician's investigation, whether it is types of pleasure, or knowledge, or anything else at all, Plato's Socrates insists on the need to be mindful of the intermediaries lying between the one and the indefinitely many, while dividing a unit into its kinds and collecting a multiplicity into a unitary form. Skipping any of the intermediary steps could be fatal to understanding the phenomenon under investigation.

The application of collection and division must begin with a unitary grasp of the one form under investigation, even if only a tentative grasp (16d). Pleasure, in our case, will be understood as perceived replenishment of a lack (31d, 33d). As I hope to show, the notion of "replenishment" here at stake is truly broad, covering not only physiological fillings, such as those that occur through eating and drinking, but also psychological ones that address our emotional needs, and, most importantly, it refers also to a metaphysical sense, whereby "replenishment" counts as the progress of our lives toward ever more thorough instantiations of the Good, by approximating ever more closely our respective normative standards of balance and well-being that correspond to the goodness of life. The broad range of meanings pertaining to the kind of replenishment that pleasure brings about reflects the large variety of pleasures we can experience and also the even wider variety of ways in which we can go astray in assessing our experiences of pleasure.

The investigation reveals first three types of false pleasures, all of which happen to be mixed with pains: false pleasures of anticipation, pleasures that are false due to misestimating the degree of pain and pleasure experienced when comparing such experiences with one another rather than by reference to a normative standard, and, finally, pleasures that are false insofar as we reduce the nature of pleasures to mere absence of pain. In the next stage, Plato's Socrates develops his account of pure pleasures, unmixed with pains, a discussion that leads into the proper articulation of true pleasures and of truth itself manifest in various degrees in pleasure and in various types of knowledge.

Under the generous umbrella of "knowledge" (*epistēmē*) or "art" (*technē*), here used interchangeably, the interlocutors reveal several types, ranging from the most imprecise of the productive arts, guided by lucky guesses (flute playing, medicine, agriculture, navigation, strategy), to the more precise productive arts (shipbuilding, house building), which make use of applied mathematics, and leading up to knowledge associated with the educational arts, such as pure geometry and arithmetic, and ending up with the most valuable and precise knowledge of dialectic, dealing with pure and unchanging realities (55c–59d).

After a thorough examination of various types of pleasure and knowledge, the culminating point of the discussion is reached when pleasures and knowledge are suitably combined with one another and when, at the end of the dialogue, we are offered a hierarchy of the ingredients that are responsible for the goodness of life (66a–c). It is here that measure (*to metrion*) comes to the fore, ranking highest in this hierarchy along with the timely (*to kairon*). As I will argue, in the *Philebus* "measure" means basically *due measure* in the sense of an absolute normative standard that functions as a moving target depending on the concrete shifting circumstances, and not a mere abstract and inert principle. The hierarchical orderings of the various types of pleasures and knowledge obtained earlier were meant absolutely, but in the concrete circumstances of our lives, it is due measure that guides from one moment to the next our prioritizing of one over another of those types of pleasure and knowledge in such a way as to reflect our continuous effort to adjust the Good to the changing circumstances of our lives. Depending on our natural inclinations and talents and on the concrete circumstances of our lives, we sometimes *rightly* find craft knowledge more fulfilling than mathematics, or the enjoyment of the mixed true pleasures more fulfilling than pure ones. Although he regards the practice of dialectic as intrinsically superior to all the other pursuits and pleasures of life, Plato's Socrates never implies that we should, for the sake of philosophical pleasures, actively neglect bodily pleasures, cutting off, say, the healthy and true pleasures of eating and rest. Due measure helps us understand what it means to say that any good mixture presupposes proportion and a harmonious combination of Limit with the Unlimited, or why, when arguing, it is important to proceed at the right pace, neither jumping too quickly to conclusions, nor arriving there too slowly after derailing detours.

Part of the special character of this dialogue resides in that, instead of focusing exclusively on either sensible things, or Forms, the conversation focuses on both and also, most importantly, on the interval and possible mediations between them. In this way, it complies with its own injunction that reasoning ought never to go from a unity to the many or from the many to the one faster or slower than it should, omitting the intermediaries, when it is these that make all the difference between dialecticians and eristic debaters (17a). I, therefore, regard the *Philebus* primarily as a dialogue about mediation, in the sense of securing the right transitions from concrete instances to universals through intermediaries. Ontologically, the Cause and the Unlimited mediate between Limit and the Mixtures, the Cause mediating from above, the Unlimited from below. Epistemologically, for one thing, the method of collection and division is to be applied orderly and gradually from the Unlimited to the one and vice versa, skipping no levels in between; for another, in a broad sense, knowledge itself is revealed to be of as many types as the kinds of objects that it takes, sensible or intelligible, thus ranging from the most imprecise opinions based on guesswork to the most exact and stable grasp of dialectic. Ethically, among the ingredients of the good human life, highest in rank are due measure (*to metrion*) and the timely (*to kairon*), which represent reflections of the Good in the realm of the changing and shifting circumstances of our lives. While it itself is neither an intelligible Form nor a random sensible thing, due measure is a normative standard that accounts for the way in which the Good can be accommodated to our phenomenal and transitory world of becoming. By placing due measure as the most important ingredient of a good human life, the *Philebus* accounts for the way in which the exact proportion and combination of the ingredients of a good life will differ from one person to another depending on the specific natural talents and inclinations and on the distinct circumstances of our lives, while remaining, nevertheless, in each of these cases, a constant normative reflection of the Good. Finally, what more eloquent way of focusing on mediation than that of showing, through the detailed analysis of pleasure that, as human beings, we are constantly somewhere in between the lowest and the best! While some of our most undignified pleasures are hardly different from those enjoyed by unreflective mollusks and beasts, our most elevated pure pleasures signal our bordering on divine status. Since pleasures are perceived replenishments of lacks, our very susceptibility to experience pleasure indicates that we are creatures of the interval, belonging somewhere between beasts and the divine.

There are several additional features that, I believe, recommend the *Philebus* as the most intriguing and complex of Plato's works. To begin with, the *Philebus* is the dialogue that addresses most explicitly the question that is constantly on Plato's mind: What is a good human life? It is in the *Philebus* that we find a most extensive discussion of the Good as the most final, self-sufficient, and the most choice-worthy object of desire, and with that, too, an understanding of the way the Good, if not accessible directly, is at least accessible through its reflection through Beauty, Proportion, and Truth. Again, it is in the *Philebus* that we can finally appreciate to its fullness the value of Plato's intellectualism or rationalism, which truly never presupposes sacrificing all pleasures, or excluding indetermination or chance from the fabric of human life. On the contrary, the rationalism here developed is robust all the more because it is built upon revealing the kinship that pleasures share with knowledge and argues for the possibility of a life ruled by reason in a universe permeated by chaos and indetermination. Furthermore, it is here that we get a most clear understanding of the interparticipation of Forms, a theme addressed also in the *Parmenides* and the *Sophist*, and a most detailed introduction and illustration of the dialectical method of collection and division, variants of which occur in the *Phaedrus*, the *Timaeus*, the *Sophist*, and the *Statesman*. Again, the *Philebus* draws at least implicitly upon a number of complex themes and theories explored in detail in other dialogues, and uses them in its own exploration of the good human life: the Divided Line, the *aporiai* of participation spelled out in the opening pages of the *Parmenides*, recollection, the science of calculating pleasures and pains first mentioned in the *Protagoras*, due measure, which receives its most extensive treatment in the *Statesman* and is mentioned also in the *Republic*, the *Phaedrus,* and the *Laws*. Drawing upon themes and views explored in other dialogues, the *Philebus* masterfully uses these insights as it proceeds to articulate the contours of a good human life: what ingredients it presupposes and why, what is their hierarchical order, and how they can combine with one another. Lest one be fooled to believe that Plato's Socrates might provide a closed systematic view prescribing a "one-size-fits-all" recipe for a good life, let it be said from the start that the presence of due measure at the top of that list of ingredients is by itself an invitation to the hardest task of a lifetime, the journey of self-discovery and responsibility.

While each of the chapters is a self-standing discussion, there are nonetheless a few threads running through all of them and unifying the work into a complex coherent whole.

A first thread concerns mediation and thinking in terms of intermediaries. Taking their clue from the advice that we should avoid advancing too quickly or too slowly from the one to the many and from the many to the one, and should, instead, make sure that we omit none of the intermediaries, the studies collected in this book emphasize Plato's concern for mediation expressed throughout the *Philebus*. Mediations take place simultaneously at different levels in our text: the dialectical method mediates between one Form and its many instances (chapter I); Limit and the Unlimited serve as mediators between pleasure and knowledge and secure the possibility of the final dialogue between them (chapter II); hybrid pleasures, which are true while being mixed with pain and false while being pure of such admixtures, mediate between pleasures that are pure and true, on the one hand, and those that are false and mixed, on the other (chapter III); due measure mediates between the Good and the particular circumstances of our lives (chapter IV) and proves to be essential in calibrating our pleasures of learning to our distinct natural talents and inclinations (chapter V); finally, the discussion developed in the last chapter attempts a different kind of mediation, one whereby what at first seem to be utterly irreconcilable views of pleasure, Plato's and Aristotle's, are in the end shown to be less at odds with one another than typically thought. I argue here that Plato's view of pleasure survives some of the Aristotelian critique, and that Plato could even incorporate Aristotle's account of pleasure as unimpeded exercise of our faculties in their natural condition as a phenomenological description of what it *feels* like to experience pleasure, while maintaining his own metaphysical understanding of pleasure as *genesis* (chapter VI).

As a second thread, a constant preoccupation throughout these chapters is integration of the discussions of specific issues—such as the distinction between mixed and pure pleasures, the possibility of true mixed pleasures or of false pure pleasures, the importance of due measure, the nature of our pleasures of learning, the nature of knowledge, the mixed pleasures of lamentation or anger, the pleasure of comic malice, etc.—into the metaphysical background of the fourfold structure of reality composed of Limit, the Unlimited, the Mixture of the two, the Cause of the mixture. Any attempt to discuss issues concerning ethics, methodology, or moral psychology independently of the metaphysical framework would necessarily be too narrow and superficial, and would compromise the teaching about the good life.

Conversely also, any attempt to study the metaphysical background for its own sake and without connection to the quest for the good life would be equally misguided and wrongheaded, as it would fall into pure abstractions detached from life.

A third thread throughout the book is the realization that the method of collection and division needs to be understood in relation to the metaphysical assumptions spelled out through the fourfold articulation of reality through Limit, the Unlimited, Mixture, and Cause of mixture. When the dialectical method of collection and division is first introduced in the dialogue it is introduced as a method that is not difficult to describe, but very difficult to use (16c). The reason for the difficulty at issue is that, discerning the joints where cuts are to be made by means of the dialectical method requires that the nature under investigation be understood in terms of the metaphysical structure of reality, here articulated in terms of that fourfold. Both a dialectician and an eristic debater might be using collection and division—the difference between the ways the two are using this method of search resides in their respective assumptions about the structure of reality and their respective metaphysical commitments. An absolute hedonist, for instance, might accept the four articulations of Limit, the Unlimited, the Cause, and the Mixture, while believing that the Unlimited is to be given priority over Limit, whereas a rationalist would see the order of priority reversed. The normative order in which we arrange the classes obtained through our cuts is determined by whether we view the universe as one in which the Cause keeps the Unlimited in check by the imposition of Limit, or as one in which the Unlimited overwhelms the rational strictures of Limit. Understanding the application of the dialectical method as dependent upon the metaphysical framework in which it is used is an essential clue for deciphering all of Plato's dialogues, and especially his late ones, in which variations in understanding collection and division from one dialogue to another depend on the different aspects of reality that constitute the focus of those dialogues.

Finally, common to these chapters is also the realization that, contrary to what traditional scholarship has been claiming, collection and division are not to be restricted either to sensible things or to intelligible Forms, but rather can be applied to both sensible and intelligible realities as long as we are clear about what we take to be the level at which the investigation is carried out each time. One and the same nature, say that of pleasure, or of the statesman, can be analyzed at various levels of comprehension. For example, in the *Philebus* the way we understand replenishments of lacks at the sensible level differs from how we understand those in an intelligible account. In the former case the replenishment is purely psycho-physiological, in the latter it is metaphysical, in the sense of revealing how the Good is instantiated in a fulfilling human life. Similarly, in Plato's *Statesman*, at a sensible level the method of collection and division discerns the nature of statesmanship strictly in terms of the statesman's provisions for food and necessary materials for the community that he rules, while at an intelligible level it reveals the nature of the statesman in terms of his art of cultivating virtue in the citizens' souls, thereby making manifest the instantiation of the Good in the life of a thriving community.

Before proceeding to specify the focus of each chapter it might be helpful to clarify that, while the relevance of Forms for the *Philebus* has been an object of controversy among scholars, I believe the text offers strong support for recognizing their presence and important role throughout. From its outset, the dialogue declares it of paramount importance to solve three *aporiai* of the One and the Many, specifying that these are meaningful as long as they are understood to be dealing with the unchanging monads of Goodness, Beauty, Man, Ox, and not with the perishable and changing attributes of particular things (14d–15b). At least two of the difficulties concerning monads raised in the *Philebus* occur also in the *Parmenides* (130b–e, 131a–c, 132b–d), where they unequivocally refer to the middle dialogues' Forms. Socrates describes the monads as nongenerated, indestructible, and always the same (15b), the same way that he characterizes Forms in other dialogues (*Symposium* 211a–d, *Phaedo* 78d–e, *Timaeus* 52a), and contrasts them with the perishable and changing things (15a). At 16c Socrates describes the dialectical method that he always admired as beginning with the identification of a single form (*mian idean*), then searching for "two or three or however many," where "three" is given in the feminine and, hence, continues the reference to *idea*. Later, in the section explicitly dedicated to the analysis of knowledge, Plato's Socrates talks distinctly about the intelligible realities that make the object of pure mathematics (56d–57d) as well as the objects reserved for dialectic "what really is forever eternally safe-same" (58a12–13), mentioning also explicitly the Good itself reflected through Beauty, Proportion, and Truth (65a). Beauty and the Good are explicitly treated as Forms in the middle dialogues (*Symposium* 211a–d, *Phaedo* 65d, 75d, 78d, 100, *Republic* 476b, 479a, 507b), and in the *Parmenides* Socrates wonders whether he should not posit also the Form of Man (*Parmenides* 130c). Whether in the *Philebus* Forms have in every respect the same meaning and function as they used to have in Plato's middle dialogues matters less than the realization that, whatever else might be true about these intelligible realities, they certainly function as universal, eternal, and unchanging principles of order and determination, and that without them we would be unable to articulate and comprehend Plato's complex understanding of the good human life.

The complexities here revealed regarding the Forms, the dialectical method, the fourfold articulation of reality, etc. make it very likely that we are dealing with a late dialogue, written at a time of mature insight and nuance. The interpretation proposed in this book does not depend on placing this dialogue among Plato's late works, though I do nonetheless find that view most plausible.[1]

Chapter I: *The Unity of the Philebus: Metaphysical Assumptions of the Good Human Life*. While scholars as astute and refined as Charles Kahn complain about the "extraordinary lack of unity" of the *Philebus*, which Kahn describes as having "a series of poorly integrated discussions,"[2] I propose a reading that reveals the interrelations between the most abstract and the most concrete moments of the dialogue. Far from the lamented disunity whereby "the course of the argument is repeatedly interrupted by problems of dialectic, cosmology and metaphysics that are very loosely tied up with the topics of pleasure, knowledge and the good" (Kahn ibid.), I propose a reading according to which the metaphysical articulation of reality accounts for the cognitive structure of pleasure and the role that pleasure and knowledge play in the good life.

Why does revealing this unity matter? To begin with, by integrating the analysis of pleasure into the metaphysical background we understand the specific hierarchy of pleasures, whereby pure pleasures are superior to impure or mixed ones, and true pleasures are superior to false ones, and we also understand why, among the false pleasures, some are falser than others. Secondly, revealing this unity also helps us make sense of the specific hierarchical order of knowledge, whereby pure knowledge that is more exact and precise is superior to the more imprecise types. Thirdly, it reveals to us the specific hierarchy of the ingredients of a good human life. And, finally, it clarifies that pleasure and knowledge share enough in common to be able to be combined as ingredients of a good human life.

Chapter II: *The Placement of Pleasure and Knowledge in the Fourfold Articulation of Reality*. Traditional interpretations place pleasure in the class of the Unlimited and knowledge in that of Limit. I challenge this interpretation and defend instead the view that pleasures, insofar as they are true, belong to the class of Mixtures, while knowledge and its cognates are among the Causes of mixtures.

To understand that pleasures, as Mixtures, are dependent on knowledge, as Cause, means to realize not only that pleasures have a cognitive structure and thus are irreducible to mere sensations of the moment or instinctual reflexes, the way *Philebus* would want us to believe, but also that, because of this, our intellectual growth and maturation will contribute to raising the quality of our pleasures and implicitly of our lives. That the type of pleasures we privilege in our lives depends on the knowledge we have and on the cluster of beliefs articulating our value judgments and commitments, is an insight that lies also at the basis of contemporary cognitive and behavioral therapy. When we understand that pleasure always presupposes a cluster of beliefs about what we value and why we value certain things in our lives, we can see how we can vary and modify the preference we give to some pleasures by refining that belief system. So too, we can become better at enjoying more true pleasures by increasing our self-knowledge and our awareness of what truly replenishes us and of the extent to which it does so.

Chapter III: *Hybrid Varieties of Pleasure: True Mixed Pleasures and False Pure Pleasures*. The third chapter stems from the need to determine whether the pairs of truth/falsehood and purity/impurity respectively overlap completely and, in case they don't, whether it is possible to have hybrid pleasures that combine the terms in the two pairs mentioned. Thus, can mixed (impure) pleasures of eating when hungry or drinking when thirsty be either true or false, or do they always have to be false? Can our pure pleasures of learning ever be excessive, or deficient, and therefore false? I argue that Plato keeps the criteria of truth/falsehood and purity/impurity of pleasures distinct and that allowing for such hybrid varieties of pleasure has significant consequences for the account of the good life here advanced.

Chapter IV: *The Nature of Pleasure: Absolute Standards of Replenishment and Due Measure*. Plato's view that pleasure is the perceived replenishment of some lack has often been subject to criticism as too narrow and incapable of accounting for some of the corporeal and all the noncorporeal pleasures. It seems at first hard, if not impossible, to specify what exactly must have been initially lacking and is correspondingly refilled through our pleasures of sight, smell, learning, recollecting pleasant memories from our past, or projecting hopes for the future, when these experiences are not preceded by any perceptible lack. What kind of replenishment are we undergoing when experiencing any of these pleasures? This difficulty seems to be only deepened when we realize that Plato suggests a reply based on objective standards in relation to which we are supposed to estimate the reality and degree of replenishment that we experience when taking pleasure in various things. For if there are objective standards of pleasure (replenishment), how can we account for the *legitimate* diversity of our natural talents, tastes, and for the correspondingly diverse ways of experiencing pleasure? In this chapter then, I explore (1) whether Plato's notion of pleasure as perceptible replenishment of a lack can account for our pure pleasures, and (2) whether and, if so, how Plato's understanding of objective standards of pleasure fits in with the recognition of a legitimate diversity of natural talents and tastes.

Chapter V: *Pleasures of Learning and the Role of Due Measure in Experiencing Them*. In the *Philebus* Socrates talks explicitly only about a very narrow category of pleasures of learning, namely, the pleasures we take in practicing dialectic (52a–b). These he describes as being always pure and true. This chapter steps beyond the letter of the text while remaining loyal to its spirit, as it attempts to explore what Plato's Socrates would say about pleasures of learning when we take "learning" in a broader sense, to include not only dialectic, but also the study we undertake in a variety of branches of knowledge, from the most imprecise to the most precise disciplines. In this vein, I am going to address a number of questions: (1) Can pleasures of learning be pure even when they emerge in response to the experience of *aporia,* which seems to be painful? (2) Once we broaden the meaning of "learning" as suggested above, can there be different kinds of pleasures of learning, some of them true, others false, some pure, others mixed? And, finally, (3) Since due measure and the timely *(to metrion, to kairion* 66a6–8) are the most important ingredients of a good human life, what role exactly do they play in our experience of the pleasures of learning?

Chapter VI: *Plato's Conception of Pleasure Confronting Three Aristotelian Critiques.* Much has been made of what appears to be Aristotle's rejection of Plato's understanding of pleasure as process and his replacement of this with an understanding of pleasure as an activity that is complete at every moment. The final chapter of this book attempts to explore whether the account of pleasure developed in the *Philebus* can survive at least some waves of criticism that Aristotle formulates in the *Nicomachean Ethics* against the understanding of pleasure as process or becoming *(genesis)*, whether Aristotle had Plato's view in mind as target of his criticism or not. While recognizing the undeniable differences between the two conceptions, I argue that Aristotle's criticism does not pose crucial threats to Plato's understanding of pleasure. In fact, I focus here on *the positive requirements for a robust understanding of pleasure* that those critical points suggest, and basically emphasize, once again, the strength and complexity of Plato's account, as one that is able to meet these requirements. I hope to show that Plato might learn a great deal from Aristotle and even adopt some of his student's insights regarding *the experience* of pleasure as an activity that is complete at every moment, while preserving nevertheless his own account of *the nature* of pleasure as perceived replenishment of a lack and his metaphysical understanding of it as a coming into being (*genesis eis ousian*).

Beyond the suggested solutions to specific problems of interpretation, this book attempts to reveal the carefully woven unity of the *Philebus* and to bring to light once again the complexity of Plato's understanding of human nature and the good life. Unlike a host of scholars who claim that, in order to pay attention to life in its immediacy, Plato had to give up the high-flown metaphysical speculations of his middle dialogues, this book argues that, in the *Philebus* Plato develops an in-depth account of the concrete phenomena and changing circumstances of life precisely by intensifying and amplifying his exploration and grasp of the underlying metaphysical reality, and not at the expense of these.

Finally, writing this book has been itself an exercise in mediation, not simply between what Plato says and how we are to understand that, but also between what Plato says explicitly and what he only hints at implicitly. As it will be obvious, on several occasions I venture beyond the letter of the text and explore the rich and complex territory of what Plato *might have said* or *might have allowed to be said* on issues he does not explicitly address. Thus, for instance, in Chapter III I discuss the possibility of hybrid pleasures, namely, true mixed pleasures and false pure pleasures, in Chapter V I explore what Plato might have said about "pleasures of learning" when "learning" is broadly construed, and exercised in fields other than dialectic, whether such pleasures can also be mixed and perhaps sometimes even false, in Chapter VI I envision what could have been some of Plato's replies to some criticisms formulated by Aristotle, and in the closing Appendix I explore the way in which the *Philebus* offers us clues for constructing a plausible reply to the *aporiai* of participation articulated in Plato's *Parmenides*.

I

The Unity of the *Philebus*

Metaphysical Assumptions of the Good Human Life

The unity of Plato's *Philebus* has often been questioned, and debates are still ongoing as to whether the dialogue's main concern is the ethical discussion of the good life, the methodological discussion of the One-Many dialectic, or the ontology of the four kinds.[1] I believe that the ethical, methodological, and metaphysical aspects, which seem to be treated disparately, are in fact harmoniously interwoven, and their joint treatment speaks for Plato's insight into the complexity of the good life. In what follows, I defend this view, by examining first the relation between the dialectical method and the view of reality articulated in terms of the four kinds of Limit, the Unlimited, their Mixture, and the Cause of the mixture, and then by showing how the dialectical method and this metaphysical worldview jointly help us elucidate the ethical concern for the good life and the classifications of different types of pleasure and knowledge. As we are going to witness, a major unifying thread of the dialogue is the realization that the dialectician's classifications of emotional and cognitive experiences cannot be separated from considerations regarding the structure of reality.

The Dialectical Method and the Fourfold Structure of Reality

The *Philebus* opens up as a competition between pleasure and knowledge: Philebus has been championing pleasure as the good, while Socrates has been maintaining that knowledge, memory, opinion, and everything of that sort are better than pleasure for those who can experience them (11b–c). Shortly after, Philebus drops out of the conversation, and Protarchus takes up the task of defending his view.[2] Upon recognizing that perhaps neither one of these two separately, but rather some combination of them, might be the good itself, the conversation turns into an examination of whether pleasure or knowledge is closer to the good (20b–23a).

Philebus's position that the life of pleasure is the good is from the start challenged by Socrates's remark that there is a great diversity of pleasures that people enjoy and some of these are opposite to others. When Protarchus steps in to defend Philebus, he argues that, although pleasures are many and of many sorts, and sometimes come from contrary sources, they are not in opposition insofar as they are all pleasures (11d–12a). After Socrates admits that his own candidate, knowledge, shares the same condition (13e–14a), Protarchus withdraws his objection for the moment, and this allows Socrates to focus their discussion on the all-pervasive issues related to the One and the Many. If both pleasure and knowledge come in many distinct types, what is there to unify each one of the two kinds?

Socrates first dismisses the One-Many puzzles related to perishable things and arising from our confusion of judgments of predication with judgments of identity, or simply concerning the unity of a whole with its parts: How can a person be at once tall and short, heavy and light? Or how can many limbs and other component parts be one single individual (14d)?[3] The serious One-Many puzzles worth investigating concern nonperishable entities, eternal monads, such as Human Being, Ox, Beauty, and the Good:

> First, whether it is necessary to suppose that there are any such monads truly in existence. Then again, how are they supposed to be: How can each one of them, always being one and the same, and admitting neither generation nor destruction, nevertheless firmly be this one unity? And after this, whether we are to suppose that, in the many things that come to be and are unlimited, this unity is dispersed and has itself become many or else that it is entirely separated from itself, which would seem the most impossible notion of all, it being one and the same to be at the same time in one and in many? (15b1–8)[4]

Before proceeding to analyze the questions here expressed, it is important to recognize that the monads here in question refer most likely to the same kind of entities that Plato's middle dialogues call Forms. In support of this view we notice that (1) there are variants of *eīdos* employed throughout the *Philebus* in reference to such monads (16d, 65a); (2) Socrates describes the monads as nongenerated, indestructible, and always the same (15b), the same way that he characterizes Forms in other dialogues (cf. *Symposium* 211a–d, *Phaedo* 78d–e, *Timaeus* 52a), and contrasts them with the perishable and changing things (15a); (3) Beauty, Proportion, and Truth, which are the unitary manifestation of the Good (64e–65a), are extensively treated as the proper objects of dialectic dealing with what is always the same (58a); (4) Beauty and the Good are explicitly treated as Forms in the middle dialogues (*Symposium* 211a–d, *Phaedo* 65d, 75d, 78d, 100, *Republic* 476b, 479a, 507b) and in the *Parmenides* Socrates wonders whether he should not posit also the Form of Man (*Parmenides* 130c); (5) at least two of the difficulties concerning monads raised in the *Philebus* occur also in the *Parmenides* (130b–e, 131a–c, 132b–d), where they unequivocally refer to the middle dialogues' Forms. It might nonetheless be reasonable not to attempt a strict identification of these monads with the Forms. As long as we recognize that they share in the most fundamental features of universality, eternity, ideality, and immutability with the middle dialogues' Forms, we do not need to show that what the *Philebus* says about monads overlaps completely with everything else that Plato says about Forms in his middle dialogues.[5] In fact, in light of the new emphasis on the interparticipation of monads or on their complex one-many structural identity, it makes sense for new aspects of eternal unchanging realities to come to light that were not recognized, or at least not emphasized, in the middle dialogues' discussion of Forms.

The first question concerns the existence of immutable monads: Do they exist as real entities or are they just thoughts (see also *Parmenides* 130b–e, 132b–d)?

The second is by far the least clear of the puzzles, and scholars continue to debate what it means, and even whether it means anything at all. A number of translations rephrase the sentence in such a way as to assimilate this part to the last question, and argue that there are in fact only two serious puzzles raised.[6] The difficulty of accepting the following formulation as a question—"Then again, how are they supposed to be: How can each one of them, always being one and the same, and admitting neither generation nor destruction, nevertheless firmly be this one unity?"(15b2–5)—stems from the fact that it is not clear why reconciling the unchangeable nature of Forms with their unity is problematic in any way. Why would a monad's immutability conflict with its unity? Though it is hard to reach a fully satisfactory interpretation, I find Hampton's solution preferable to others, since, although not that easy to square with Socrates's formulation, at least it resonates with Socrates's discussion and use of dialectic throughout the dialogue. Hampton writes:

> Clearly no conflict would exist if what is meant by unit here is absolute simplicity. But if what Plato means by *mian tautēn* (this one, 15b) is a whole of parts, then a conflict could occur between a Form as a whole and the parts of which it is composed. So the contrast Plato is drawing in the second question is between a Form as a self-identical, immutable, timeless, and unified entity on the one hand, and on the other, a Form which differs from, and even opposes, other Forms, including Forms which are its parts. In other words, the contrast is between the emphasis Plato put upon the simplicity and independence of a Form from everything else including other Forms, and the stress he is now (in the *Sophist* and *Statesman*, as well as in the *Philebus*) putting on the "weaving" or interrelations among the Forms. (Hampton 1990, 19)

If we follow this line of interpretation, the question in effect asks how can Forms be imperishable and unchangeable monads while they themselves are present in other, more specific Forms, and how do specific Forms preserve their nature and unity despite partaking of other Forms?[7] To illustrate this situation: How can Shape, for instance, which is one, be present both in the Curved and the Straight, which are contraries? Or how can Man preserve its unity and nature in spite of partaking of Beauty, Measure, and the Good?

Finally, the third question focuses on the relation between Forms and sensible things: How is one Form present in many things at once since, if the sensible things partake of it by partitioning it, the Form will lose its universality, and if the Form is present wholly in each and every particular participant in it, the Form will shed its unity and self-identity and become plural (see also *Parmenides* 131a–c)?[8]

Nowhere in the *Philebus* is either one of these questions explicitly and directly answered, and yet each one of them is answered at least implicitly and indirectly through the investigation of pleasure and knowledge that unfolds in light of metaphysical considerations about the fourfold structure of reality.

Right after formulating these issues of the One and the Many, Socrates introduces a dialectical method meant to help us address them. The dialectical method is introduced in a most reverent way, as a gift of the gods to men, a path that Socrates himself has always admired, one responsible for *discoveries* made in every art. It is characterized as an approach that, while easy to describe, is extremely difficult to use (16b–c). It begins by assuming that

> there is in each case one form (*mian idean*) for every one of them [i.e., for every one of the things that are ever said to be], and we must search for it, as we will indeed find it there contained. And once we have gotten hold of it, we must look for two, as the case would be, or if not, for three or some other number. And we must treat every one of these further again in the same way, until it is not only established of the original unity that it is one, many, and unlimited, but also how many it is. (16c9–d7)

Socrates illustrates the concrete application of this method for the cases of linguistic and musical sound. Linguistic sound is treated in two complementary passages, the first of which illustrates the method's progress primarily, though not exclusively, by identification of subdivisions within a unity, and thus discerns the intermediates *en route* from the one to its infinitely many instances or subspecies (17a–b), while the second illustrates primarily, though not exclusively, the complementary direction, from the infinitely many to the one, by collecting a plurality within corresponding units (18a–d).[9] While division is explained in the passage quoted above, Socrates describes the complementary account of collection as follows:

> Just as someone who has gotten hold of some unity or other should not, as we were saying, immediately look toward the unlimited nature but first look for some number, the same holds for the reverse case: if one is forced to start with the unlimited, he should not head immediately for the one, but should in each case grasp some number that determines every plurality whatever, and from all of those finally reach the one. (18a7–b4)

When he applies division to linguistic sound, Socrates says that we do not become literate unless we have divided sound into its subclasses and are in the position to say how many kinds of vocal sound there are and what their nature is. Though he does not specify the intermediaries' nature when he proceeds downward by division, Socrates identifies them as vowels, semi-vowels, and consonants when he ascends to their common form by collecting them from their dispersion in an indefinite and unlimited plurality (18b–c).[10] In the final stage of the analysis, the grammarian collects all the items discerned under their well-defined unitary nature as "letters" (18c5–6), and this last move derives from his realization that letters cannot be known independently of one another, but only as part of the entire alphabet.[11] The focus is not strictly or primarily on identifying each separate unit, but rather on realizing that to understand one of them we need to understand it in its interrelations to others and to understand all of them as part of one unitary system or art (18c–d).

The analysis of spoken sound brackets in between its two parts the collection and division of musical sound. The analysis of musical sound starts from an initial unity and discovers the high, low, and even pitch as intermediaries between this unity and the indefinitely many instances encountered in experience (17b–e). And as with letters, so also with musical sound, one does not become an accomplished practitioner of the art unless he masters knowledge about how many intervals in high and low pitch are, what is their nature, which musical notes define each interval, and what combinations result in harmonious rhythms and modes (17c–e). It is by using due measure in operating collections and divisions that we make sure not to skip intermediaries in a classification, thus going through the steps at the right pace, neither faster nor slower than we should.

In two seminal works Mitchell Miller provides detailed accounts of how Socrates's dialectical analyses of letters and musical sounds reveal the field of possible instantiations of the original unit of sound on a continuum that stretches between maximal and minimal release of breath and between high and low pitched sound respectively, and persuasively argues that the focus is not on simply distinguishing and identifying the separate units, but on discerning the interrelations among them (Miller 1990, 330–39; Miller 2010, 62–72). Miller discerns two phases in which collection and division are applied in the two illustrations: a first one, in which we obtain a preliminary set of distinctions laying open the field of the initial form as a whole, and a second one, in which more refined distinctions disclose the determinate many (2010, 65–66). The cuts obtained in the first phase disclose the "single form's field of possible instantiations as a continuous range or series" (ibid., 65). Thus, when musical sound was divided into low, high, and equal pitch falling between the first two,

> even as we set one group over against the other as its opposite, we see that at a deeper level "low" notes and "high" notes are

also, like the "equal-toned" in each case balances of high and low, with each note differing from each other by virtue of their differing proportions of high to low. What the initial trifurcation reveals, thus, is a continuum stretching from balances in which, say low predominates through balances that are relatively equal to balances in which high predominates. (Miller 2010, 66)

The same thing happens with the threefold classification of spoken sound into sounds that are voiced, those that are not voiced but make a certain noise, and those that are both noiseless and unvoiced and are called mutes (18c):

More than just collections of sounds they mark out three contiguous regions on a gradient of spoken sound leading from that which requires the most open-mouthed, least fricative release of breath to that which requires the most closure and stopping of the release of breath. (Miller 2010, 67)

It is important to notice that in practice division and collection are never strictly separated. Thus, although the predominant procedure in dealing with musical sound is division, as the analysis moves from the unity of sound to its three classes of high, low, and intermediate pitch, and from there to individual sounds, collection is also employed as the analysis moves from individual notes to their combinations (17d1–2). Similarly, *en route* to collecting the many into a more or less defined unity, the grammarian also applies division, as he divides each of the intermediates, vowels, semi-vowels, and consonants, into the letters that correspond to each (18c2–5).

Socrates's illustrations confirm his earlier remark that the dialectical method of collection and division has proved to be useful in discoveries made in any field of art (16c2–3). Linguistic and musical sounds are excellent choices for Socrates's illustration for a number of reasons. For one thing, both illustrations pertain to systems within which understanding one element means understanding its placement and interrelation to all the others that are part of the same system or network.[12] Secondly, the order in which the two illustrations are introduced is significant, letters being easier to follow since they do not require the extensive reliance on mathematics that intricate musical rhythms and intervals do. Finally, linguistic and musical sound can be treated either as sensible or as intelligible objects in a classification, depending on whether we choose to focus on their empirical manifestations or on the underlying intelligible mathematical ratios of high-low pitch or of the greater or lesser amount of breath used to voice them. As such, they serve as excellent paradigms that illustrate the application of a dialectical method that is responsible for discoveries made in all the arts, from the most imprecise ones based on guesswork to the most precise dialectical art based on complete knowledge.

In both cases, of letters and music, we start from the indefinitely many, which means from the basic level where we use strictly our senses to notice the amount of breath that is used to utter sounds and the bodily movements that specify rhythms of music.[13] Then, we refine our accounts insofar as a thorough classification of various musical intervals requires mastery of mathematics, and the understanding of the possible combinations of letters requires the sophisticated knowledge of a linguist or a grammarian. Whether literacy and music are regarded under their sensible or intelligible aspect depends on the extent to which the method is pursued. The farther we pursue it, that is, the deeper we go in discerning the metaphysical grounds justifying the natural joints at which a unity is divided in natural kinds, the more we depart from sensible and head toward intelligible considerations. Application of the method does not have to start from discerning as its initial unit a fully defined intelligible Form, but it certainly attempts to reach that stage. While the method of divisions is actually applied in grammar and music, as well as in many other arts, from the point of view of philosophy the method's application is not carried far enough within the confines of these disciplines. This is not due to a failure of music as music, or of grammar as grammar, but simply because these arts do not require as comprehensive an account of their objects as dialectic does. While in their theoretical investigations both grammar and music reach a level of abstraction and sophistication where they deal with numerical ratios and intelligible Forms of Harmony, Beauty, Proportion, and so on, the expert musicologist or grammarian is not expected to analyze the connection between these Forms and everything else there is, nor to explain Beauty and Numbers with reference to the rationality or goodness of the universe. Such tasks the dialectician alone takes up in his use of the method. If this is correct, Plato's view seems to be that the grammatical and musical applications of collection and division are to be pursued farther by the dialectician until we understand not only how intelligible eternal Forms are present in sensible things (the third puzzle above) and how some Forms relate to one another, but also grasp the interrelations among all the Forms and comprehend their nature as manifestations of the Good (the second puzzle above). This finds support in Socrates's suggestion that divisions and collections are to be applied repeatedly in dealing with one theme of investigation (cf. *palin*, 16d5).[14] In the dialectician's hands, the method promises to explain ultimately the plurality of intelligible Forms as a unitary manifestation of the Good, similar to the way in which Beauty, Proportion, and Truth are described later on (65a).[15]

It is also worth noting that the present mention of music and letters as paradigms for the illustration of the dialectical method is only a first instance in a series, as music and letters keep showing up, in one shape or another, like a leitmotif throughout the conversation.[16] Thus, the next time when letters and the art of literacy are alluded to is through the image of the soul as a book containing a scribe (*ho grammatistēs*) and a painter inside (38e–39c). Later on, the art of literacy shows up as art of persuasion developed by Gorgias (58a6–b3), on the one hand, and as dialectic proper, which is the truest and the most precise art (57d6–58a), on the other. Music, too, resurfaces in the context in which Socrates talks about the pure pleasures that fill imperceptible lacks, as he talks about the pleasure we take in the beauty of mathematical shapes, colors considered in themselves, and the pleasures stemming from the "smooth and bright sounds which produce one pure note" (51d6–e2), and then again, toward the end of the dialogue, when flute playing is said to be based on guess work, allowing for a lot of imprecision and very little reliability (56a). What are we to make of these recurrences of letters and music throughout the text? In a number of ways the recurrence of the two illustrations draws our attention to relations existent among the various arts: the superiority of dialectic over the arts of literacy and of music; the continuity existent among these arts, whereby musicology is more precise than linguistics, since the former depends more directly on mathematics, while flute playing is less precise than the linguist's or the grammarian's art; dialectic remains all along the most reliable art and the most precise. Thus, the reemergence of the two illustrations reveals a gradual progression in exactness and reliability from flute playing to literacy, to musicology, and finally, to dialectic. Furthermore, that the same dialectical method is applied in all these arts, from the most imprecise to the most precise, tells us something essential about the usefulness of this method when properly employed, and also about the risks of misusing it when, for instance, we might lose track of whether we collect and divide sensible fluctuating items or intelligible unchanging realities.

The manner in which the dialectical method is supposed to help us solve the serious One-Many puzzles is not immediately obvious. And the fact that, instead of applying it directly to the elucidation of pleasures and knowledge, Socrates seems to put the method aside and replace it with his revelation in a "dream" that, after all, neither a life exclusively dedicated to pleasure nor one exclusively dedicated to knowledge is the best life for a human being (20b–22d), has given scholars reason to question the method's usefulness. Doubts in this regard are often amplified by the incomplete and apparently random classifications of pleasure and knowledge that Socrates provides. I believe that these considerations signal difficulties only on a superficial understanding of the method's procedure and task. Once we understand, however, that the method's ultimate purpose is to give us access to the most comprehensive and profound understanding of reality and that, for this reason, it must proceed by taking guidance from the nature of reality itself, the method proves its general usefulness and its success in its application to the cases of pleasure and knowledge in our text.

To clarify the kind of guidance and influence the structure of reality has on the method's application, let us begin by noticing that divisions and classifications can be made within alternative metaphysical frameworks, and the specific framework within which they are made justifies ultimately the joints and criteria according to which divisions and collections are operated. It is for this reason that the above quoted passage that describes the main thrust of the dialectical method is prefaced by assumptions about the nature of the reality that the method attempts to disclose more fully:

> The things that are ever said to be are composed, on the one hand, of one and many (*ex henos men kai pollōn*), and, on the other hand, have within themselves limit and unlimitedness. Since this is the structure of things we must assume that there is in each case one form (*mian idean*) for every one of them [i.e., for every one of the things that are ever said to be], and we must search for it, as we will indeed find it there contained. (16c9–d2)

And if the method's application finds its ultimate justification in the structure of reality, then the latter must itself be amenable to being approached and dealt with by means of that method. That this is how Plato's Socrates also regards the issue is reflected in the following lines, where the four basic articulations of reality and the corresponding members of each are reached by means of collection and division:

> First, then, let us take up three of the four, and since we see that two of them are split up and dispersed each into many, let us collect each into a unity again, so that we may understand how

each of them is in fact one and many. —If you could explain all that more clearly, I might be able to follow you. —I am basically saying that the two kinds that I posit are the ones I referred to just now, the unlimited and what has limit. That the unlimited is in a way many I will try to explain now. (23e3–24a4)

The model of reality presupposed by this dialectical method has a fourfold structure, which Socrates introduces by saying that "all the things that are now in the all" (*panta ta nūn onta en tō panti*, 23c4)[17] can be divided into four kinds: Limit (*to peras*), the Unlimited (*to apeiron*), the Mixture (*to meikton*) of the two, and the Cause (*hē aitia*) of their mixture. Let us take a look at each of these four.

The Unlimited is a domain of indefiniteness and indetermination (24a–e), whose members are in permanent flux between contrasting features (24d2–5). It contains several pairs of mutually relative and gradient opposites that frame continua which are governed by the more and less, the stronger and milder, and the too much, as structural principles (24e7–25a1). Thus, the hotter and the colder, the dryer and the wetter, the high and the low, the fast and the slow all belong to the Unlimited, insofar as each of these continua is governed by at least one of the structural principles mentioned, such that more of one term in the pair implies less of its opposite, and too much of one implies too little of its opposite (see also Harvey 2009, 10; Miller 2010, 73–74; Garner 2017, 44–50).[18] The members of the Unlimited are indefinite and hence cannot be identified as distinct individual things. So, when, in addition to the indefinite ranges of continua that he mentions, Socrates also includes in this class blizzards and heat waves (26a6), as well as excessive pleasure and pain (27e, 31a, 52c), which should not be taken as individual sensible instances, but rather as states of excess in which weather and our emotional states respectively have lost their proper balance and are distorted to the point of no longer preserving their nature. Excessive pleasure, as we later find out, is in fact no pleasure at all, it is false pleasure (52c), and its nature is better characterized as a pleasure-pain continuum, with no definite nature of its own (see Benitez 1989, 75–76).[19]

Limit is a principle of measure, order, and determination. The class of Limit comprises the equal, the double, and "all that is related as number to number and as measure to measure" (*prōton men to ison kai isoteta, meta de to ison to diplasion kai pān hotiper an pros arithmon arithmos ē metron ē pros metron*, 25a7–b1). I take this to mean that its members are elements that act as ordering causes when applied to the Unlimited, bringing about the harmony of the fluctuating opposites by imposing definite numbers on them (25d11–e2). Since the members of Limit explicitly mentioned are the equal, the double, and "all that is related as number to number and as measure to measure" (25a7–b1), it is plausible to think that all the members of this class are mathematical ratios imparting measure, order, and harmony to the Unlimited.

If this is right, it is natural to ask where in relation to Limit and to the fourfold in general are we to place the Forms, which, we have seen, are alluded to as monads earlier on (15a, 16d) and will be mentioned explicitly at a later stage (58a, 64e–65a). Scholars have argued for each and every imaginable case: that the Forms are included in the class of Mixture, in that of the Cause, or of the Unlimited, that the Forms are present in none of the four classes and are in fact irrelevant for the dialogue as a whole, or, alternatively that they are present simultaneously in every one of the four classes.[20] But Forms clearly cannot be members of the Unlimited class, since Forms are by definition sources of definiteness and determination, whereas the Unlimited pulsates with indetermination (15b). Forms cannot be members of the Mixed class since the latter admit generation and change while Forms do not (15a–b). Nor can Forms be included in the category of the Cause of mixtures, since that Cause is described as a mind (*noũs*), whereas Forms are objects of mental activity (16b–19a). Consequently, Forms cannot be present simultaneously in every one of the four classes.[21] If we accept, as I do, that Forms are relevant to our dialogue, the only remaining possibilities are either that Forms are in the class of Limit, or that they are outside the fourfold, acting as sources of Limit and of its members, a position insightfully defended by Miller (Miller 2010, 72–78). I believe it is safest to assume that Forms act as sources of Limit and of its members, since Socrates mentioned explicitly only mathematical relations as members of Limit. If this is correct, then the Form of Health, for instance, is to be understood as expressing itself through distinct ratios that vary in terms of the kind of organism whose health is at issue (e.g., the health of a human being, a horse, a cat, or any other animal) and the types of balances measured by ratios corresponding to ranges in arterial pressure, height, weight, etc. These ratios are the limits that structure the indefinite continua of the high and low, the quick and slow, the hot and cold, etc. that pertain to the Unlimited. To say then that Forms are sources of Limit means that each Form prescribes the norms for what it is to be an instance of that Form and this norm is expressed in definite measures by the corresponding members of Limit.

The class of Mixtures includes sensible entities, both as sensible features shared by a plurality of individuals, as suggested by the collective designation of its members as things that come to be (*gignomena* 26e3, 27a11, *symbainein,* 25e4) or are produced (*poioumenon,* 27a1, a6).[22] The instances of the mixed class that Socrates mentions are: health, strength, beauty (26b–c), living things (32b1), and the good human life combining knowledge and pleasure (27d1–6). These are all instances of good, harmonious, and proportionate mixtures, but nothing in the text requires that all the members of this class need to be perfectly harmonious mixtures. In fact, Socrates's declaration that this is an overwhelmingly abundant and diverse class (26c8–9, 27d9) seems to suggest otherwise. I believe it is reasonable to think that the mixed class is broad enough to include a variety of combinations of limit and the unlimited all of which are still within normal limits, and to exclude only those instances that are excessive to the point of having their own natures distorted. It is indeed difficult to see what determines the range of normality and thus of mixtures, but we can at least say negatively that what determines the range of complete irregularity is complete absence of limit.[23] Excessive instances are so much lacking in measure that they fall, like the false pleasures and the blizzards mentioned above, in the class of the Unlimited (see also Benitez 1989, 83). While change characterizes both members of Mixture and of the Unlimited, the change that characterizes the former allows nonetheless for a relative permanence and preservation of their nature, for the presence of Limit in them ensures that their becoming is a *genesin eis ousian* (26d8) and not a random indefinite fluctuation of the sort that characterizes the members of the Unlimited.

The main reason why Socrates chooses to illustrate the third kind with examples of fine and harmonious combinations is probably that he is thus preparing his introduction of the fourth kind, the Cause of the mixture, reason (*noûs*). Since reason is intrinsically valuable, so too are its effects. As it becomes obvious, however, reason or wisdom can operate in various degrees at the divine and human levels respectively, and this helps us understand that the fluctuation in the degree of rightness and harmony in the mixtures is a function of the degree to which reason presides over the combination of Limit and the Unlimited in a particular case. Socrates suggests that, while at the cosmic level a divine universal reason presides over the mixtures of Limit and the Unlimited, and ensures the cosmic manifestation of measure and proportion,[24] at the level of our individual lives, a reason with similar function though of weaker power is responsible for the proper combination of Limit and the Unlimited in the good human life (28e–30e). Human reason emulates the divine sort and thus its own agency, knowledge, is a way of discovering the intelligibility of what there is: Forms in themselves, the intelligible formal aspect of mixtures, as well as its own intelligibility through self-reflection. The method of collection and division is proposed in our dialogue as dialectical procedure to assist and aid us in emulating the divine.

The four classes are articulations in terms of which we are to understand, interpret, and analyze "all the things that are now in the all" (23c4). I take this to mean that the good life, its ingredients, the various types of knowledge, the varieties of pleasure, and indeed everything else there is to be understood, are to be mapped onto this structure and explained in terms of this fourfold.

Let us now take a closer look at some additional indications of Plato's conception of the intimate relationship between the dialectical method and the above-sketched framework of reality. Socrates's remark, when he embarks upon the introduction of the fourfold model, that for adjudicating the priority between reason and pleasure they will need partly the same and partly different weapons from the ones used in the methodological discussion remains somewhat cryptic. While it is not difficult to accept that by preserving partially the same weapons Socrates must mean that they will still use the notions of limit (*peras*) and unlimited (*apeiron*) in the fourfold model, it is not quite clear whether he uses these terms with the same meaning and application in both cases. In the context of the dialectical method *apeiron* refers to the unlimited plurality of individual instances, which the method can no longer analyze (16d–18c). The method's application ends with *infimae species*, in which a unitary form can still be discerned, and then lets the unlimited plurality of instances flow indefinitely. In the context discussing the fourfold model, on the other hand, *apeiron* refers primarily to the indefinite and unlimited degree of more and less, hotter and colder, etc. (23c–25a). Something similar happens with the use of *peras* (limit). While in both contexts it preserves its general meaning of definiteness, in the context of the dialectical method "definiteness" refers to the finite and specifiable number of intermediary subdivisions of a Form, whereas in the context discerning the basic articulations of reality, it is the main characteristic of intelligible Forms insofar they preserve their nature and function as paradigms of measure.[25]

The fact that there is an overarching common meaning of both *peras* and *apeiron* in the two contexts prompts us to look for an explanation of the use of the same terms with slightly different applications in the two passages as, the way the method of division identifies species within a common genus.[26] I believe that the predominantly quantitative sense in which both *peras* and *apeiron* are used in discussing the method is grounded in the predominantly qualitative sense they have in the context of the fourfold. In other words, we are not supposed to draw a definite line between the quantitative and the qualitative uses of *peras* and *apeira* in the two contexts. For in order to make its divisions and to arrive at *infimae species* the method must consider qualitative differences among natural kinds, and thus the quantitative sense of the instances it discovers depends on the quality of the monads under consideration. Thus, the fact that, for instance, one can discern a definite number of subdivisions of beauty is a reflection of the qualitative definiteness that pertains to intelligible Beauty insofar as it can combine with other Forms. Correspondingly, the fact that one can no longer treat accidental similarities or differences among an indefinite number of individual things as constitutive criteria of a rigorous classification is a reflection of the indefinite quality of the unlimited manifest in these particular and changeable occurrences. The connection between the senses of *peras* and *apeiron* in the two contexts is, again, an expression of the rationalist assumption that the dialectician's divisions mirror the natural kinds that are in reality.

A closer look at the overarching ethical theme under investigation in the *Philebus* shows that the dialectician's classifications of various types of pleasure and knowledge are not done independently of the question of value. As we shall witness in greater detail below, Socrates not only classifies various kinds, but he also adjudicates the superiority of some over others: of pure pleasures over impure pleasures, of dialectical knowledge over mathematical knowledge, and so on. The dialectical method of division can justify a hierarchical ordering of its classes only if it is carried far enough to reveal its own reliance on the model of the four kinds, since that model is intrinsically axiological. The ultimate standard and source of value is the Good, since it alone is perfect and self-sufficient (20d–e). By the characterizations it receives, and in perfect consistency with the *Republic* 508e–509b, the Good of the *Philebus* reigns supreme over the other Forms (64e–65b). All the Forms are sources of Limit. Reason (*noūs*), as the cause of right orderings, is the cause of the presence of limits in the mixtures and is, therefore, closer to the Good than the mixtures. In turn, members of Mixture themselves can be hierarchically arranged depending on the extent to which reason presides over the combination of Limit and Unlimited in each of them. This is why we can speak of some mixed things being more beautiful or more harmonious than others. Last in this hierarchical order is the Unlimited with its own members, all in flux and lacking determination. The hierarchical order of various types of pleasure and knowledge, which we will be witnessing in detail in the next section, as well as the superiority of knowledge over pleasure become intelligible in light of this metaphysical background.

Another indication that Plato's Socrates conceives of the philosopher's need to use the divine method always in correlation with the fourfold model of reality is that, while the method of division is said to be applicable and useful in all sciences and all crafts (16c), including the imprecise arts of music (56a) or navigation (56b), the dialectician's concern is with eternal and immutable objects (58a, 59a–b).[27] Correspondingly, then, the specific mark that distinguishes the philosophical from the nonphilosophical use of divisions and collections is that the former alone is aware of the ultimate assumptions on the basis of which collections and divisions are operated. Crafts make classifications without inquiring into their own ultimate presuppositions, while the dialecticians are always explicitly preoccupied with discerning and legitimizing their own and others' presuppositions. Socrates's earlier remark that the method is not very difficult to describe but extremely difficult to use (16c) makes full sense in light of this interpretation. The difficulty here at issue concerns the discovery of the natural joints, which prevent random cuts within unitary kinds.[28] While the difficulty in finding natural joints is encountered to some extent also in crafts and less precise types of knowledge, it is not as acutely present there as in philosophy, since the latter alone aims at offering an account of the classifications in terms of the ultimate structure of reality.

Finally, it makes perfect sense for a dialectical method to be connected to an understanding of the structure of reality in the way suggested above, even outside of the *Philebus*. In various dialogues Plato illustrates this relation, although he chooses to introduce different dialectical methods or, perhaps better, to specify varying aspects of the same, and to emphasize distinct but nonetheless complementary aspects of reality. Thus, in the *Meno* and the *Phaedo* Socrates uses the method of hypothesis upon the background of the three-terms model of reality disclosed through recollection: Forms-soul-sensible things. In the *Phaedrus*, Socrates applies a variant of collection and division within the same framework disclosed by recollection.

Taken together all these aspects invite the conclusion that the fourfold structure is not introduced to replace the divine method, or to complicate it in unnecessary ways, but rather to deepen the investigation of the good life and to reveal the method's fundamental metaphysical assumptions.

Using the Method and the Fourfold Model to Analyze Pleasure and Knowledge

Before we launch into Socrates's classifications of various types of pleasure and knowledge respectively and see how the dialectical method and the fourfold ontology are jointly involved in these, let us first clarify whether we have a unifying account of pleasure in the *Philebus* or not. Socrates starts off by identifying what I believe is the unifying aspect (*mia idea*) of all pleasures, namely, that they are perceived replenishments of lacks or perceived returns to our natural state (33d), and then proceeds to distinguish various types of pleasure. Some scholars, however, dispute the claim that this account is meant to hold for all pleasures. Thus, Gosling and Taylor (1982, 140), Hampton (1990, 73), and most recently Fletcher (2014, 113–42, and 2017, 179–208, esp. 195–206) have argued instead that Socrates does not provide a general unifying account for all pleasures and that he assumes that different types of pleasures have radically different natures. In a first phase, Gosling and Taylor rejected the restoration model as a general definition of pleasure on account that this model is only applicable to pleasures caused by an actual restoration of the body, and as such excludes anticipatory, emotional pleasures, and pure pleasures (Gosling and Taylor 1982, 136, 138). In an insightful and compelling article, Tuozzo significantly weakened the force of this worry by slightly amending the general account, while staying strictly aligned to the spirit of the dialogue, to say that pleasure is "a conscious psychic process caused either by a restoration of a natural harmony in body or soul, or by entertaining a representation of oneself as in the conditions that cause such restorative pleasure. To put it more briefly and only slightly misleadingly: pleasure may be caused by the image as well as by the reality of bodily or psychic restoration" (Tuozzo 1996, 513).

More recently, Fletcher attempted to resuscitate the view that there is no general account of pleasure in the *Philebus* by arguing that, while mixed pleasures are merely remedial and as such at most necessary ingredients of a good human life, pure and true ones are not merely necessary ingredients of a good life, but actually genuine goods for us and also an intrinsic component of the divine life itself. Consequently, Fletcher takes the characterization of pleasures as perceived replenishments of lacks at 31d, 32b, 33d to apply only to mixed bodily pleasures, not also to the pure ones. As evidence for this view she mentions (1) that the illustrations that Socrates gives of destruction (*phthora*) are all cases of physical imbalance, whether the organism is emptied of liquid or food, or excessively heated or cooled; (2) that right after his analysis of bodily pleasure and pain, Socrates states that this is "one kind (*hen eîdos*) of pleasure or pain" (32b6–7), thereby implying that there are other kinds too; and (3) that Socrates does not provide examples of how the restoration account could apply to the pleasures of anticipation or to other psychic pleasures (Fletcher 2014, 117). Fletcher's more recent work takes this view farther and argues that the absence of a unitary account of pleasure is responsible for the failure of the dialectical method to provide a systematic and complete division of pleasures (2017, 179–208).

In response to these arguments, note first that the dialectical method, which is applied throughout the dialogue to the classification of all pleasures, requires us to discover the one nature (*mia idea* 16d) that is the same among many, and throughout the dialogue there simply is no alternative account of pleasures to the one offered at 33d. Thus, *prima facie* at least, we have no reason to assume that there might be several accounts. Besides, Socrates never promised or attempted to provide a *complete* classification of all types of pleasures, but merely to illustrate the method's capacity to organize distinct varieties of one nature, and this he succeeds to do well. Furthermore, Socrates does *not* "state" that the account of pleasure as perceived replenishment belongs to one kind (*hen eîdos*) of pleasure or pain; he is *asking* Protarchus whether *he* believes that to be so, hence 32b6–7 is at most inconclusive regarding Socrates's commitment to there being different natures (*eidē*) for the various types of pleasures. Finally, the fact that, when the account of pleasure is first introduced all the examples provided are instances of physiological replenishments does not mean that this is the only kind of filling or replenishment possible. Most likely, Socrates provides illustrations of physical pleasures because these are the easiest type to grasp and as such most suited for that opening stage of the discussion. In fact, psychic pleasures are introduced immediately after (35e–36b, 47d–48a), and I see no obstacle in the way of conceiving of these as psychic replenishments. The fact that Socrates does not provide explicit accounts and illustrations of how psychic experiences can count as replenishments is not a reason to imagine that we cannot do so or that Plato would not want us to. Aside from the fact that the very experience of pleasure is soul-dependent insofar as it is never reducible to bodily motion, but rather requires explicitly *the awareness* or *perception of* that motion as a case of filling or restoration of balance (33d, 43a–c), it is in fact always the case that our replenishing is never strictly physical or physiological, but rather psycho-physical. For physical fillings or replenishments have an emotional echo, whether by awakening pleasant memories, or by stirring hopeful anticipations. Such emotional responses generate their own characteristic pleasures that fill our emotional needs and reestablish our emotional balance along with the physical one (35e–36b). As psychophysical beings and conglomerates of mixtures, bodily replenishments affect our emotional state and our psychic replenishments or depletions have an impact on how we perceive our bodily motions of filling or emptying. The memory of enjoying eating watermelon in the past is responsible for our pleasant anticipation of such replenishment in the future and the anticipation itself feels fulfilling to us.

Furthermore, pleasures of the soul alone, independently of the body, such as those connected with love, longing, laughter, or anger, for instance, may also be described as replenishments insofar as they satisfy our emotional needs and return us to a state of harmony and balance that had been previously disrupted. It is not accidental that Socrates characterizes pleasures interchangeably as perceived replenishments (*plērōsis*) of lacks (33d) and as restorations of balance (31d5). Their characterization as "restorations of balance" is wide enough to cover emotional along with physical pleasures, when "perceived fillings (*plērōsis*) of lacks" seems less apt to do so. If the specific illustration of the malicious person's experience of comedy reflects a false pleasure and, as such, a depletion rather than a replenishment (48a–50b), the text provides hints to see what a true experience of comedy and healthy laughter could feel like. Thus, early on Socrates refers to the lighthearted experience of joking that counterbalances seriousness when doing philosophy ("joking is a relief from seriousness," 30e), and talks about the way in which he might rightfully look ridiculous on account of the discrepancy between his modest rational means, on the one hand, and his high aspirations to uncover the ultimate articulation of reality (23d1–3), on the other, and later on we get a giggle or two on account of the way in which getting lost in abstract speculations can render philosophers oblivious to concrete circumstances (62a7–b9). These are all illustrations of pleasures of comedy that a well-disposed character can experience. In all these cases the pleasure experienced comes upon our perceiving a restoration of balance between the too light and too serious. As the complex conglomerate of mixture that we are as human beings, we need the right ratio of light- and heavy-heartedness just as much as we need the right ratio between full and empty stomach or too much or too little of drink. Witnessing a hilarious situation is pleasant insofar as it generates our awareness of relief from a tensed or too serious mood and, as such, it fills us with the needed amount of relaxation and light spirit.

Pure pleasures too can be regarded as restorations of balance and fillings of lack. Translating *plērōsis* as *re-plenishment* is somewhat misleading. *Plērōsis* means, literally, "filling," while re-plenishment (*anaplērōsis*) means a re-filling, but Plato never uses *anaplērōsis*. Talk about *re*plenishment makes us presuppose that the experience occurs after a prior depletion, and as such it is most adequate to characterize physiological pleasures such as eating or drinking, but causes difficulties in understanding how it could apply also to our pure pleasures, given that those are by definition not preceded by pain: What must have been first present, and then absent, to be *re*-plenished by our *pure* pleasures of smell, of pure colors and sounds, or of learning? Sensitive to this nuance, Garner wisely chooses to translate the original more literally as "fulfilments" rather than "replenishments" and to envision re-plenishments as derivative sense characteristic primarily to reoccurring experiences that we get through eating, drinking, or sleep, etc. (Garner 2017, 71–78). While I think that it might be best to translate *plērōsis* literally as *filling*, avoiding thus also the sense of completion or finality that is present in the notion of "fulfillment," I will be using both filling and replenishment for it throughout this book. Once we think about pleasure *primarily* as *perceived filling*, we have no difficulty applying this characterization to our pure pleasures. They fill in us unperceived lacks. As finite beings we are always in a condition of lack on account of our finitude. Pure pleasures are experiences whereby we are aware of gradual returns to a natural balance, gradual transitions toward closer approximations of our normative state of well-being.

Ultimately, there is a metaphysical sense of replenishment at play in the *Philebus*. A fuller discussion of this metaphysical sense will be saved for chapter VI, yet it is important to sketch, if only in outline at this point, the gist of that notion. As finite beings we are constantly in the condition of lack and constantly eager to get closer to our normative state. Our experiences are fulfilling when they are perceived as getting us closer to that state and are depleting when they get us farther afield from it. The ratios that represent our respective normative states differ from one person to another and are taking into account the whole project of our life as a whole. That Plato's Socrates is primarily concerned with the project of our life as a whole emerges clearly in a number of passages (11d6, 20b–23b, 43c8, c13, d7–9, e8, 66a–c). It is then relative to the ultimate aim of a good life that we are to determine what is truly filling or replenishing and to what extent, and what is depleting. The metaphysical sense of replenishment at stake, then, is one according to which feeling replenished means being aware of coming ever closer to instantiating the Good in our lives, which means approaching the ratio of mixtures that qualifies as the normative state of well-being that we can have given our specific strengths, weaknesses, and circumstances in life as such.

Our earlier discussion of Socrates's analysis of musical and linguistic sound showed that the application of the dialectical method does not have to start by identifying as the unitary aspect or form (16d1) an eternal and immutable paradigm, and can instead start with a provisional account. Hence, this is all we need to assume at this point about the identification of pleasure as perceived replenishment of a lack.

It might surprise us at first that, instead of starting with a classification of what are properly called pleasures, Socrates begins by discerning types of false pleasures and only afterward proceeds to examine their true and pure counterparts. One reason why Plato's Socrates proceeds this way is probably connected to his attempt to offer a persuasive account to someone like Protarchus who, as heir of Philebus's position, privileges bodily pleasures, and it is some of these that will turn out primarily, though not exclusively, to be false. Another reason has perhaps to do with the gradual dialectical transformation of the understanding of pleasure, which we are witnessing throughout the dialogue and which will be examined in full detail in the next chapter. This transformation requires that, by the time Socrates can offer a satisfactory account of true pleasures, he must have already revealed a number of criteria for excluding their false counterparts.

The three types of false pleasure are not discovered through an application of the dialectical method to pleasure itself, precisely because false pleasures fall short of sharing in that unitary aspect of a perceived replenishment of a lack that collectively characterizes pleasure as pleasure. Rather, they are discovered through an application of that method to falsehood itself as it is manifest in pleasures, in beliefs, fears, and expectations (36c). Since falsehood as such can be defined as taking the unreal for the real or the real for the unreal (*Sophist* 261a), the three cases of false pleasures are cases of mistaking nonreplenishments for presumed replenishments. The types of false pleasure that Socrates identifies are: the falsity that infects our pleasures of anticipation, the falsity regarding the estimation of the degree of pleasure experienced, and the case in which we mistake pleasure for a neutral state of neither pleasure nor pain. Let us take a brief look at each of these types of false pleasures, following that more detailed analyses of these pleasures will be given in chapters II and IV.

False pleasures of anticipation occur when we experience pain simultaneously with pleasure, as for instance, when our body suffers pain and our soul enjoys the pleasant anticipation of the filling needed by the body. In some of these cases, Socrates argues, our anticipatory pleasures are false (36c–40e). Scholars have often interpreted the falsehood at issue as due exclusively to the falsehood of our *factual* beliefs about the future (Waterfield 1982, 23–24; Irwin 1995, 328–30; Gosling 1975, 214–18; Frede 1993, 444–46; Guthrie 1978, 220; Oghihara 2012, 308). On that account, if I believe that I will get a large amount of money when in fact I will not, not only my belief, but also the pleasure I currently take in the expectation that my belief will turn out true, is false. But, as I will argue in detail in chapters II and IV, Socrates's point here is not, or at least not primarily, that anticipatory pleasures are false because our belief about the future event will turn out not to correspond to the facts. Rather, his point is that they are false due to the falsity of our assumption that the expected object, whether it actually occurs or not, is in fact pleasant or will bring about the expected replenishment. On this interpretation, both a good and a wicked person may enjoy the prospect of earning a sum of money, whether their factual beliefs will turn out true in the future or not. The difference between the good person's true pleasure and the wicked person's false pleasure resides in that the former enjoys the prospect of earning money within legitimate limits and for legitimate reasons (e.g., as a means to secure for themselves a decent life and/or as a means to benefit others), whereas the latter does not (e.g., he/she regards it as a means to become utterly rich and/or to make other people envious of their wealth). True pleasures originate in one's ability to identify proper objects of desire, while false pleasures originate in failure to do so (Hampton 1990, 57–59; Moes 2000, 140–41; Harte 2004, 111–28; Carpenter 2006, 5–26).

A second type of false pleasures arises from deceptions regarding the intensity of pleasure and pain when they are assessed on account of the immediacy or remoteness of their corresponding objects (41a–42c). Just as we are inclined to mistake the actual size of things when we see them from too close by or from afar, so too we are inclined to mistake the actual intensity of our pleasures and pains when they are compared only relative to each other and relative to the immediacy or remoteness of their occurrence, and not evaluated for their intrinsic worth by appeal to an absolute standard.

Finally, the third type of false pleasures here addressed makes even more explicit than the previous cases that the truth or falsity of our pleasures depends on whether or not the object enjoyed is in fact an object worthy of being enjoyed. False pleasures of the third type occur when we mistake a neutral condition of absence of pleasure or pain for genuine pleasure (42c–44d). Those who think they experience pleasure when they are simply not in a condition of pain experience a false pleasure. And those who believe they are experiencing pain simply because they are not experiencing pleasure experience a false pain, a situation discussed also in *Republic* 584e–585a.

Let us now see how the application of the dialectical method in the horizon of the metaphysical fourfold articulation helps us understand Socrates's classifications of various types of pleasure and knowledge in the *Philebus*. Applying the dialectical procedure of collection and division to pleasure, once we discover the unitary form of *perceptible replenishment of a lack* to cover all pleasures, we are to seek the two or three or however many subdivisions of it, and to continue the same operations until we reach the *infimae species* beyond which we let individual pleasures run loosely in their indefinite plurality.

Socrates thus starts by dividing pleasures into two: mixed and pure, depending on whether what is filled is a perceptible or a nonperceptible lack, respectively. Thus, while all pleasures presuppose a lack to be filled by them, only mixed or impure pleasures presuppose our earlier conscious experience of that lack as painful, while pure pleasures do not. Mixed pleasures are in turn subdivided into: pleasures of the body alone, of the soul and body, and of the soul alone (46b–c). Of the first, Socrates mentions the experience of itching and scratching and sexual pleasures (46d–47a). As instances of mixed pleasures of body and soul Socrates invokes the examples of the body's condition of pain in situations of hunger or thirst and the soul's simultaneous pleasant anticipation of a filling with food or drink (47c–d, 31e–32c). Finally, of the mixed pleasures of the soul alone Socrates mentions those we experience in wrath, fear, longing, lamentations, love, jealousy, and the state experienced in watching comedy or tragedy (47e–50d). As for pure pleasures, Socrates mentions here the pleasures of learning (51e–52a), those we take in the beauty of geometrical shapes accessible through diagrams drawn with the ruler and compass (51c–d), pleasures we take in smooth and bright sounds (51d), or those associated with smells (51e).

A schematic representation of these classes has the following look:

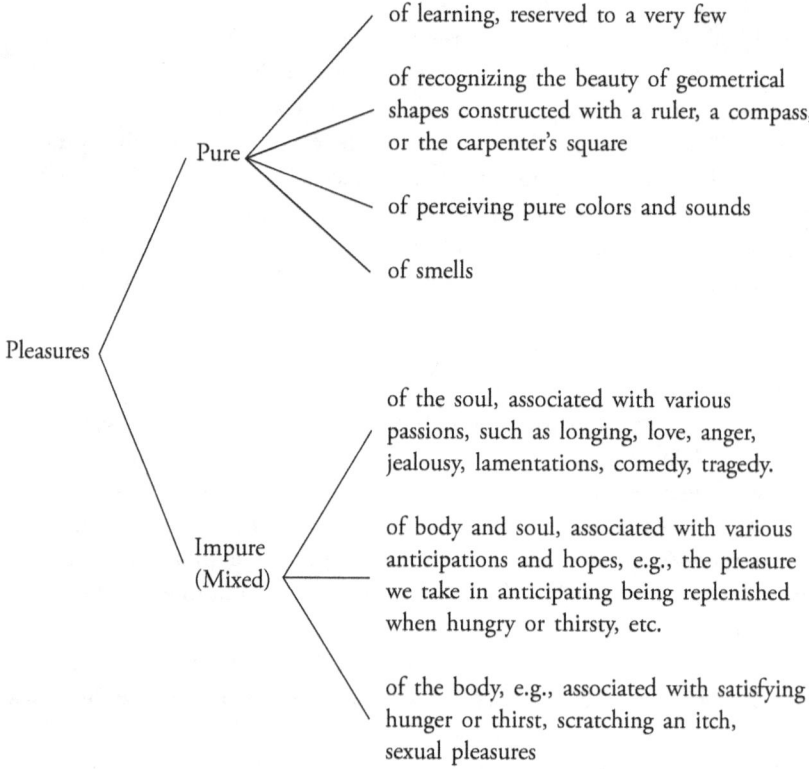

The fourfold model of reality is presupposed in the background of this analysis. Although, as I will argue in the next chapter, all true pleasures belong to the class of Mixtures (52c–d), they are not all of equal value. The axiological difference among members of the mixed class depends upon the degree to which reason (*noûs*) presides over the combination of Limit and the Unlimited in various cases. Thus, since the pleasures of learning and of contemplating the beauty of geometrical shapes are more akin to the activity of a divine reason (*noûs*) than the pleasures of smell, the former are superior to the latter (51c–e). Furthermore, the fact that, within the class of true pleasures, which includes pure and some of the mixed pleasures, the pure ones are superior to the mixed ones is again understandable in light of the same general assumptions. Pure pleasures are always measured and manifest the presence of limit; mixed pleasures often grow wild and lose measure and limitation and are thus easily threatened by falsehood. Nevertheless, as we shall see in chapter III, Socrates does not consider all the mixed pleasures to be false. When he discusses the three types of falsehood that can infect our pleasures associated with pain Socrates does not say or imply that every time we experience a mixture of pleasure and pain we experience false pleasures. Both a bulimic and a healthy person can enjoy eating after having suffered from hunger. The difference between the former's false pleasure and the latter's true pleasure is a difference in the aspects of eating that they enjoy: bulimic individuals falsely enjoy the overstimulation caused by excessive amounts of food, whereas healthy people rightly enjoy the natural replenishment through the moderate amounts they consume.

The classification and hierarchical ordering of various types of knowledge is made by reference to the nature of the objects of our cognitive experiences (55c–59c). Socrates rates as lowest the knowledge associated with the less precise of the productive arts, guided by lucky guesses (flute playing, medicine, agriculture, navigation, strategy), followed by the more precise productive arts (shipbuilding, house building). Next in the order of value is the knowledge associated with educational arts. In this category we discern first applied, vulgar mathematics (the "arithmetic of the many," who "compute sums of unequal units, such as two armies or two herds of cattle, or any two units regardless whether they are very small or huge" (56d9–e1) and, higher still, pure mathematics (56e–57a). In fact, it is admittedly unclear whether Socrates means to offer a distinctive place to vulgar mathematics among the educational arts or regards it as merely the part responsible for precision in the more productive arts such as shipbuilding and house building. We need not be too unsettled, however, by this ambiguity, which might very well be intentional. It suggests that there is continuity among the branches of knowledge listed, each of them exhibiting varying degrees of precision. Educational arts are superior to the productive sort by virtue of their greater share of measure or proportion and thus implicitly certainty and precision. Most valuable of all is the knowledge of dialectic, since it is the discipline "concerned with being and with what is really and forever in every way eternally the same . . . by far the truest kind of knowledge" (58a1–5). The classification of these branches of knowledge is not meant to be exhaustive. What matters most in it is identifying dialectic as the highest among all the branches of knowledge, and understanding that the various types of knowledge differ from one another in terms of degrees of certainty and precision. Correspondingly, while the branches remain distinct, the gap between them is *in practice* bridgeable, in the simple sense that moving from one branch of knowledge to another is a matter of increasing the certainty or precision of the respective art. It is in this sense that the ambiguous placement of vulgar mathematics somewhere between practical arts such as shipbuilding, house building, and the educational art of pure mathematics is relevant for emphasizing the continuity in practice between the various arts.

The hierarchy of types of knowledge in the *Philebus* generally follows the *Republic*'s Divided Line (509d–511e) and its educational curriculum (514a–534c). The lowest crafts based on guesswork and conjecture (*eikazein*) have a direct correspondent in the Divided Line's lowest section (*eikasia*); the more precise crafts (shipbuilding and house building) correspond to belief (*pistis*); the pure mathematical studies correspond to the level of thought (*dianoia*); dialectic fits with reason or understanding (*noēsis*). Vulgar or applied mathematics is distinguished from pure mathematics in the *Republic* as well (525b–527c), and both types of study straddle the line between belief (*pistis*) and understanding (*noēsis*). Although throughout *Philebus* 55c–58a Socrates uses the terms for crafts (*technai*) and branches of knowledge (*epistēmai*) interchangeably, the dialogue maintains the epistemological distinction between knowledge proper (restricted to dialectic) and opinion (assigned to the crafts) as drawn in the middle dialogues, and specifies their objects as Being and becoming, respectively (58e–59b).

In a schematic presentation, then, here is the classification of knowledge that Plato's Socrates provides in the *Philebus*:

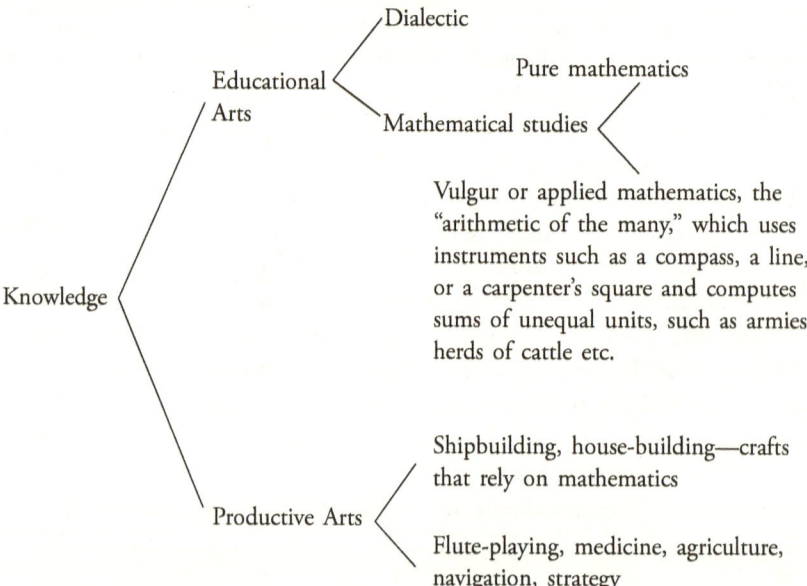

That the application of the dialectical method is directed throughout by guidelines imposed by the structure of the reality to which it is applied is strongly supported in the last part of the dialogue, where the highest Forms through which the Good discloses itself—Beauty, Proportion, and Truth—become active criteria employed both in the discovery of natural joints for each kind and in adjudicating the superiority of some kinds over others. Thus, the criteria used to assess the superiority of pure over impure pleasures are Purity, Beauty, and Truth (52d–53c); those used to establish the superiority of the pleasure attendant upon our contemplation of the beauty of mathematical shapes over the "less divine" pleasures of smell are Measure or Proportion and Truth (51c–e); those used for adjudicating superiority among various kinds of knowledge or crafts are Purity (55c), Truth (55c, 57 d), Certainty (*saphesteran* 57b), Precision (*akribeia* 55a, 57d), and the use of measure and number (56e, 57d). Dialectic is declared superior to Gorgias's type of rhetoric on account of its Clarity, Precision, and Truth, which Socrates explicitly opposes to the alternative criteria of grandeur, nobility, and usefulness to us (58a–c). Finally, the criteria for assessing the superiority of knowledge over pleasure are again Measure, Beauty, and Truth (65c–e). Clearly, then, the dialectical method of divisions is intimately connected with the assumptions about the reality that the dialectician collects and divides. A nonphilosophical view, say one according to which Pragmatic Usefulness and Grandeur would be more dignified than Beauty, Proportion, and Truth, would recognize more prestige and value in Gorgias's rhetoric than in dialectical reasoning. But then, again, the "good" that would express itself primarily through Pragmatic, as opposed to rational, value would no longer be the Good of a rational universe that allows for "sufficient limit" amid the plenitude of limitlessness (30c4).[29]

The divine method helps us not only to discern the classes of pleasure and knowledge and their axiological hierarchy, but also to understand how pleasure and knowledge can be combined as ingredients of a good human life (61d–66d). When Socrates sets himself to combining various types of pleasure with knowledge as parts of a good life, he refuses to go about it by randomly mixing every kind of knowledge with every kind of pleasure (61c–d). Once the classes of pleasure and knowledge are mapped onto the fourfold model of reality we see that true pure pleasures, the only ones that are welcomed in the final combination as ingredients of the good life, pertain to the class of mixtures (52c–d).[30] Knowledge, for its part, is most akin to the rational cause of the mixtures (*noũs*). In a sense, then, both pleasure and knowledge mediate between Limit and the Unlimited, knowledge mediating on the side of Limit, and pleasure on that of the Unlimited. There is obvious kinship between the purest pleasures of learning and the highest Forms of knowledge, and there is affinity in general between true pleasures and the various types of knowledge by virtue of their common share in Proportion, Beauty, and Truth. Their common share of intelligible aspects is metaphorically depicted through their personified dialogue in which types of both welcome each other (61d–64a). It is obvious that the pleasures that enter this dialogue are only the true ones, since it would be impossible for a member of the irrational class (*apeiron*) to express itself through rational discourse, let alone to welcome through discourse the most pure and elevated types of knowledge, including self-knowledge (63b–c). In dialogue with reason, pleasures themselves agree with knowledge in disparaging their own false counterparts, which stand in the way of a good life. The situation is telling for Plato's insistence on the need for a fully integrated soul within which appetitive, emotional, and rational parts speak in unison.[31]

Finally, let us return for a moment to the three One-Many puzzles that prefaced the introduction of the dialectical method. The questions concern the existence of Forms, the possibility of Forms preserving their unity and self-identity in relation to other Forms, and the possibility of Forms preserving their unity and self-identity in relation to the sensible things that have a share in them. Notice that Plato acknowledges the perennial nature of these puzzles (15d). Hence, we should not assume that he intends to solve them here once and for all. What Socrates criticizes is not the presence of the One and the Many in discourse, for this simply reflects the nature of reality, but the misuse that eristic debaters make of it and their way of abusing *logos* generally (16e4–17a3).

To the first puzzle the answer is that Forms, which have been disclosed as absolute standards of reality, must be assumed to have real, and not just conceptual, existence if we intend the classifications and hierarchical orderings of pleasure and knowledge to have objective and universal value. In the absence of universal and absolute Forms, our divisions proceed randomly, and every time we return to divide one subject we cut it at arbitrary joints. The dialogue does not offer a demonstration for the existence of Forms, but it presents us with an architectonic that is coherent and meaningful only on the assumption that Forms are real as sources of Limit, and not mere thoughts.

The second puzzle focuses on systematic relations among Forms. By contrast to the practitioners of less precise arts, the dialectician's task is to keep applying the method until he reaches the ultimate metaphysical assumptions that validate a classification. The dialectician discovers this ground only by studying the interrelations among Forms themselves in light of the Good. Thus, while for instance the musicologist rightfully distinguishes among themselves low, high, and equal pitch, respectively, and advances as far as to study the mathematical relations among them, the dialectician alone can provide an ultimate justification of the musicologist's procedure, by revealing the natural kinds as articulations of the overall Goodness or rationality of the whole.

Finally, the third puzzle concerns the presence of Forms in sensible things: If the Form is wholly present in each sensible thing that partakes of it, the Form becomes plural and thus loses its self-identity, while if the Form is only partly present in things, the Form is partitioned and thus no longer a universal. In the *Phaedo*, the *Republic*, and the *Parmenides* Plato has Socrates approach this problem in terms of participation of particulars in the Forms. In the *Philebus*, he approaches it in terms of Forms being sources of Limit and the rational Cause (*aitia*) bringing Limit to the Unlimited. The fourfold structure of reality guards us against assimilating properties of Forms to those pertaining to mixtures: it helps us avoid confusing the way in which Forms can be present in sensible things with the way in which sensible things or properties can be present in other instances of the same rank. This explanation dissolves the initial paradox, since it opens up the possibility that Forms can be wholly present in each particular partaking of them yet without losing their self-identity and unity, since they are intelligible and not sensible components of things. For on this new understanding Forms are present in instances of Mixtures insofar as Forms are sources of the ratios that prescribe the normative range of balances corresponding to one or another nature or type of thing. The Form is then fully present in the particular thing the way in which a recipe is fully present without partition in a cake that embodies it or the way a mathematical equation is expressed through an individual object embodying those measures and ratios.

The unity of Socrates's treatment of the good life in the *Philebus* rests upon the idea that the dialectical method needs to be carried far enough to disclose its own ultimate metaphysical presuppositions. But if this is so, the method both takes its guidance from and is supposed to discover the ultimate structure of reality. The apparent circularity here, however, is not a vicious one, but one that discloses the typical nature of dialectical progress. Application of the method explains our access to an understanding of the fourfold model, and that model in turn justifies the natural joints at which the method divides categories into subclasses. The dialectician does not start with absolute mastery over either one of these ends; he proceeds by refining each of them gradually while making use of both. Plato's own nondogmatic approach to philosophy is an excellent example of how an open-ended view of the method and the reality it applies to can work positively for dialectic.

II

The Placement of Pleasure and Knowledge in the Fourfold Articulation of Reality

As already witnessed in the previous chapter, the *Philebus* develops around the question as to whether pleasure or knowledge is more akin to the good and ends up identifying the place of each of these two competitors among the ingredients of a good human life. Two major instruments are introduced and used in this investigation: the dialectical method of collection and division and the fourfold structure of reality, consisting of Limit, the Unlimited, the Mixture of these two, and the Cause of their mixture. Traditional interpretations have typically placed pleasure in the class of the Unlimited and knowledge either in that of Limit or, sometimes, in that of the Cause of mixtures, a view defended, among others, by Frede, Hackforth, A. E. Taylor, Irwin, Russell, and Vogt.[1] The aim of this chapter is twofold. It attempts (1) to challenge the received interpretation and to defend instead the view that pleasures, insofar as they are true, belong to the class of Mixtures, while knowledge and its cognates are among Causes of mixtures; and (2) to explore some of the major consequences that the right placement of pleasure and knowledge on the metaphysical map have for the good life. I am going to argue that the proper metaphysical placement of the two ingredients helps us understand that for Plato pleasure is causally dependent upon and structured by knowledge. Thus, throughout this chapter we are going to witness how a mediation between pleasure and knowledge is possible, so much so that by the end of the *Philebus* we find the two in dialogue with each other, while at the start they appeared to be completely foreign to each other, separated by an unsurpassable gap.

To this end, after a brief reminder of the fourfold articulation of reality, which we discussed in more detail in the previous chapter, we take a close look at the textual passages relevant for the placement of pleasure and knowledge (I); and then we look at the implications of the placement of pleasure in the class of Mixtures and of knowledge on the class of Cause (II). I am going to argue that Socrates's identification of pleasure as a Mixture and of knowledge as Cause of mixtures accounts for the fact that we witness throughout the dialogue a gradual progression from the initial unbridgeable gap between pleasure and knowledge to an intimate collaboration between them that culminates in the personified dialogue, whereby types of pleasure welcome the relevant types of knowledge, and knowledge in turn invites pleasure in the good human life. I suggest that this shift, or better, dialectical development of the nature of pleasure, reflects a transition from the Phileban conception of pleasure as thoughtless thrill or sensation to the Platonic understanding of pleasure as cognitively structured experience that depends on our beliefs not only about factual situations, but also about the meaning and value of such situations for life generally.

The discussion here developed will not only offer some insights into the complex nature of pleasure as causally structured by knowledge, but will also address some of the voices woefully lamenting the "disunity" of the *Philebus*, by showing how the classification of pleasure and knowledge and the whole ethical discussion fit into the fourfold articulation of reality and can only be understood in relation to that.[2]

As witnessed already, Socrates proposes that "all the things that are now in the all" (*panta ta nūn en tō panti*, 23c4) can be divided into four kinds: Limit (*to peras*), the Unlimited (*to apeiron*), the Mixture (*to meikton*) of the two, and the Cause (*hē aitía*) of their mixture. The Unlimited is a domain of indefiniteness, indetermination, and excess, containing as members continua governed by the more and less, the stronger and milder, and the too much, as structural principles (24e7–25a1). Limit, by contrast, is a principle of measure, order, and determination, and as such its members act as ordering causes when applied to the Unlimited, bringing about the harmony of the fluctuating opposites by imposing definite number on them (25d11–e2). In the context of our present concern with pleasure, imposition of order on the Unlimited aspect of pleasures is said to save pleasures from ruin (26b7–c1). I take that to mean that the presence of Limit is responsible for the preservation of nature among the things it limits.

The class of Mixtures includes things that come to be (*gignomena* 26e3, *to gignomenon* 27a11), or are produced (*poioumenon* 27a1, a6), hence things that manifest a relative degree of order, and proportion that ensures that they preserve their nature as coming into being (*genesis eis ousian*, 26d8). Unlike the members of the Unlimited, which are in permanent flux, members of Mixture enjoy a relative permanence.³ Finally, the fourth kind, the Cause of mixtures, maker of the universe, responsible for the production of all these (*to panta tauta demiourgoūn* 27b1), presides over the mixture of Limit with Unlimitedness. Just as a divine universal reason ensures the cosmic manifestation of measure and proportion, so too our own human reason is responsible for the manifestation of measure and proportion in a good human life (28e–30).

The four classes constitute the horizon of meaning and intelligibility within which the various types of knowledge and the varieties of pleasure are to be understood.

The Placement of Pleasure and Knowledge on the Fourfold Metaphysical Map

The received view is that pleasure pertains to the class of the Unlimited, while knowledge either to that of Limit or to that of Cause. Three passages seem to support the placement of pleasures in the Unlimited: 27e–28b, 31a, and 65c–d. When we take each of them in turn and read them in their respective contexts, we see, however, that these passages in fact refer only to sybaritic pleasures, and therefore we have good reasons to resist the relegation of all of our pleasures to the Unlimited.

The first passage runs as follows:

> Do pleasure and pain have limit or are they the sort that receive the more and less? —Certainly the sort that receive the more, Socrates! For how else could pleasures be all good, if they were not by nature unlimited in multitude and in intensity? —But nor would pain be all bad, Philebus. So that we need to look for something other than the unlimited nature that would provide pleasures with a certain measure of good. Thus, *for you* (*soi*) however, pleasures are assigned to the unlimited. (27e5–28a4)

Though this passage has sometimes been cited as evidence for the view that Socrates places pleasure in the Unlimited, it constitutes in fact a rejection of that view.⁴ Note that Socrates stresses the second person singular pronoun in his reply to Philebus: "Thus, for you (*soi*) however, pleasures are assigned to the unlimited" (28a3). Socrates proceeds here by means of a *reductio* argument, according to which, if pleasure's goodness were due to its share in the Unlimited, then pain, which admits of the more and less, should also be good on that account (27e–28a). Pain, however, is obviously bad. And the more unlimited it is, the worse it is. Hence, since the Unlimited cannot be both cause of goodness (in pleasure) and cause of badness (in pain) it must be that something other than their unlimited character is responsible for the goodness inherent in pleasures. Pleasures, then, certainly have a share of the Unlimited, but their constitution is not confined to that kind. Notice also that in this exchange Socrates appeals to a notion of the "unlimited" different from the one he introduced in the earlier conversation with Protarchus (24a–25a). In the earlier passage (24a–25a), the Unlimited referred to several pairs of mutually relative and gradient opposites, where the more of one implies the less of the other, whereas in the present argument, the "unlimited" simply means absence of an upper boundary, more and more. What happens is that Socrates appeals here to Philebus's own notion of the "unlimited" precisely in order to show that the sybaritic pleasures which he defends lack the required measure and moderation provided by limit. All the more then, this passage cannot be taken at all as evidence that Socrates assigns pleasure to the Unlimited, in the sense introduced at 24a–25a.

The second time when pleasure is explicitly assigned to the Unlimited is when Socrates declares, "Let us then keep in mind these things about both, that reason is akin to a cause and of its kind, while pleasure, on the other hand, is unlimited and neither has nor will ever have either beginning, or middle, or end" (31a7–10). This declaration comes, however, at the end of a stretch of conversation in which the interlocutors have only been dealing with the hedonist, Phileban conception of pleasure, while Socrates has not yet had the chance to introduce what he takes true pleasures to be. Indeed, the passage just quoted (31a7–10) summarizes the conversation at lines 27e–31a, which addressed exclusively Philebus's view of pleasure, and hence only the sybaritic pleasures, with their supposed boundlessness, and does not invoke in any way Socrates's own view. Therefore, I suggest that the passage we are looking at reflects at that stage only a tentative and provisional view, one that, as we shall see, is going to be refined in what follows.

In addition, we might also read the reference to the unlimitedness of pleasures at 31a7–10 as a phenomenological description of the experience of pleasures, and not a reference to their ontological status.[5] If so, the passage simply acknowledges that our experience of pleasures *feels* somehow indefinite and unlimited. There might well be implicitly at play throughout the dialogue a distinction between a phenomenological account of the way we experience pleasure and an ontological account of what pleasure means when mapped onto the fourfold articulation of reality. Phenomenologically, our experience of at least some pleasures could well be described as lacking beginning, middle, or end, thus being unlimited, and Socrates too could accept that characterization; ontologically, nevertheless, true pleasure is placed in the class of Mixtures, and not in that of the Unlimited. Philebus can recognize only the phenomenological aspect of pleasures, his anti-intellectualism making the idea of an ontological model unavailable to him. Protarchus starts off by defending Philebus's view of pleasures and thus it makes perfect sense that Socrates has to address also the phenomenological aspect of our experience of pleasure alongside the ontological aspect of its proper metaphysical placement. As long as we know each time whether we are talking about the way we experience pleasure or about what pleasure strictly speaking means for the project of a good human life, there should be no confusion, and the accounts are to be seen as complementary sides of a complex view. Since Mixture is an especially densely and diversely populated class, with members varying from some that border on Limit to others that border on the Unlimited, it makes a lot of sense to say that to us, mixtures bordering on the Unlimited might already *feel* altogether unlimited. Ontologically, pleasures are mixtures, while phenomenologically at least some of them *feel* unlimited, especially when we assess them by comparison and contrast to other, more limited experiences that we have.[6]

Finally, at 65c–d, close to the end of the dialogue, we hear Protarchus speak about pleasures as the greatest impostors of all due to their lack of limit and measure. It seems, however, by the way he refers to them as "greatest impostors" and compares them with "children lacking even the least bit of reason" (65d1), that Protarchus has in mind the pleasures that Socrates has just shown to be false, or else that he must have missed much of Socrates's point throughout the conversation.

As we now turn to the following three passages, we see that Socrates has been associating throughout true pleasures with mixtures.[7] To begin with the first:

> The goddess herself, fair Philebus, recognizes how excess and all kinds of wickedness allow for no limit to pleasures and their fulfillment, and she therefore places instead law and order as a

limit on them. And while you say that this ruins them, I, by contrast, say that this is their salvation. (26b7–c1)

The text contrasts Socrates's with Philebus's understanding of pleasure by showing that partaking of Limit is responsible for pleasures' maintenance of their own nature.

A second text along similar lines is even more explicit in recognizing pleasures among the members of the mixed class:

> Pleasure and pain seem to me to come to be both together by nature in the common kind. —Remind us again, dear Socrates, which one of the kinds mentioned do you wish to indicate as the common kind? —I will do so as best as I can, my amazing Philebus. —That is noble of you. —We named common the one that we listed as third out of the four. —You mean the one that you introduced after the Unlimited and the Limit, the one in which you placed also health and I believe also harmony? —Excellently stated. (31c2–d1)

A third passage spells out clearly that true pleasures are in the class of Mixtures, while excessive ones in that of the Unlimited:[8]

> We will place those pleasures which admit the great and the intense, whether frequently or rarely, to the class of the Unlimited, the more and less, which affects both body and soul; and we will assign the other pleasures to the class of things that possess measurement. (52c4–d1)

In addition, the generic characterization of pleasure as perceived replenishment of a lack or return to a natural balance of an organism (31d4–10, 33d) also supports the placement of pleasures in the category of Mixtures rather than in that of the Unlimited, for it associates pleasure with balance and regards it as something perceptible.[9]

With the textual ground cleared up as far as pleasure is concerned, turning toward knowledge, we see it as a function of reason and, thus, most properly counted as part of the Cause of mixtures together with reason (*noũs*) and wisdom (*phronēsis* 28a4, *sophia* 30b4, c6). When he starts off the investigation of the fourth kind, the Cause, Socrates asks to which of the natural kinds we should assign reason (*noũs*), knowledge (*epistēmē*), and wisdom (*sophia*) 28c. At the very end of the argument, whose main aim is to identify the Cause of mixtures as the fourth kind, Socrates declares that this stretch of reasoning served also toward identifying the kind to which knowledge, reason, and wisdom belong (30e). The argument proceeds along these lines:

a. Elements like fire and earth are present both in our own individual bodies and in the universe as a whole. (29b)

b. The fire and earth and all the other elements pertaining to the universe are purer at the cosmic level than at the level of our own bodies. (29c)

c. The cosmic elements act as source of the elements in us. (29c–e)

d. Our own body is also ruled by a soul. (30a)

e. Our own soul must then, similarly, have its own source and origin in a soul that pertains to the cosmos at large. (30b)

f. While the universe as a whole is ruled by a divine rational mind, our own lives too are ordered and arranged by reason, though our own reason has weaker power and lower degree of purity than the cosmic reason. (30b)

g. This cosmic soul then possesses the wisdom that acts as an ultimate Cause arranging all mixtures. (30c–e)

h. Hence, knowledge or wisdom belongs to the fourth kind, that of the Cause of mixtures, and the various degrees of wisdom account for the more or less harmonious combinations of Limit and Unlimited in mixtures. (30e)[10]

The Relation between Pleasure and Knowledge in Light of Their Placement on the Metaphysical Map

Let's proceed now to examine the implications of the right placement of pleasure and knowledge on the metaphysical map. I believe that Socrates's identification of pleasure as Mixture and of knowledge as Cause of mixtures accounts for the possibility of the progression that we witness throughout the dialogue from the initial unbridgeable distance between pleasure and knowledge toward a more and more intimate collaboration, culminating in the personified dialogue between them, whereby types of pleasure welcome the relevant types of knowledge, and knowledge in turn invites pleasure along in the good human life. Let us go through the main moments of the dialectical development of the concept of pleasure. This development marks a transition from Philebus's conception of pleasure as thoughtless thrill or momentary sensation to the Platonic understanding of pleasure, as intentionally and cognitively structured experience that depends on our beliefs about the meaning and value of such experiences for life generally.[11] There will be ten such moments for us to survey that will help us configure the trajectory mentioned above. It is worth paying close attention to the gradual transitions from one step to the next. Here goes the first:

[1] The dialogue opens up with a clear separation between pleasure and knowledge, as if to suggest that they have nothing whatsoever in common with each other. Thus, in Socrates's formulation:

> So, Philebus, on the one hand, says that what is good for all the living beings is to enjoy themselves, and to be pleased and delighted, and all the other things that harmonize with these. For us, however, on the other hand, it is not these, but rather knowing, understanding and remembering, and all the things akin to these, right opinion and true calculation that are better than pleasures and more agreeable for all those who can partake of them. (11b4–c1)

From the absolute separation between pleasure and knowledge declared in this passage the conversation will move to reveal gradually an intimate connection between them. It is precisely because he assumes this complete separation between the two that Philebus, the extreme hedonist who champions sybaritic pleasures, drops out of the conversation after a mere few lines of dialogue, inviting Protarchus to adopt and defend his view. Perhaps even more adequate than calling him an extreme hedonist, we ought to call Philebus a merely would-be-extreme-hedonist, since he has no understanding whatsoever of what pleasure really is. Philebus's refusal to engage in argument, his dropping out altogether of the conversational scene dramatically, illustrate his commitment to the view that pleasure has no affinity whatsoever with knowledge and has no cognitive component whatsoever.

[2] The connection between pleasure and knowledge is made for the first time in the text in a negative manner, revealing at first the false, exces-

sive pleasures that the eristic debaters, newcomers to the use of arguments and discourse generally experience when they misuse arguments:

> Whoever among the young has gotten a taste for it [for the condition of discourse that makes each thing one and many] is as pleased as if he has discovered a treasure of wisdom, he is possessed by pleasure and takes delight in moving every argument, now turning it to one side and rolling it up into one, then again unrolling it and dividing it up, throwing first of all and most of all himself into confusion (*aporia*), and then also whoever else happens to be around, whether younger or older, or of the same age, sparing neither his father nor his mother or anyone else who might listen to him. (15d8–16a1)

This passage is not yet showing positively the contribution that knowledge has to pleasure, as it talks only about ignorance with its associated false pleasure and it also leaves ambiguous whether the confusion is the result of the "pleasure," or rather the source thereof, or both. Suffice it to say that we witness early on in the text a connection between the two, a connection that will be explored and deepened in the conversation to follow.

[3] The next instance in which pleasure and knowledge are shown to be connected is when Socrates launches a thought experiment meant to help adjudicate whether pleasure or knowledge is the good. If we were to compare a life of pleasure that has no share whatsoever in knowledge to a life of knowledge that has no share in pleasure, would either one of the two turn out to be a sufficient, perfect, and most choice-worthy life (20e–21a)?[12] When the portraits of the two one-dimensional lives are drawn, a certain asymmetry strikes us right away: knowledge turns out to be necessary for pleasure, whereas pleasure is not necessary for knowledge. A life of pleasure that is entirely devoid of cognitive components, namely, the kind of life that Philebus advocates as ideal, turns out not to be in fact truly a life of pleasure, for it is impossible for a human being to enjoy something without being able to recall the enduring character of the self that is enjoying it and the self-sameness of the object responsible for that pleasure. A life of knowledge, however, devoid of all pleasure, is not a logical impossibility. In fact, that is the kind of life that the gods have and is an ultimate ideal for us to aspire to.

Here, then, is the passage outlining the thought experiment for what it would feel like to have pleasure unaccompanied by knowledge and its cognates:

> Since you would not have either understanding, or memory, or knowledge, or true opinion, is it not obviously necessary that you'd be ignorant first of all about this very question whether you are enjoying yourself or not, given that you were empty of all intelligence? —Yes, necessarily so. —And since you won't have memory, it is obviously necessary that you won't remember that you ever enjoyed yourself, and it would also be impossible for any pleasure to endure from one moment to the next, since it would leave no memory. Then again, not having right opinions, you would not realize that you are enjoying yourself even while you do, and, being unable to calculate, you could not figure out any pleasures to follow for yourself at a later time. You would thus not live a human life but the life of a mollusk or of one of those beings in shells that live in the sea. (21b6–c8)

The experiment suggests that pleasure is intrinsically structured by knowledge and thus depends on it, while knowledge does not depend on pleasure. Pleasure without knowledge is not really pleasure; knowledge without pleasure to follow it remains nonetheless knowledge. Pleasure needs knowledge as a causal structural element for its own production, while knowledge, when it is humanly achievable knowledge that is at stake, sometimes has pleasure following upon its own realization. The causal relation between knowledge and pleasure begins thus to emerge.

[4] The connection between pleasure and knowledge appears next in the context of the argument designed to show, contrary to Philebus's assumptions, that pleasure and desire generally are experiences of the soul, not of the body (33c–35d). In short, the argument proceeds by showing that, since desire is structured internally and intentionally by knowledge, and since desire is presupposed by (many, if not all, of) our pleasures, pure as well as mixed, (most, if not all, of) our pleasures must be causally dependent on knowledge. When we unfold it, the argument goes like this:

> a. As far as some experiences of pleasure are concerned: We experience a certain pleasure even while our body is emptied, and when we experience such a pleasure, we have a desire for something that could bring about the filling of our body. Such are for instance our pleasant anticipations of filling with drink when we are thirsty, with food, when we are hungry.

b. If we have a desire for something that could bring about the filling, something in us is in touch with what brings about the filling.

c. If something in us is in touch with that which brings about the filling, it is either the body, or the soul.

d. The body itself cannot be in touch with that which brings about the filling, since the body is now empty.

e. Therefore, the soul in us is in touch (through memory) with that which brings about the filling. (from b, c, and d)

f. If the soul in us is in touch (through memory) with that which brings about the filling, desire is not a matter of the body, but of the soul.

g. If desire is a matter of the soul, desire is cognitively structured, that is, knowledge and memory are constitutive to it. Hence a new born baby's cry of hunger, prior to the baby developing the memory of the nourishment that would replenish him or her, signals pain, but not yet strictly speaking a desire for food, the new born baby's memory being unable to be in touch with the object that could bring about the desired filling, since the baby had never experienced that object before (35a–c).

h. At least some [if not all] of our pleasures presuppose desire for replenishment.

i. Therefore, at least some of our pleasures are cognitively structured. The argument has two additional implicit steps:

j. Our desires can be conscious or unconscious [implicit assumption].

k. Both mixed and pure pleasures presuppose desire: mixed pleasures presuppose conscious desires following upon painful lacks, while our pure pleasures presuppose unconscious desires following upon preexistent lacks not felt as painful (58d4–5)[13] [implicit assumption].

l. Hence, many (if not all) of our mixed as well as pure pleasures are cognitively structured [from (g), (j), and (k)].

The example used in the early stages of the argument sketched above—that of replenishing our bodies with food or drink when thirsty or hungry—illustrates the case of a pleasure mixed with pain, replenishment enjoyed on account of a previously felt lack. It might thus at first seem that only pleasures mixed with pains presuppose desire for replenishment, not also pure pleasures, that is, pleasures that are independent of pains, replenishments of unfelt lacks. But this is not the case. By its definition, pain, whether of a bodily or spiritual nature, is strictly empirical as it refers to lacks that we are conscious of, that is, perceived lacks. Desire, however, is not restricted to conscious experiences, but extends also to unconscious, implicit, or tacit pursuits. In the *Philebus*, Socrates talks about an innate desire and love that we have for truth (*tis pephuke tēs psuchēs hemōn dunamis erān te toũ alethoũs* 58d4–5). Pleasure itself occurs in response to explicit or implicit desires as replenishment of a lack, whether the lack is explicitly felt as painful (in which case we have mixed pleasures) or not perceived as painful (in which case we have pure pleasures). The pleasure we get in response to our tacit love and desire for truth by replenishing our lack though contemplation of eternal realities is pure pleasure and hence most intensely cognitively structured. If, then, there is in us an inborn desire for truth (58d), and if all desires require memory's contact with the object that satisfies that desire (35a–c), it follows that our memory must have been in touch a priori with the truth that we now desire to learn, and, hence, our soul must have been in touch with the Forms prior to being embodied. It is impossible not to hear Plato's theory of recollection echoed in all this. In fact, there was a hint at it even earlier, when Socrates talked in one breath about two types of recollection, empirical, whereby a previously forgotten perception (*aesthesis*) is called up in memory, and a priori, whereby a previously forgotten piece of knowledge or of learning (*mathematos*) is recalled (34b10–c1). Benitez formulates the same idea when he writes:

> There is, of course, a big difference between an innate ability to know and pre-natal knowledge, but the ability is compatible with pre-natal knowledge. We should note, moreover, that the ability Socrates mentions is virtually identical to the ability of souls in *Republic* 518b–c. . . . [I]f the ability described in *Republic* 518b–c presupposes the doctrine of recollection, the same ability described in *Philebus* 58d may do so as well. But there is a stronger reason to suspect that 58d presupposes the doctrine of recollection. Socrates claims that the cognitive ability of souls responds

> to an innate desire for what is true (here "what is true" refers to stable, unchanging realities, i.e. the Forms). Unless Socrates is being exceedingly careless, his analysis in 35a and following must apply in 58d as well. By the earlier argument then, the soul must have some contact with coming-to-know Forms (the replenishment for ignorance) through memory. And, if the desire for knowledge is present in souls from birth (*pephuke*, 58d4), the memory of the desired replenishment would have to be prenatal. Thus the ability of souls Socrates describes appears to presuppose the doctrine of recollection. (Benitez 1999, 116–17)[14]

Since, then, knowledge and memory are necessary for desire, and desire is required for most, if not all pleasures, we see, once again, that knowledge itself is constitutive of most (if not all) of our pleasures. The argument focuses attention on the beliefs we entertain as constitutive of the experience of pleasure, emphasizes the dependence of the body's well-being on the soul, and helps us recognize the priority of the soul over the body even in matters regarding our bodily pleasures. All these contribute to stressing the plausibility of the view that knowledge has a causal role to play in relation to pleasure.

[5] Socrates next proceeds to prove to Protarchus that pleasures can be false. He constructs his argument on the analogy between false pleasures and false judgments: just as judgments can be true or false, so too pleasures can be true or false. Though it starts by relying simply on the parallelism between judgment and pleasure, the argument eventually proceeds to show that the veracity of our judgments is in fact causally responsible for the veracity of our pleasures. This further step is not fully spelled out in the argument based on analogy, but it will become explicit through the discussion of the three types of false pleasures. Here is how the analogy proceeds:

a. We distinguish between an act of judging and what the judgment is about.

b. Similarly, we distinguish between taking pleasure and that which pleasure is taken in (37a).

c. Our judgments are true if their content corresponds to reality (if we characterize their object correctly) and false if it doesn't (if we mischaracterize it). Our judgments depend on perception and memory in our text symbolized by the scribe

(38e–39b). When looking from a distance, for instance, we can be easily deceived in taking what we see near a rock under a tree to be a statue instead of a man (39c–d).

d. Similarly, our pleasures, symbolized by the painter we have in the soul,[15] are true if we characterize their object correctly, and false if we don't.

e. Therefore, just as judging remains judging, whether the judgment made is right or not, so too taking pleasure remains taking pleasure, whether one takes pleasure rightly or not.

There has been ample scholarly debate as to whether Socrates's argument is successful at proving, contrary to Protarchus, that pleasures can be false. Gosling reads Socrates to be arguing that a pleasure is false if it is accompanied by a false belief. If this is all that Socrates means, then it is only in a loose sense that pleasure can be called false. For in that case, strictly speaking, only the belief in question is false, not also the pleasure. Hence, for Gosling, Socrates does not succeed in his attempt to refute Protarchus (Gosling 1959, 44–53).[16] Contrary to Gosling, Penner and Frede argue that Socrates's argument is in fact successful, insofar as Socrates means that a pleasure can be said to be true or false in the primary propositional sense if it not only accompanies a belief, but is also *taken in that belief*. To illustrate this, we can compare the following two situations. Case (1): Pleasure merely *accompanying* a false belief: "I enjoy P as a painting. By the way, I also believe that the artist who painted P happens to be Van Gogh." In this case, if I am mistaken about the painter's identity, then my belief accompanying my enjoyment is false, but not also the pleasure. Case (2): Pleasure *being taken in* a false belief: "I enjoy P as a painting painted by Van Gogh." In this case the falsity of the belief infects the pleasure itself which turns out to be false (Frede 1985, 165–79; Penner 1970, 166–78).[17] For both Frede and Penner then, only Case (2) counts as relevant illustration of Socrates's view on false pleasures. I believe that Frede and Penner correctly emphasize the cognitive structure of pleasures insofar as they show that pleasures have propositional content, but in the end their interpretation falls short of showing that pleasures are truth-apt. This is the case, first, because the falsity of the propositional content in which one takes pleasure still shows only that the beliefs on account of which we enjoy X are false, but not yet that the enjoyment itself is false;[18] and secondly, on Frede's view, because Socrates is successful in proving the possibility of false pleasures only at the expense of reducing pleasures to judgments, and moreover to judgments of fact. In the end then, Frede and Penner provide a reductionist account that restricts the cognitive component of pleasures to propositions stating facts and declares propositions to be the sole place of truth.[19] The problem with that is that propositional truth does not allow for degrees, while, in fact, the classification of the various types of knowledge is meant to stress exactly the multiple degrees of truth relative to the varied degrees of purity of the intentional objects (55c–59d). Correspondingly, there are degrees of falsehood at issue as well, and that is why some pleasures are said to be "even more false" than others (42c6). Hence, a refined account of false pleasures needs to be given. I will attempt to sketch the contours of such an account in the discussion of false pleasures of anticipation below.

The analogy between pleasure and knowledge breaks down at two points and indicates a rather asymmetric relation between pleasure and judgment, and it is on the basis of this asymmetry that we can begin to understand the causal role of knowledge vis-à-vis pleasure. First, (1) judgments influence the truthfulness of pleasures directly, while pleasures don't influence directly the truth value of our judgments; secondly, (2) whether true or false, judgments always remain judgments in the end, whereas pleasures can at times be so false as to no longer be pleasures at all. The first point is easy to understand: pleasure depends on there being a scribe (memory and perception), not the other way around. Pleasure can and, of course, does all the time influence what the scribe will scribble in the book, but pleasure's influence is not a sine qua non for the scribe's note taking, whereas the scribe's activity is a necessary condition for any experience of pleasure. The second point becomes relevant as we understand that there are degrees of falsehood present in our pleasures, and that, while some false pleasures still allow for a measure of truth even while mixed with falsehood, thus still remaining pleasures to some extent, others are so radically false that they are, in fact, no pleasures at all. There are, for instance, pleasures that are false due to our misidentification of the degree or intensity of pleasure enjoyed: even though the overall intensity of filling might be misjudged, there might be some amount of pleasure that is true. But there are also false pleasures we experience when we simply take absence of pain to be pleasure itself (this is the third type of false pleasure discussed in our dialogue and said to be "falser" than the other false pleasures discussed). In such cases there is no pleasure whatsoever to enjoy, while false judgments always remain judgments, no matter how false they may be.

[6] As we proceed to examine the three types of false pleasures analyzed in the text, we not only see that pleasures depend upon some

cognitive element, but we also identify more exactly the kind of beliefs that are mainly responsible for the truthfulness of pleasures. The *Philebus* discusses three types of false pleasures: false pleasures of anticipation, false pleasures due to misestimating the degree of pleasure, and false pleasure due to misidentifying pleasure with a neutral state, of neither pleasure nor pain.[20] Let us take each of them in turn.

False pleasures of anticipation (39d–40e) cover cases of deception regarding our expectations for the future. We often experience pain simultaneously with pleasure, as, for instance, when our body suffers some lack and our soul enjoys the pleasant anticipation of the filling needed by the body. In some of these cases, Socrates argues, the pleasures we take in anticipating our future replenishment are false. Socrates's discussion of the false pleasures of anticipation can be interpreted at both a superficial and a deeper level, respectively. Protarchus likely understands only the surface meaning of the falsity infecting these pleasures, but, upon reading the text in light of subsequent elucidations, we catch a glimpse of a deeper meaning intended. Arguing from a hedonistic perspective, Protarchus claims that pleasures can only be true, since they are identical to sensations, and thus, to speak of false pleasures makes no sense at all.[21] Socrates challenges this position by arguing that, just as our judgments about things seen at a distance may prove to have been false once we are looking at them up close, so too can be the case with our pleasures of anticipation, since they depend upon our beliefs.

As witnessed in the previous chapter, on the standard interpretation Socrates's point is that our present pleasures anticipating events in the future are false whenever the events we anticipate do not happen the way we expect them to happen (see Frede 1993, 444–46; Waterfield 1982, 23–24; Irwin 1995, 328–30; Gosling 1975, 214–18; Guthrie 1978, 220; Oghihara 2012, 308). On the reading that I am advancing, on the other hand, Socrates's primary point here is not that anticipatory pleasures are false because our belief about the future event turns out not to correspond to the facts, but rather that they are false due to the falsity of our assumption that the expected object, whether it actually occurs or not, is in fact pleasant, that is, whether it can bring about our expected replenishment or return to our natural condition that the definition of pleasure talks about (31d4–10, 32b2–4). In other words, the belief that determines the truth-quality of our pleasure is not the factual belief about how things are going to turn out, but rather the value judgment about the meaning and value of the expected event for our lives, the judgment that identifies a certain expected event as an occurrence capable to replenish us or to lead to the restoration of our natural balance. Thus, for Plato, a person's anticipatory pleasure of winning the lottery could be true or false depending not on whether they will in fact win, but more on what they take winning the lottery to mean. The anticipatory pleasure of the money lover who thinks that boasting and bragging about his luck will be replenishing some lack in him and will reestablish his balance is false, even if that person actually wins, while the anticipatory pleasure of the generous donor who hopes to win the lottery so that he may donate more money for a good cause is a *truer* pleasure, replenishing in him the need to be generous to others, whether or not he ends up actually winning the lottery.[22]

In support of this reading, we need only to look at the moral language used to show that good people have typically true painted images of pleasure because they are loved by the gods, whereas bad people have typically false painted images because they are not loved by the gods (40b).[23] What sense would it make to say that the good person tends to make correct predictions about the future, while the morally corrupt person fails in this? Has Plato ever encouraged us to believe that merely anticipating correctly future events, that is, prophesying, even in the absence of understanding the meaning and significance of the future events prophesied, is a mark of a good character or of someone loved by the gods?

It is important to realize that the dramatic context of the conversation invites both a surface reading of the falsity of these pleasures and a deeper one, the former meant to persuade at this stage Protarchus along with others sharing his views, the deeper meant for readers more exercised in philosophy. On the surface reading, Socrates rejects Protarchus's view by showing him that anticipatory pleasures can in fact be false, in cases where we make false judgments about the future: the falsity of our factual judgments about the future infects our current pleasures of anticipation. On a deeper reading, Socrates's discussion invites the suggestion that false pleasures of anticipation arise due to the falsity of our assumptions about the structure of reality: mistakes about the structure of reality infect our apprehension of the expected object's worth and thus we often end up taking as pleasant something that in fact is not, that is, something that, whether it occurs or not, cannot in fact bring about replenishment. True pleasures originate in one's ability to identify what are proper objects of desire, while false pleasures originate in failure to do so.

We see how the present discussion goes beyond the painter and scribe analogy: the painter and scribe analogy was confined to the empirical level accounting for empirical judgments that we make based on perception and imagination; the ignorance infecting our pleasures of anticipation, however, transcends the empirical level as it concerns the meaning of what we deem to be replenishing, and not simply the future absence or occurrence of what we take to be replenishing. Most likely, Protarchus accepts Socrates's argument insofar as he misinterprets it to be limited to the superficial empirical statement that our pleasures of anticipation are false whenever our prognostications (scribbled and painted in the soul) turn out not to correspond to the facts, and not insofar as he would have penetrated the full ethical and metaphysical implication of identifying what replenishment and natural balance mean given the fourfold structure of reality. And most likely also, the main reason why Socrates chooses to discuss anticipatory pleasures prior to the other types is precisely because Protarchus can at least accept the falsity of these pleasures, albeit in this superficial and limited sense. Socrates can keep Protarchus engaged in the conversation even if Protarchus has not yet grasped the full meaning and implications of this argument for false pleasures of anticipation. What we deem to be replenishing or helping our return to the natural state depends on our understanding of human nature in the context of the fourfold model of reality developed in the *Philebus*. If the good human life is to be one of the most harmonious and valuable members of Mixture, then the ratio of Limit to the Unlimited mixed in that life must heavily weigh the scale in favor of the former. The good person's life ruled by reason tends to set limits on illimitations, and thus identifies as replenishment everything that brings us closer to Limit and away from the Unlimited. The morally corrupt person, on the contrary, mistakes depletions for replenishments.[24]

A second type of false pleasures originates in our misestimating of the degree of pleasure or pain that we experience (41a–42c). Such situations occur when the intensity of our pleasures or pains is assessed by comparing them only relative to each other and relative to the immediacy or remoteness of their occurrence, and not by appeal to an absolute standard. Here, again, appealing to an absolute standard for measuring the degree of replenishment involves mapping out the situation on the fourfold metaphysical background and assessing it in that context. And again, the kind of knowledge that is constitutive and causally responsible for the truthfulness of our pleasures is not merely empirical cognition of facts, but rather metaphysical reflection on the implications and significance of facts for the quality of our lives.

Finally, a third type of false pleasures results from reducing pleasure to mere absence of pain (42c–44d). Those who think they experience pleasure when they are simply free from pain experience a false pleasure. Similarly, those who believe they are experiencing pain, simply because they are not experiencing pleasure, experience a false pain. Socrates's main intent in the discussion of this type of false pleasures is to rebuke the mediocrity of a life content with a general feeling of bodily satiety and well-being and not driven to experience any of the higher pleasures available, pleasures that fill in us a lack not perceived as painful. If all pleasure is reduced to mere absence of pain, it becomes impossible to account for any of the more elevated pleasures that do not rest on a previous conscious experience of pain as, for instance, some of our pleasures of learning or of artistic contemplation (51b–53c). In other words, to develop pure pleasures we need to develop a taste for the kind of replenishment they provide, a replenishment that fills an unperceived lack in us, a taste whose development requires higher levels of knowledge. These are pleasures we have upon replenishment on account of our inborn desire and love for truth (58d), our a priori memory being in touch somehow with intelligible objects whose lack is experienced by us only implicitly and is not consciously perceived as painful.

That Socrates's main intent in rejecting this sort of false pleasures is to rebuke the mediocrity of a life content with a general feeling of bodily satiety and bodily well-being emerges from Socrates's repeated claim that he is rejecting people's prospect of guiding *their whole life* by the identification of pleasure with absence of pain (43c8, 43c13, 43d7–9, 43e8), and by his rejection of the natural scientists' position, which reduces all pleasures to freedom from pain (44c1–2)—it is these people, who share a harsh nature, that are the real enemies of Philebus, for it is due to positions such as theirs that we eliminate the positive effects of pleasure in our lives. Socrates is fully entitled to reject the equation of pleasure with mere absence of pain since, as we are well aware, attainment of more elevated pleasures in life often requires us to endure pain.

In each one of the three cases of false pleasures examined above, ignorance of one sort or another was responsible for the falsity of these pleasures: (1) ignorance of what is truly, as opposed to merely apparently, replenishing us; (2) ignorance of the degree to which we are replenished; (3) ignorance of the higher truth that our soul desires beyond immediate satisfactions that alleviate pain.[25] Conversely, then, the knowledge that constitutes the counterpart of such ignorance must be responsible for turning false pleasures into true ones. The third type of false pleasures analyzed was described by Socrates as "even more false" than the preceding ones (42c). Correspondingly, the connection between the knowledge that would turn these false pleasures into true counterparts progressively tightens as we go from the knowledge needed to correct the first types of false pleasures to making sure that we don't reduce pleasure to mere absence of pain. Indeed, the first two types of pleasure assume the right understanding of the nature of pleasure, but err in identifying its objects, while the third type of false pleasures misidentifies both the object of pleasure and the nature of pleasure as such. Hence, knowledge is constitutive to pleasure both insofar as it secures our understanding of pleasure as replenishment of a lack and insofar as it identifies correctly the objects that can fill this lack.

[7] After the discussion of these three types of falsity that can infect our pleasures, Socrates moves on to examine pleasures mixed with pain and considers in detail the case of comic malice as an example of emotional pleasure. Self-ignorance often makes one appear ridiculous. When exposed and joined with powerlessness, self-ignorance regarding one's looks, or riches, or wisdom (48e), that is, thinking oneself more handsome, richer, or wiser than one truly is, can trigger a malicious person's laughter. The laughter it triggers in the malicious person combines pleasure with pain. The malicious person suffers pain on account of his envy of the self-ignorant person's assumed goods, and experiences pleasure upon realizing that the self-ignorant fellow did not in fact possess those presumed goods in the first place.[26] And this goes both for fellows the malicious person witnesses on stage and for those he witnesses in life. The experience of the malicious person is indicative of a false pleasure. In fact, his laughter is an indicator of the malicious person's own self-ignorance and personal insecurity. In laughing at a fellow's misfortune, the malicious person reveals his own self-ignorance, which is much more significant than that of the ridiculous person he laughs at. For, unlike the self-ignorant ridiculous person who is simply unaware of his own ignorance, the malicious person thinks himself superior to his fellow and, as such, takes his depletion to be a replenishment, his worldview turned upside down. This is also why Socrates describes the malicious experience as an "unjust (*adikos*) pleasure and pain" (49d).

Most interesting for our purposes is reconstructing the positive counterpart of comic malice, the healthy laughter in reaction to what is funny, the healthy Socratic irony, and even self-irony being cases in point. Self-knowledge gives us the right assessment of when to laugh and what to laugh at and thus fuels the pleasure we rightly take in things laughable. Socrates's irony prompted by other people's ignorance is worlds apart from malicious laughter. Though it too mixes pleasure with pain, Socratic irony selects the intentional objects of pleasure and pain differently than the way the malicious person does, insofar as Socrates's irony combines pain on account of the ignorant person's ignorance with pleasure on account of recognizing *aporia* as an opportunity with potential beneficial effects on the interlocutor (Wood 2007, 89; Miller 2008, 263–88, Austin 2012, 130–33).

Socrates treats even himself with irony as he recognizes the ridiculousness involved in his own practice of philosophy. The practice of philosophy oftentimes rightfully makes us look ridiculous, for it reveals the discrepancy between the lofty nature of the task and our limited resources and capacities for accomplishing it. Essential is how we react in response. When faced with the prospect of dividing the metaphysical articulations of reality, Socrates admits that he might well look ridiculous undertaking such an enormous task (23d1–3). As long as we acknowledge this discrepancy, we are saved as philosophers. When, however, we don't, we take ourselves too seriously and become dogmatic. Later on, when listing the ingredients of a good human life, the philosopher's need to heed particulars also, to be aware of our immediate surroundings, is also introduced on a comic note, poking fun at the philosopher's natural tendency to dwell in the medium of eternal truth while neglecting the obvious, the immediate, the simple (62a7–b9).

The connection between pleasure and knowledge is complexly rendered by the discussion of these mixed pleasures: while malicious laughter combines false pleasure and false pain, the philosopher's irony, and, even more so, his self-irony illustrate the tight connection between true pleasure and true pain. It takes a truly humble and philosophically refined spirit to delight in self-irony, for the philosopher's self-irony presupposes taking pleasure in awareness of our own ignorance *insofar as* this awareness *is* an experience of self-knowledge. Simply put, by coming to recognize my ignorance I become aware of an aspect of my own cognitive state; I am *pleased by my self-discovery*, while still pained at the realization of my lack. In this case, not only knowledge of what replenishes us, but also knowledge of what depletes us is *constitutive* to the true pleasure experienced.

[8] The next occasion that reveals the connection between pleasure and knowledge occurs in the context discussing the unmixed, pure pleasures (50e). In reaction to Socrates's declared intention to turn toward pure pleasures, Protarchus asks Socrates to specify the kinds of pleasure that could rightly be regarded as true (51b), thus presumably assuming that pure pleasures must also be true. A certain ambiguity lingers, as to whether we are to understand that pure pleasures are always true or not. In the next chapter, I argue that Socrates does not assume that all pure pleasures must be true and

that his argument allows for the possibility of false pure pleasures. All that the argument establishes is that pure pleasures are always truer than impure ones, but not also the stronger claim that pure pleasures are always true.

The examples of pure pleasures discussed are those of the pleasure we take in perceiving pure colors, shapes, smells, and sounds insofar as they are based on imperceptible and painless lacks (51b). The beauty that we appreciate in a musical note or a simple shape all by itself presupposes a more intense cognitive involvement, refinement, and epistemological sophistication than the beauty we appreciate in one animal or picture relative to some other (51c–d). The beauty inherent in a pure musical tone or shape or even in a pure patch of color that has no admixture captivates us, so that our sight and hearing linger in perceiving these pure objects. Insofar as this kind of appreciation of filling requires a subtle and sophisticated involvement of our cognitive capacities, these pure sensible pleasures mark a turning point from the pleasures we take in perceiving toward those we take in the sort of learning whose objects are intelligible realities. As Miller puts it:

> Indeed, the more perfectly these sensible "pures" bring their natures into palpable presence, the more powerfully do they provoke the intellect to distinguish these natures, as such, from the sensibles as their embodiments and, further, to explore them in terms of their purely intelligible relations to one another. This, however, is precisely the work of "the studies" (*ta mathēmata*, 57e7), and the learning (*toũ manthanein*, 52a20) that Socrates introduces by naming the fifth kind of pleasure. (Miller 2010, 85–86)

Socrates argues that pure pleasures are always pleasanter, truer, and more beautiful than their impure counterparts (53b–c). The argument proceeds by analogy with the case of whiteness: purity resides not in quantity or amount, but in the absence of any admixture of something foreign. Purity makes something truer than impurity by preserving the thing's genuine nature (53b). It emerges by analogy that pure pleasures must be truer than impure ones, since the former, unlike the latter, admit of no admixture of pain.

[9] There are, then, also pleasures of learning (52a–58e). The pleasures of learning that Socrates considers here explicitly are the true and pure pleasures of learning that deal specifically with dialectical knowledge (52b). Since there are many types of knowledge that Socrates identifies, from the most imprecise ones, based on guesswork, to the most precise one of dia-

lectic (55c–59d), we are probably right to expect a broad array of pleasures associated with "learning" in the various fields. Of course, this presupposes that we broaden the understanding of "learning" itself and, from its restrictive use synonymous to "contemplation of intelligible objects," we come to view it as equivalent of a generic sense of "studying." In this broad sense, "learning" is used to indicate the exploration of everything, from the most imprecise arts of flute playing, medicine, agriculture, and navigation, to the more precise practical arts of shipbuilding and house building, and up to pure theoretical mathematics and finally to dialectic itself.

Our epistemic sophistication is directly responsible for the kinds of pleasures of learning that we enjoy. In other words, the more attuned to reason and rationality we are, the more elevated the learning we delight in. To the person who feels at home with abstract thinking, studying mathematics and philosophy is truly enjoyable; however, to those who don't feel quite at home in the realm of abstractions, exposure to complex mathematical or philosophical truths will not be conducive to pleasure, or, at least, not right away.

If we are right to say that learning in each and every one of the fields of knowledge can bring about pleasure, there are two main coordinates to consider: (1) whether we are talking about pure or about mixed pleasures of learning; and (2) whether the learning in question is a filling with Being or with becoming. When the pleasure of learning is experienced in response to ignorance that is painful, the pleasure of learning is mixed with that pain—as, for instance, when solving a problem that we have been trying to figure out for a while, or when remembering something we had forgotten and have been trying hard to recall. There are, however, also pleasures of learning of a superior sort, when the replenishment we experience is intrinsically filling and does not simply come in response to a lack felt to be painful. The more stable and universal the object of learning, the more replenishing the pleasure we feel in response. Socrates classified the kinds of knowledge by the criteria of purity, truth, certainty, and precision (55c–56a, 56c, 57b–d, 58a–c, 59c). The degree of truth and purity of our pleasures of learning is directly proportional to the degree of truth or purity pertaining to the objects of the respective types of knowledge.

The discussion of these pleasures of learning seems to have prompted a certain concern about an apparent contrast between the accounts of the *Philebus* and the *Republic* regarding the philosopher's pleasures, insofar as the *Philebus*, presumably, unlike the *Republic*, cannot recognize the pleasures of philosophical contemplation, but only those of philosophical learning.

As Frede puts it:

> Intellectual pleasures are here strictly limited to learning, because only learning is a process. Learning is pleasant because it is the filling of an unfelt lack. That this is the point is confirmed by the insistence that neither the acquisition, nor the loss of knowledge is accompanied by pain. That knowledge itself does not provide pleasure is assured at 55a, where the life of pure thought is assigned to the "third life." Plato has given up the notion, defended in *Republic* IX with so much fanfare, that the philosopher outdoes everyone in the amount of pleasure he gains. He obviously came to realize that this is incompatible with the generic definition of pleasure as a process. (Frede 1993, 52n3; see also Frede 1992, 425–63, esp. 453)

But Plato does not give up on the idea that the contemplative knowledge that philosophers can have can be enjoyed or accompanied by pleasure. That "third life" of a divine sort, completely dedicated to knowledge and with no admixture of pleasure whatsoever since it lacks nothing, surpasses even the most dedicated human philosophical life. The philosopher's contemplative knowledge is not equivalent with this third type of life, if only because the philosopher cannot sustain such contemplation continuously and knows that all too well. The knowledge that philosophers attain is always still in a way limited and, hence, compatible with the pleasure of learning more. As long as we talk about being human we assume a condition in which lack too is always present: even while we are knowledgeable we can still experience the enjoyment of holding on to the knowledge we have, of maintaining it while we know we could lose it at any moment or over time given our own limitations. Gods are perfect and completely contemplative, and therefore have no reason to worry about losing their knowledge, forgetting, or about discovering later on that they did not know what they thought they knew. As humans, however, we worry about finding out that what we took to be knowledge is not really knowledge, that is, that we are ignorant and also ignorant of this very ignorance. Hence, in a fundamental sense, all there is to knowledge for us is a process of learning, since no absolute and inalienable possession of knowledge is ever achievable, but this does not mean that the act of sustained contemplation of Forms, the filling with Being that we experience in the most elevated moments, cannot itself be experienced with joy or accompanied by pleasure.

[10] Once the various species of pleasure and knowledge have been examined, Socrates and Protarchus position themselves like builders with ingredients ready to use, ready to combine the ingredients of a good life. They start mixing the ingredients allowing first the truest and the purest ones and continuing for as long as the ingredients are still congenial and orderly arranged in relation to these foremost ones. Thus, after the truest knowledge, that is, dialectic, comes knowledge of the divine circle and the divine sphere and also the rather impure and imprecise kinds of knowledge of the human circle and human yardsticks. There is no damage done accepting the imprecise and lower types of knowledge *as long as* the highest kinds have already been included. Next, they turn toward pleasures, allowing in first the pure pleasures and then all the necessary ones. At this point Plato personifies the pleasures and knowledge themselves to engage them directly in dialogue with each other. From this point on, the mixing of the ingredients no longer looks like the philosopher's doing from outside, but rather more like the ingredients' own needful call for their complements. Pleasures welcome the kind of knowledge that understands not only other things but also each and every one of the types of pleasure, "as far as this is possible" (63c3), while knowledge welcomes pleasures that are of its own kin, pure pleasures, as well as pleasures of health and temperance and all those that commit themselves to virtue, and rejects the foolish and intemperate sort of pleasures, which impede knowledge. We notice, however, again the same pervasive asymmetry that recognizes knowledge as causally constitutive to pleasure. For it is pleasures that declare it "neither possible (*oute panu ti dunaton*), nor beneficial (*out' ōphelimon*)" for one kind to remain alone, unmixed with the other (63b7–c1), whereas knowledge stresses the kinship it has with the true and pure pleasures, but nowhere does it imply its own existential dependence on pleasure. The dialectical development of the notion of pleasure throughout our text shows how far away we have moved from the reductionist hedonistic view of pleasure as sensation and glow with no cognitive component whatsoever to it, the view that Philebus put forth at the beginning.

To conclude, then, we started from an examination of the textual support for including pleasure and knowledge in the classes of Mixture and Cause of mixture, respectively, and then moved on to survey several instances in which this reading reveals the close intimacy between the two. As the above analysis has shown, pleasure and knowledge are intimately connected: knowledge is causally responsible for the imposition of limit upon the unlimitedness that is constitutive to each and every instance of pleasure, while our pleasures of learning especially contribute to stimulating our capacity and desire to know. Knowledge grounds pleasure ontologically, while pleasure contributes psychologically to strengthening our knowledge and understanding generally. The roles are, clearly, asymmetrical: knowledge is causally constitutive to pleasure, while pleasure is influential for, yet not necessary to, knowledge. None of these claims about the intimate relation between the two could have been harmonized with the traditional assignment of all pleasures to the Unlimited and of knowledge to Limit. For, on that reading, pleasure and knowledge would have remained forever distant and foreign to each other. Far, then, from the image of an overly intellectualistic Socrates, dismissing pleasures in favor of reason, we have come upon Socrates's thoughtful attempt to reveal the complex cognitive scaffold that makes pleasure possible. And far from regarding the *Philebus* as the disjointed work that it has often been thought to be, we came to see an impressively unified work in which the ethical and metaphysical discussions are interwoven.

III

Hybrid Varieties of Pleasure

True Mixed Pleasures and False Pure Pleasures

Socrates uses the dialectical method of collection and division first to discern three types of false pleasures and then to classify pleasures into pure and mixed (impure), each with its respective subspecies. Problems of interpretation arise when we attempt to integrate and coordinate the discussion concerning the truth/falsehood with that concerning the purity/impurity of pleasures. More specifically, difficulties arise in connection with the assumption that scholars have sometimes made, that truth/purity and falsehood/impurity, respectively, are overlapping criteria and that all the mixed (impure) pleasures are false while all the pure ones are true.[1] If this were the case, it would seem that much of even the most virtuous person's life is permeated by false pleasures, for the pleasures arising from satisfying our bodily needs and most of those associated with our emotional life would need to be false, since they clearly are mixed with pain. In addition, the view that all pure pleasures must be true also precludes the possibility of someone's ever overestimating or underestimating the degree of pleasure experienced through our senses (e.g., smelling a rose) when such experiences are not preceded by perceptible lacks, for such pleasures are pure and would then also need to be always true. In this chapter, I am going to argue that Plato keeps the truth/falsehood and purity/impurity criteria distinct in his assessment of pleasures, and thus leaves room for the possibility of hybrid pleasures in the form of true mixed (impure) pleasures and false pure pleasures. As we shall see, allowing for hybrid varieties of pleasure is an essential way of stressing the importance of mediation in the *Philebus*.

Distinct Criteria for Classifying Pleasures: Truth/Falsehood and Purity/Impurity

After providing his account of pleasure as perceived filling or replenishment of a lack (33d), Socrates gradually, and at first only implicitly, introduces the two sets of criteria for the classification of pleasures, first truth/falsity, and later purity/impurity. He begins by discerning distinct types of false pleasures: false pleasures of anticipation, false pleasures due to misidentification of the degree of pleasure experienced, and false pleasures that arise through mistaking for pleasure a neutral condition of neither pleasure nor pain. As witnessed in our examination of the three types of false pleasures in the previous chapter, the truth and respective falsity of our pleasures depend on whether the object of our enjoyment replenishes a lack *and* whether we perceive correctly the degree to which replenishment occurs. Implicit throughout this account is the view that there are objective standards in relation to which we can assess the kind and degree of replenishment/depletion that we are experiencing. Notice that Socrates does not claim that he has thus offered an exhaustive list of possible types of false pleasures, but only that he has shown Protarchus that pleasures can sometimes be false. Consequently, while Socrates illustrates the three types of false pleasures explicitly discussed with cases of mixed pleasures, it is not in principle impossible for some pure pleasures to fall prey to some of these or perhaps other kinds of falsehood.

While all the pleasures presuppose a lack to be filled by them, only mixed (impure) pleasures presuppose our earlier conscious experience of that lack as painful. When experiencing pure pleasures, on the other hand, we are enjoying the perceived replenishment but are not experiencing the lack thus filled as painful, that is to say, pure pleasures fill an unperceived lack.

Socrates begins by dividing the class of mixed pleasures into pleasures of the body (of itching and scratching, sexual pleasures, 46a, 46d–47b), of the body and soul (mixing the body's painful lack with the soul's pleasant anticipation in cases of hunger, thirst; 36b, 47c–d), and of the soul itself (involved in longing, love, anger, jealousy, lamentations, malice, the experience of tragedies or comedies; 47e–50d):

> There are then, on the one hand, mixtures that belong to the body and are confined to it, and, on the other, those pertaining to the soul and confined to the soul. And then we will also find mixtures of pleasure and pain that involve both soul and body,

and at one time their combination will be called pleasure, at another pain. (46b8–c4)

Itching and scratching along with sexual pleasures are given as illustrations of the first type:

Take as example of a case in which pains predominate over pleasures the one which we have mentioned just now, of itching and scratching. Whenever the irritation and the inflammation are inside and cannot be reached by rubbing and scratching, there is only a relief on the surface. Sometimes exposing the parts affected to fire or to the opposite of fire, going from one extreme to the other, produces intense pleasure. At other times this leads to an inner state that is opposite to the outer, mixing pleasures with pains, the balance may turn now one way, next time the other, separating by force what was mixed, or mixing what was apart, and this way pains appear alongside pleasures. (46d7–47a1)

Now whenever the mixture contains a preponderance of pleasure, the admixture of pain gives rise only to a tickle and a mild irritation, while the predominant part of pleasure causes contractions of the body making it sometimes to leap and producing in it sensations of colors of all sorts and shapes of all sorts, and palpitations of all kinds, driving the person out of his mind and making him shout out like a madman. (47a3–9)

Mixed pleasures of the soul in combination with the body arise in situations earlier referred to as pleasures of anticipation, where the body is emptied and the soul experiences in either hope or despair the anticipated filling of the body, thus, situations in which "the soul and the body are not in agreement, and the final result is a single mixture that combines pleasure and pain" (47d).

When it comes to mixed pleasures of the soul alone, Socrates associates these with a plethora of emotions including wrath, fear, longing, lamentations, love, jealousy, malice (46d–e), and provides a detailed discussion of the malicious person's enjoyment of comedy (48b–50d). Interestingly, Socrates restricts his account here only to the malicious person's experience of comedy and does not consider the pleasure that everyone else takes in comedy. The experience of comedy is said to combine pleasure and pain, and thus be a mixed pleasure. The malicious person takes delight in his fellow's misfortune, and, specifically, in the misfortune that arises due to self-ignorance. When, upon being self-deluded, the self-ignorant imagines himself much better looking, richer, or much wiser than he is, only to then discover he does not have these qualities, he is ridiculous. The malicious person's reaction to this is a mixture of pleasure and pain: pain at viewing and envying in the first place his fellow's *imagined* good looks, riches, or wisdom, and pleasure at the later realization that, in fact, his fellow doesn't actually have those goods. This happens both on stage as well as in life (48b–50d). In fact, the reference to the ridiculous as "friends" (49d, 50a), makes it clear that Plato's Socrates is interested primordially in real-life situations, and only secondarily in situations produced on stage, for we don't typically have either friendship or enmity with the actors on stage. And indeed, malicious people find the ridiculous situations of others all the more pleasing to them when they happen to their fellows in life, not merely on stage. It is clearly a false pleasure they enjoy!

Pure pleasures are classified into (1) pleasures we take in the beauty of pure colors (51b–d, 53a–c), (2) of geometrical shapes (51c), (3) of sounds that produce one pure note (50d–e), (4) the "less divine tribe" of pleasures associated with smells (51e1), and (5) the pleasures of learning (51e7–52a2). Socrates emphasizes that the beauty of geometrical shapes constructed by means of a compass, a ruler, or a carpenter's square is absolute, not relative, as he describes these shapes to be "by their very nature forever beautiful by themselves" (51c6–7) and opposes their intrinsic beauty to the relative beauty that is present in a picture or in a living being. Consequently, the pleasures that these objects bring about are by nature inherent to them:

> By the beauty of shapes I do not mean what the many might assume, namely the beauty of a living being or of a certain picture, but rather, as the argument goes, something straight, or round, and what is constructed out of these with a compass, a carpenter's ruler or square, such as surfaces and solids, if you see what I mean. For these things are not beautiful in a relative sense, the way others are, but rather by nature always beautiful by themselves, and they provide their own specific pleasures, which are completely unlike those of scratching. And there are colors too of the same kind. Do we understand this now, or what do you think? —I am really trying to understand, Socrates. But

perhaps you too could try to make it a bit clearer. —What I am saying is that those among smooth and bright sounds, that produce one pure note, are beautiful not in a relative sense, but in and by themselves, and are accompanied by their own pleasures, that belong to them by nature. (51c1–d9)

The beauty of pure colors is said to be analogical to that of these geometrical shapes, and pure colors are said to import their own kinds of pleasures (51d). I take this to mean that lack of admixture of something foreign is intrinsically beautiful and has the effect of replenishing lacks in those perceiving such pure objects. The pleasures we get upon perceiving pure colors are analogical to, but not identical with those experienced upon contemplating the beauty of these geometrical shapes, more specifically of their diagrams, since they are said to be constructed by means of ruler and compass, not of the intelligible objects themselves represented in these diagrams. Unlike the objects of the pure pleasures of learning, which Socrates explicitly restricts to learning of the most exact sort "experienced only by a very few" (52b8), the objects of these other pure pleasures mentioned—the beauty of shapes constructed with a compass or the carpenter's square, the beauty of pure colors and tones—are sensible, not intelligible. Nevertheless, the objects of these more precise crafts such as music and geometry contain a more pronounced trace of the intelligible realities than the pleasures we take in the less precise sensible occurrences, and so too do their corresponding pleasures. Pleasures of smell, however, are said to be "less divine" than the other pure pleasures mentioned (51e5), which I take to mean that there is less rigor in setting the parameters for all the features that render a smell free of all possible admixtures of something foreign than there is in the case of pure white or of a geometrical shape. When talking about the way we experience smells, a host of external associations through memory and expectations can easily intrude and mar the purity of an odor as object of pleasure. It is harder to point out exactly the inherent quality of one odor that is responsible for pleasure than it is to point out the quality of one musical note or of a patch of white unmixed with anything else. Note, however, that the discussion of these pure pleasures has seamlessly made use of a dual sense of "purity." On the one hand, "purity" here characterizes the *lack of admixture of pain in the pleasures we take,* which are replenishments of previously unperceived lacks, on the other, it characterizes the *lack of admixture of extraneous factors in the objects of these pleasures themselves*—the purity of white means that there is no other hue mixed in it, the purity of a sound is that it is just the note that it is.[2] The importance of this dual use of "purity" will become evident later on.

A schematic representation of all the types of pleasure mentioned above, pure and mixed, has the following look:

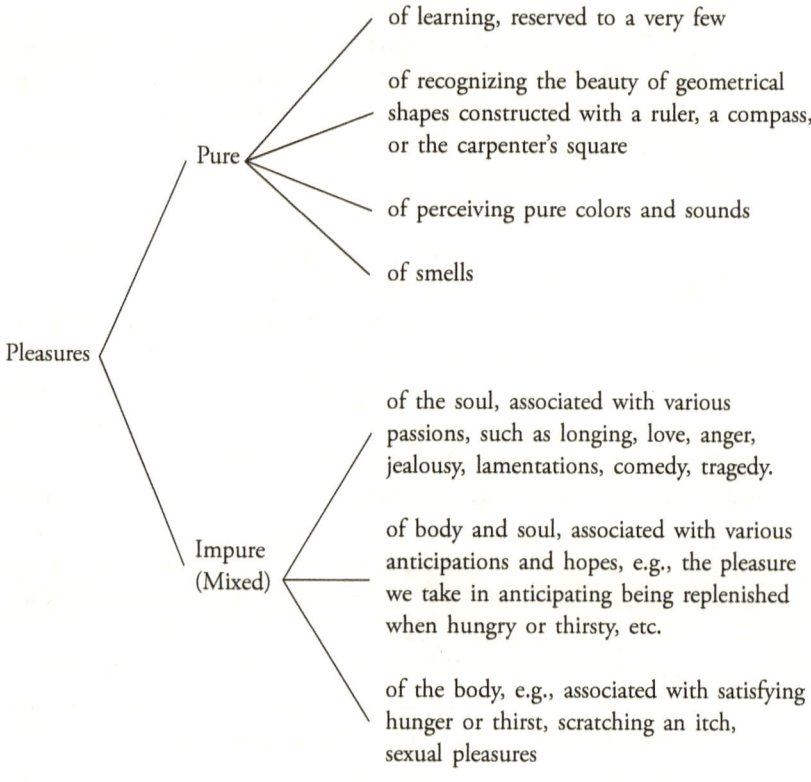

The criteria involved in the classifications reviewed above are clearly distinct: truth/falsehood refers to whether the object enjoyed does in fact replenish a lack, and, if so, to what extent, while purity/impurity refers to whether the occurring replenishment is of a perceived or unperceived lack.[3] So far, however, we have established only that the two pairs of concepts involved in the two criteria are not synonyms and answer distinct questions. Yet, the more intriguing and interesting question remains whether truth and purity, falsehood and mixed character, respectively, are coextensive even if their intensions differ, that is, whether they pick out the same set of pleasures, even if based on distinct considerations. It is to this that we turn our attention in the next section.

Hybrid Pleasures

Can Mixed Pleasures Be True?

Far from the text precluding the possibility of true mixed pleasures, it in fact provides evidence supporting such a possibility. When discussing the mixed pleasures of the body, Socrates used for his illustrations extreme cases—itching and scratching and the excessive sexual pleasures—which most likely are false. They are false, however, not because they are mixed with pain, but because they are excessive to the point where they cease to replenish and begin to deplete us by disrupting our balance. This point is well captured in Socrates's description of the profligate's pleasures as "making it [the body] sometimes leap and producing in it sensations of colors of all sorts and shapes of all sorts, and palpitations of all kinds, driving the person out of his mind and making him shout out irrationally" (47a6–9). The reason why Socrates studies these pleasures in their most intense forms is that he is currently reasoning under the guidance of "the real enemies of Philebus" who, equating pleasure with mere relief from pain, deny that there is any genuine reality or truth to pleasures. To make their point, these natural scientists turn toward the most intense and extreme examples. Socrates explicitly disagrees with their complete rejection of truth from the domain of pleasure (44c–d) and follows their guidance only to prove the point about the unreality of pleasures as far as the most intense, excessive pleasures are concerned.

Let us take distance for a moment from the extreme cases and consider possible mixed pleasures that are true. Even if Socrates does not mention them explicitly, we can imagine true mixed pleasures related to the body, such as those of moderate cooling after much heat or of heating after much cooling, of moderate eating when hungry, or the pleasures of sex when they restore the balance of our organism. Such mixed true pleasures seem to be exactly the kinds of pleasures recognized as worthy ingredients of a good life as pleasures of health (63e) or necessary pleasures (62e). What could be wrong with enjoying eating the right amount of a healthy meal when hungry, or drinking the right amount of water when thirsty and in need of hydration, or of enjoying a relaxing time after a lot of stressful and intense stretch of work?

When giving examples of mixed pleasures of the body and soul, Socrates refers back to cases discussed earlier on: the body's current painful experience of lack and the soul's pleasant anticipation of replenishment needed by the body in cases of hunger and thirst (35e–36c, 47c). Here again, we have good reason to think that sometimes such experiences will turn out to be false, for instance, in situations of pathological dysfunctions of the nutritive system (e.g., bulimia) or due to some grave imbalances manifest in the soul of vicious individuals who dedicate their lives to the satisfaction of appetites. There is, nonetheless, also good reason to think that one could enjoy such pleasures in moderation, measuring their intensity by appeal to an absolute standard, and not by comparing pains to pains, pleasures to pains, or pleasures to pleasures, or being overly influenced by the nearness or remoteness of their occurrence. True, the fact that *we* can imagine these kinds of mixed pleasures to be true does not yet mean that Plato also regards them as such. Nevertheless, we can at least declare that Plato's account is complex enough to accommodate the inclusion of mixed true pleasures of the body, even if he may not have considered this possibility. None of the things that Socrates says in the *Philebus* excludes the possibility of such pleasures. In fact, the text gives us indications that Plato has likely thought of mixed pleasures being sometimes true, or at the very least necessary pleasures as being worthy of inclusion in the good life (62e–63e). In the context of the discussion regarding the ingredients to be allowed in a good life, Socrates welcomes the pleasures of health along with those of temperance and of the other virtues (63e), and regards them as akin to reason and knowledge, as opposed to all the false pleasures attendant upon vice and excess, which are a clear impediment to reason and knowledge. Most likely, our measured pleasures of eating the right amount when hungry and drinking the right amount when thirsty can be naturally subsumed under these pleasures of health that sustain and encourage our intellectual pursuits by securing the right balance in our organisms.

Mixed pleasures of the soul alone receive a more extended treatment. After mentioning mixed pleasures associated with anger, longing, love, jealousy, lamentations, malice, and the experience of watching tragedy (47e–48a), Socrates takes a closer look at the pleasures of comedy enjoyed by the malicious person (48a–50d). We have good reason to think, however, that Socrates does not mean that pleasures associated with all these emotions, from love to longing, to anger and everything else, are necessarily always false. In fact, earlier on he suggested that fear and anger and "all the other things of this sort," presumably other emotions, "are *at times* (*eniote*) false" (40e). The implicit suggestion is that they can also be true *at (other) times*. Even if Socrates thus admits that fear and anger can be true, can we be sure that the pleasures associated with them can also be true? It is not too difficult to see that we can. The *Timaeus* shows that anger can be an essential catalyst leading to the restoration of our balance and, I believe, we are to conclude that, in such cases anger and the pleasure associated with it must both be true. Anger can be positively used to help us reestablish our overall balance as it provides reason with the most persuasive medium for communicating its message to our appetites:

> The heart, then, which ties the veins together, the spring from which blood courses with vigorous pulse throughout all the bodily members, they set in the guardhouse. That way, if spirit's might should boil over at a report from reason that some wrongful act involving these members is taking place—something being done to them from the outside or even something originating from the appetites within—every bodily part that is sensitive may be keenly sensitized, through all the narrow vessels, to the exhortations or threats and to listen and follow completely. In this way the best part among them all can be left in charge. (*Timaeus* 70b, trans. Donald J. Zeyl)

The experience of anger in these situations presupposes a mixed pleasure (*Philebus* 47e), which often is true, in cases in which we undergo pleasure, at the realization that reason's command has been restored over the appetites, and pain, insofar as we perceive the depletion caused by the resistance that our appetites oppose to reason. Again, while Socrates does not say so explicitly, I believe we can safely expect that the pleasures we take in love, longing, lamentation, etc. can nonetheless be true, even while mixed with pain, when their object is truly filling us and when our assessment of the extent of our filling is accurate. In fact, in the *Philebus* Socrates talks explicitly about our soul's natural "love of truth" (58d), clearly echoing the *Republic* 501d, 582e, and the *Symposium* 210d–212b. While love is a mixture of pleasure and pain in all these cases, it is clear that Socrates deems the dialecticians' pleasures involved in their "love of truth" as being always true, since dialectic truly replenishes us with Being (*Philebus* 58a; *Republic* 585b–e), and our awareness of this, as shall be further explained, can only be truly pleasant. Such pleasures, however, are worlds apart from the excessive "pleasures of love" mentioned at 65c, which owe their falsity to their excess and are completely devoid of reason.

The detailed discussion of comedy invites the suggestion that, while comedy always presupposes a mixture of pleasure and pain, the comedic pleasure felt by the virtuous person is most often true, whereas that experienced by the malicious person is false. Socrates deals here explicitly strictly with the pleasure of the malicious person and gives only implicit hints regarding a virtuous person's pleasant experience of comedy.[4] The ridiculous nature of a comedic character springs from self-ignorance, whether in regard to one's own wealth, beauty, or wisdom (48d–49a), when such ignorance is combined with weakness. When, however, combined with strength it becomes dangerous and threatening instead of ridiculous (49b–c). When witnessing something ridiculous both a virtuous and a malicious person could experience a mixed pleasure, but there is a significant difference between the ways these two individuals experience the mixture of pleasure and pain. They will find different objects replenishing or depleting, since they have radically different conceptions of the good. The malicious person experiences pain at seeing other people thriving and pleasure at their misfortune. Thus, he will rejoice at seeing the ridiculous person suffer misfortunes due to his ignorance.[5] Yet, the main thing the malicious person fails to realize is that in humiliating and mocking the ignorant person, he is showing himself to be at least as ridiculous as the target of his laughter, since he too is self-ignorant (Wood 2007, 82). The malicious person's self-ignorance is of the most serious sort since it is in regard to wisdom that he deceives himself, thinking himself wise when he is not (48e). The virtuous person finds comedy and the ridiculous pleasant primarily on stage and derives pleasure in part from knowing that this is not happening in real life. The virtuous person experiences pain in reaction to another person's misfortune and pleasure upon recognizing that it is only happening on stage.

But what about Socrates's irony, which is directed at his self-ignorant interlocutor, in life rather than on stage? True, Socrates often ironically laughs down his interlocutors' self-ignorance, yet his experience differs from that of a malicious person. The malicious person laughs at the self-ignorant person as a way to assert his own superiority on the basis of the other's deficiency. Socrates appeals to irony and sometimes mocks his opponent's ideal of life in order to improve his interlocutor's soul and, ultimately, his life. Moreover, as character in a Platonic dialogue, Socrates's irony is meant to diminish in our eyes as readers the attractiveness of a life lived in ignorance, vice, and the comfort of false pleasures.[6] Socratic irony can serve as effective instrument for education insofar as it can generate his interlocutor's feeling of shame. For in light of that shame one can recognize his self-ignorance and ridiculousness and start working on overcoming these. Although it too mixes pleasure with pain, Socratic irony combines pain derived from witnessing a person's ignorance with pleasure derived from recognizing the experience of *aporia* as an opportunity of self-discovery with potential beneficial effects on the interlocutor.[7]

Most importantly, Socrates treats also himself ironically, as he understands that self-irony can be an excellent instrument for self-improvement. Socrates understands that the discrepancy between the lofty aims of philosophy and our modest resources for attaining those often rightfully makes us look ridiculous in our very practice of philosophy, for we aim to attain too much with the limited intellectual resources that we possess (23d1–3). Similarly, the comic aspect of the philosopher's natural tendency to dwell in the medium of eternal truth while neglecting the obvious, the immediate, the simple, is also derided in the same spirit. For, as Socrates prompts Protarchus to point out, in addition to the highly pure knowledge associated with the "divine circle or sphere," a good life must also include the crafts associated with concrete manifestations of geometric shapes in tridimensional objects (the "false yardstick and circle"), if one is to ever "find his own way home" (62b), and likely also the even more imprecise arts of music, that is, playing an instrument on account of hearing, rather than on account of the precise ratios of harmonies and principles of music, whose content is based on lucky guesses and imitation, if one is supposed to live a *life* (62c)!

As readers of Plato's dialogues, what we laugh at and how we laugh at those matters a great deal and reflects how little or how much we've learned from his work. Laughing down Socrates's interlocutors while arrogantly thinking ourselves superior to them generates false pleasures, whereas using their experience as an opportunity to reflect our own ignorance leads to healthy self-irony and generates true pleasures that we take in increased self-awareness and self-knowledge.[8]

It is only reasonable that Plato wants to leave plenty of room for true mixed pleasures of the soul itself, since many of these pleasures are necessary not only for our survival, but also for our rational development and spiritual growth. Given the wide variety of emotions that Socrates includes in this class, love, envy, jealousy, anger, longing, lamentation, we can speculate that Socrates envisions most of the pleasures accompanying them, for example, love, longing, anger, lamentation, as capable of both truth and falsehood, yet the intrinsically vicious emotions of envy, jealousy, and malice (*phtonos*) can only be accompanied by false pleasures.[9]

Can Pure Pleasures Be False?

Once he finishes the examination of mixed pleasures, Socrates declares that they will next proceed to the discussion of *pure* pleasures (50e). In response, however, Protarchus asks Socrates to specify the kinds of pleasure that could rightly be regarded as *true* (51b), thus presumably assuming that pure pleasures must always also be true. Socrates replies by listing the perceived replenishments related to pure colors, to shapes, smells, and sounds insofar as they are based on imperceptible and painless lacks (51b). Is Socrates's list an unqualified reply to Protarchus's question about pleasures that are true, or is it rather only the follow-up of his own plan to turn to the discussion of pure pleasures? In other words, is Socrates thereby committing himself to the view that all the pure pleasures are always true? I incline to think that he is not, and the main textual support for this is that it is only after this exchange and after providing a more extended list of pure pleasures that Socrates addresses explicitly the question about the relation between purity and truth as applied to pleasures:

> After these there is still another thing to examine about them.
> —What is it? —What is more closely related to truth: the pure and unmixed or the intense, abundant, and large? (52d)

As we shall see, what emerges from Socrates's argument is only the modest claim that pure pleasures are always *truer* than the impure ones (53b–c), not also the stronger claim that pure (unmixed) pleasures are always true and cannot be false. The argument proceeds by elucidating the nature of purity in the case of whiteness, and will apply analogically to pleasure the new insight here obtained. Purity resides not in quantity or amount, but in the absence of any admixture of something foreign. Purity, then, makes something *truer* by preserving the thing's genuine nature.

> We are then in every way right to say that a small portion of pure white is at the same time whiter, more beautiful, and truer than a large portion of mixed white. —Perfectly right. (53b)

By analogy, pure pleasures must be *truer* than impure ones, since the former, unlike the latter, admit of no admixture of pain. The argument assumes degrees of truth and claims only that pure pleasures are *truer than the mixed ones,* not also that all the pure pleasures are necessarily true. This leaves open the possibility that some pure pleasures are less true ("less divine," 51e) than others—a point that Socrates makes also in the *Republic* by pointing out that pleasures of smell are pure (*Rep.* 584b), yet less true than the pure intellectual pleasures, which fill us with Being (*Rep.* 585b–e)—and also that some of them can at times be false.

What would count as false pure pleasures? There certainly are situations when we exaggerate or underestimate the degree of pleasure we take in an object, even when there is no pain inextricably mixed with it, as it happens, for instance, in cases in which we estimate the intensity of a pleasure we feel by comparing it to other pleasures (41e) or when we let our assessment be influenced by the nearness or remoteness of the object enjoyed instead of appealing to an absolute standard. I could thus be exaggerating the pleasure I take in smelling roses when I assess my experience in light of the closeness or remoteness of the experience or based on a relative comparison when I turn to smelling roses from having just smelled the subtler scent of daffodils. We can imagine similar cases for other pleasures not preceded by perceptible lacks. Take, for instance, the experience of pleasure that someone passionate about art would have upon learning about a new painting by his favorite artist when he assesses this experience *by contrast to and under the influence of* his distaste for having spent the previous two hours bored by something of no interest to him whatsoever: he will be very much prone to exaggerate the delight he takes in contemplating the artwork.

If what we said above is right, and some of our pure pleasures can at times be false, would we also want to say that all pure pleasures, whether sensible or intelligible, can sometimes turn out to be deceptive and false? Plato is not addressing directly this question, hence the response I propose will require a reconstruction of details. A number of hints provided by the text protect our speculations from randomness. Throughout the *Philebus*, Socrates uses the notion of purity to mean different things. When applied to pleasures, purity (*katharon*)[10] designates essentially the painlessness of pleasures, the fact that these pleasures are unmixed with pain. When used with reference to the structure of the universe (29b, 30b) and to the various kinds of knowledge (55c–d, 57c, 58d, 58d, 59c) purity is used in an ontological sense as expression of reality and truth.[11] Here are two of these passages in which "purity" is used in its ontological sense:

> That the amount of each in us is small and insignificant and never has the purity (*eilikrines*) and power belonging to its nature. Let's

take one example to illustrate them all. There is such a thing as fire in us, and there is fire in the universe. —Indeed. So, what about that? —And isn't the fire that is in us small and weak and poor, whereas the fire in the universe is amazingly vast in amount and beauty and the whole power that belongs to the nature of fire? —Indeed, that is very true. (29b6–c4)

Of the body that belongs to us, don't we say that it has a soul? —That is obviously what we will say. —But where does it come from, dear Protarchus, unless the body of the universe happens also to be ensouled, possessing the same properties as ours, yet in a better way in all respects. —Clearly from nowhere else, Socrates. —For we cannot believe, Protarchus, regarding those four classes of limit, the unlimited, their mixture and the cause which is present in everything, that this is recognized as comprehensive wisdom, which provides soul for us and is responsible for the development and healing of our body, and in other cases provides structure and order, that it should fail to be responsible for the same things on a larger scale, with things that are in addition beautiful and pure (*eilikrines*), and that it did not fashion the finest and most honorable nature. —That would not make any sense. (30a3–30c1)

"Purity" here is a feature that pertains to the highest and noblest of realities insofar as they display supreme causal and ontological power. A similar, ontological, sense of "purity" appears in a number of passages dealing with knowledge and the various degrees of purity of the arts. The kinds of knowledge are classified in proportion to the degree of purity and truth pertaining to their object and thus in direct proportion to the certainty and precision of the various branches of knowledge. Starting off with the most imprecise crafts, such as flute playing, medicine, agriculture, navigation, and strategy, moving on to the more precise ones like shipbuilding and house building, then to the applied, vulgar mathematics, next to the pure mathematical studies, and ending up with dialectic, which attains the highest degree of precision and truth (55c–59b).[12]

As used in the hierarchical ordering of the types of knowledge, purity characterizes a thing's reality and stable determination of its nature. At first glance, the meaning of purity as painlessness of pleasures and its ontological meaning as stable determination of a thing's nature, changelessness, and reality seem to be unrelated. But if we think about the wider context of the discussion we can see the link between them. The central theme of the *Philebus* concerns the nature of the good human life. The investigation proceeds by distinguishing various kinds of pleasure and knowledge and then discusses the right way of mixing them that leads to a fulfilling life. Socrates insists on the importance of proceeding correctly in discerning which types of knowledge and of pleasure should be combined in this final mixture (61b–64a). Two main factors determine the righteousness of the mixture: (1) the intrinsic worth of the elements combined, and (2) the inner harmony and cohesion of a soul in which pleasures and reason can carry out a conversation. The second aspect suggests that not every kind of pleasure is compatible with every kind of knowledge, and vice versa. To put it positively, the type of pleasure must be proportional to the degree of purity and truth pertaining to the knowledge that is effective in a person's soul. The strong correlation between the purity of knowledge and the truthfulness and purity of pleasure is rooted in the way that pleasure and knowledge relate to each other in terms of the fourfold structure of reality. Pleasure, we have seen, is in the class of Mixtures. Knowledge, for its part, is in the class of the Cause of mixtures, alongside reason (*noūs*) and wisdom (*phronēsis* [28a4]; *sophia* [30b4, c6]). Naturally, then, the purity of knowledge, that is, the purity of the specific object of knowledge, has a direct influence on the truthfulness and purity of the pleasure taken in the acquisition of the type of knowledge in question. Consequently, the purity of the intelligible objects contemplated through dialectic determines and is responsible for the truthfulness of the pleasures we take in such learning. Having the sensitivity required for taking pleasure in intelligible, stable objects presupposes that one knows these objects, for taking pleasure is not just replenishment, but perceived replenishment. Thus, in order to be capable of perceiving replenishment we must have a cognitive grasp of the object replenishing us. The stability and reality of intelligible objects responsible for our replenishment rule out the possibility that we might be misestimating the replenishment we are experiencing. Cases in which one mistakes the degree of replenishment brought about by intelligible objects are cases in which what we were enjoying proves after all to have been a replenishment not with Being, but with some imitation thereof.

The pleasures of learning referred to in the text, on the other hand, are always true, not simply because they are free from pain, but because the objects that replenish us in the experience of these pleasures are real, stable, and unchanging. The context clearly suggests that Socrates here refers strictly to the learning practiced by the very few engaged in dialectic 52b. Hence, experiencing such pleasures presupposes that we have knowledge of these objects and thus cannot mistake the intensity of replenishment.

Our elucidations so far also explain why mixed pleasures are more prone to being false than unmixed (pure) ones. The reason for this is that the admixture of pains in our experiences of pleasure makes it easier for us to be misguided in assessing our experiences and thus miss their real nature. The mixing of pleasures with pains drives our experiences away from Limit and closer to the indefiniteness and lack of measure characteristic to the Unlimited, to the point where Limit will no longer have sufficient control over the Unlimited to maintain the nature of real pleasures. Though it is not impossible to mistake the degree of some of our pure pleasures (those that involve the senses), it is much more likely to fall prey to such deceptions when experiencing mixed pleasures.

Why Hybrid Pleasures Matter

The separation of the two sets of criteria of truth/falsehood and purity/mixture (impurity) and, with it, accounting for the possibility of hybrid pleasures are important in a number of ways. First, by keeping the two sets of criteria distinct, Plato can recognize the positive function that some of our emotions have in promoting our rational maturation, and he is not forced to condemn as false our mixed pleasures intrinsic to these emotions. Love, fear, longing, anger, etc. can and often do work as essential catalysts that help the conversion of our soul through its reorientation from the sensible to the intelligible realm. *Republic* 518c points out the importance of a full conversion where spirited and appetitive parts of the soul are consonant with reason's turn from sensible particulars toward the Forms. The same point of a well-integrated soul is made in the *Philebus* through the personified dialogue between pleasure and knowledge (63a–64a). That episode shows the emotional and rational aspects of the soul speaking in unison and welcoming each other—once the most intense, false pleasures have been excluded, not simply because they are enemies of reason, but also because they are a hindrance to their own true counterparts (63d–e). Other dialogues also openly acknowledge the positive role that emotions have in assisting and supporting our rational part. Thus, in the *Phaedo*, arguably the most austere and intellectualist of Plato's dialogues, Socrates talks at length about the importance of persuading "the child in us" (77d–78b), supposedly our emotional part, and concludes the defense of the immortality of the soul with a myth (107d–114c), called in to complement and aid the limitations of rational arguments offered thus far. In the *Symposium*, Socrates talks about the love of Beauty being responsible for the lover's ascent from sensible to intelligible realities, and in the *Phaedrus*, the white horse in charge with true opinions and honor clearly assists the charioteer in taming the black horse. Hence, recognizing the existence of these hybrid pleasures confirms the multilayered nature of our *psyche* and the textured nature of the moral realm.

Second, it might seem at first that the *Philebus* reaffirms the strict dualism and separation between Being and becoming, knowledge and opinion (58a, 58e–59b, 61e) put forth at the end of book V of the *Republic* (476a–480a) and is thus threatened by all the adjacent difficulties related to the impossibility of advancing from opinions to knowledge or of making knowledge in any way relevant to the realm of particulars. In fact, however, Plato is careful in the *Philebus* to suggest at least implicitly that, while the ontological distinction between Being and becoming remains in place as strong as ever, the divide is not unbridgeable *in practice*. One way in which he signals the continuity between them is by discussing all the various skills and crafts as types of knowledge (57b1, 57e3, 58c1, 58e2) distinguished among themselves by *degrees* of precision, purity, certainty, and truth (55c–58e). Another major way in which Plato signals the possibility of gradual transitions *in practice* from one level to the other is by allowing room for these hybrid pleasures. The structure of reality proposed in the *Philebus* impresses through its gradations and mediations at various levels. Not only are the four main articulations arranged in hierarchical order, with Limit at the top, followed by the Cause of mixtures, Mixtures, and then the Unlimited, but even the members within each one of the four classes (or, better, perhaps, within three of the four, the Unlimited being an exception since it is too indefinite to allow for such order) are prone to hierarchical orderings. The ranking takes the Good as its highest standard since it alone is perfect, complete, and self-sufficient (20d–e). Since the Good, as supreme Form, is the ultimate source of the class of Limit, as a class, Limit will be the highest in status among the four. Cause is the rational principle that brings Limit to the Unlimited, and thus follows next in the hierarchical order. Mixture comes third, since it combines Limit and the Unlimited, while the Unlimited is the last in axiological order, since it is defined by indefiniteness and illimitation. Correspondingly, then, among mixtures, true pure pleasures are superior to their impure true counterparts, since the former exhibit a more measured combination of Limit and the

Unlimited than do the latter. Also, the transition is not simply from false to true pure pleasures, but rather has a more modulated texture, going through true mixed pleasures, that can be either true or false.

Finally, by keeping the two sets of criteria—truth/falsehood and purity/impurity—distinct, Plato's Socrates provides an account that can accommodate the objective, absolute hierarchy of types of pleasure and of knowledge respectively to a specific individual's talents and circumstances of life. While intellectual pleasures are intrinsically superior to, say, pleasures of eating, this does not mean that in every concrete circumstance pursuing an intellectual task is preferable over the experience of true mixed pleasures of eating when hungry, sleeping when tired, drinking when thirsty, etc. When eating a healthy meal restores the necessary balance of an organism, it does not impede the enjoyment of intellectual pleasures, but rather facilitates it. At the heart of knowing exactly when to choose one activity or one type of pleasure over another is the need for due measure. It is to the examination of this very notion of due measure that we turn in the next chapter.

IV

The Nature of Pleasure

Absolute Standards of Replenishment and Due Measure

The main thrust of this chapter is to show how it is possible to mediate between the absolute standards of pleasure we aim to realize in our lives and the concrete circumstances in which we experience pleasure. As witnessed already, throughout the *Philebus*, Plato's Socrates defends an understanding of pain and pleasure as perceived processes of depletion and filling or return to our natural state, respectively (31d, 33d). Hunger and thirst, for instance, are destructions or disruptions, and thus painful, while eating and drinking are corresponding restorations of the proper balance in the organism, and thus pleasant. Plato distinguishes between pure and impure (mixed) pleasures: while all the pleasures presuppose a lack to be filled by them, only impure pleasures presuppose our earlier conscious experience of that lack as painful. When experiencing pure pleasures, on the other hand, we are enjoying the perceived filling or replenishment, but are not experiencing the lack thus filled as painful, which means that pure pleasures fill an unperceived lack.

The view that pleasure is the filling or replenishment of some lack has often been subject to criticism as too narrow and incapable of accounting for some of the corporeal and all the noncorporeal pleasures. For it seems difficult, if not impossible, to specify what exactly must have been initially lacking and is correspondingly filled or replenished through our pleasures of sight, smell, learning, recollecting pleasant memories from our past, or projecting hopes for the future, when these experiences are not preceded by any perceptible lacks.[1] What kind of replenishment are we undergoing when experiencing any of these pleasures? To avoid this difficulty, commentators have sometimes argued that Plato restricts the definition of pleasure as perceived restoration of a lack to bodily pleasures[2] or that the definition of pleasure here proposed is intended by Socrates *ad hominem,* to signal merely the fact that Socrates opposes the hedonist view, and not as the definition that Plato himself endorses.[3] As argued however in chapter I, the dialogue does not seem to support any of these proposed solutions, and the characterization of pleasure as perceived filling or replenishment of a lack is, rather, intended as a generic account for all pleasures.

The difficulty signaled seems to be only deepened when we realize that Plato suggests a reply based on objective standards in relation to which we are to estimate the reality and degree of replenishment that we experience when taking pleasure in various things. For the idea that there might be universal and objective standards of pleasure seems to make it difficult to account for the legitimate diversity of our natural talents, tastes, and corresponding ways of experiencing pleasure. Would Plato suggest that, for instance, since the pleasure of dialectical contemplation is superior to the pleasure of any other pursuit, a gifted shoemaker, ought to get initiated in dialectic, instead of taking delight in the craft at which he is so skilled?

The present chapter explores these two issues: (1) whether Plato's notion of pleasure as perceived filling or replenishment of a lack can account for our pure pleasures, and (2) whether and, if so, how does Plato's quasi-objective understanding of standards of pleasure fit in with the recognition of a legitimate diversity of natural talents and tastes. I will argue that, when integrated in its proper metaphysical horizon, Plato's understanding of pleasure is perfectly able to accommodate both apparent difficulties. The chapter is structured in two parts, corresponding roughly to the two questions just mentioned. The first part starts off with a discussion of false pleasures in order to explore how we are to understand the idea of replenishment first in the more obvious cases of mixed pleasures, and then in the less obvious cases of pure pleasures. The second part deals primarily with the issue of accommodating absolute standards to the legitimate diversity of our natural talents and tastes.

Pleasure as Perceived Replenishment of Some Lack

In the first half of the *Philebus*, Socrates is trying to show Protarchus that some of the experiences that people usually call pleasure are false pleasures. The cases discussed include: the falsity that infects our pleasures of anticipation, the falsity regarding the estimation of the degree of pleasure experienced, and the case in which we mistake a neutral condition, a state of neither pleasure nor pain, with one of pleasure.

False Pleasures of Anticipation (36c–40e)

In some of the cases in which we experience pain simultaneously with pleasure, when, for instance, our body suffers pain and our soul enjoys the pleasant anticipation of the filling needed by the body, our anticipatory pleasures are false. This happens when we misidentify the experience and take as replenishment something that in fact is not. As argued already in chapter II, the discussion of this type of false pleasures is meant at different levels, a superficial and a deeper one. On the surface reading, Socrates simply argues that anticipatory pleasures can, in fact, be false in cases where we make false prognostications: the falsity of our factual judgments about the future infects our current pleasures of anticipation. On a deeper reading, Socrates's discussion invites the suggestion that false pleasures of anticipation arise due to the falsity of our assumptions about the structure of reality: mistakes about the structure of reality infect our apprehension of the expected object's worth, and thus, we often end up taking as pleasant something that in fact is not, something that, whether it occurs or not, cannot in fact bring about replenishment.

Neither Protarchus nor first time readers of the *Philebus* are expected to comprehend the deeper meaning of the discussion of false pleasures, since it is only in light of the dialogue's subsequent elucidations that we can see this meaning embedded in Socrates's discussion of falsehood. However, identifying Protarchus's grasp as superficial does not imply that this surface reading is inessential, redundant, and could just as well have been left out of the text. On the contrary, that reading is crucial for enabling everything that follows. For without an effective argument that could persuasively show Protarchus and us (on our first encounter with the text) that pleasures can sometimes be false, none of the discussion that follows could have ever gotten off the ground.

Much of the discussion at 36c–39e is dedicated to drawing an analogy between pleasures and judgments: pleasures, just like judgments, can be either true or false, and the common cause of falsehood in both judgments and pleasures resides in mistakes about the object of our judgments and pleasures respectively (37e). Socrates's general formulation, that what is at stake here is a mistake about the object of judgment/pleasure (37e), is broad enough to cover the possibility of mistakes in both factual judgments (e.g., taking a man for a statue) and axiological beliefs (e.g., taking something bad for a good thing). Accordingly, two distinct interpretations of the following illustration are possible, corresponding, on the one hand, to the more superficial and, on the other, to the deeper reading signaled above. Socrates illustrates his point by saying that, when looking at it from close by, we may discover we have been deceived about an object when we saw it at a distance: what from a distance appeared to be a statue might turn out to be a man (38c–e). The parallel between pleasure and judgments suggests that it is similarly possible to be deceived regarding the pleasure we experience when anticipating that we would take pleasure in an object in light of the disappointment experienced when the object is close by.

That Plato intends the deeper reading is supported by several indications. As the dialogue develops, it becomes ever clearer that truth is inseparable from considerations of value and thus not reducible to statements of fact. Notice, for instance, that while the Good itself, the ultimate standard of value, cannot be given a satisfactory elucidation in itself, it will be revealed through its reflection in Beauty, Proportion, and Truth (65a2); as a reflection of the Good, truth itself is inherently structured by value. Furthermore, within the hierarchy of various kinds of knowledge, dialectic is said to rank highest of all since it is "truest" (58a), and dialectic's truth-character resides primarily in the nobility and value of its objects. Moreover, when Socrates sharply distinguishes dialectic from Gorgianic persuasion and asserts the superiority of the former over the latter, he admits that the latter might have ranked higher than dialectic if the criterion of evaluation had been practical usefulness to us rather than clarity, precision, and truth (58c). The distinction between pragmatic usefulness and truth invites us to reflect retrospectively on the illustration we have used above: the falsity of a pleasure of anticipation cannot be reduced to the mere fact that the future disappoints our prognostication of what will happen. Pragmatically, I will always be better off with the future turning out such that I do earn a lot of money. But as far as truth is concerned, it all depends on my motivation for wanting to earn that money, and this rests ultimately on my understanding of the Good. Finally, in the passage dealing specifically with false pleasures of anticipation, Socrates already explicitly recognizes a direct connection between virtue and true/false pleasures generally when he says that good people, in general, enjoy true pleasures, while wicked people enjoy false ones (39e–40b). Though Socrates does not elaborate at this point on what he means, Plato might legitimately expect his readers to be familiar with his elaborations in the *Republic*, where Socrates argued extensively that the just man's pleasures are superior to those of the unjust due ultimately to the intrinsic worth of the objects enjoyed (580a–583e). Later elucidations in the *Philebus* suggest that good people are right in identifying what counts as a real object of pleasure, that is, an object that truly replenishes a lack, while vicious people are not (45d–47b, 55a–b). If the suggested reading is correct, the ultimate assumption underlying Socrates's analysis of false pleasures of anticipation is that false pleasures in general, including false pleasures of anticipation, are the result of false beliefs about what is valuable, that is, about the Good.

Socrates then continues the discussion of false pleasures signaling deceptions regarding the degree of pleasure and pain we enjoy when we assess their intensity on account of the immediacy or remoteness of their corresponding objects, and not by appeal to an absolute standard (41a–42c). Our immediate experience of pleasure may cause us to underestimate or overestimate the intensity of the future pain we anticipate or of the pain we have experienced in the past. Similarly, our immediate discomfort may cause us to underestimate or overestimate what we anticipate as future pleasure or what we have experienced as pleasure in the past. Here again, the ontological assumption upon which Socrates's identification of this type of false pleasure rests is that there are absolute standards in relation to which we can legitimately recognize the true degree of pleasure and pain experienced. These standards measure the intrinsic worth of the objects we find enjoyable and are independent of the temporal and spatial closeness or remoteness of the experiences we have. They are objective standards measuring the extent to which an object replenishes a lack.

A third type of false pleasures occurs when we mistake a neutral condition (absence of pleasure or pain) for genuine pleasure (42c–44d). Socrates says that this type of "pleasure" is in a sense *even more false* than the earlier one (42c). What he means is probably that, when we are only mistaking the degree to which an experience is pleasant, we are still enjoying some legitimate amount of pleasure, but when we are altogether mistaken about the object of pleasure and take the absence of pleasure and pain for pleasure itself, there is simply no pleasure whatsoever experienced. Those who think they experience pleasure when they are simply free from pain experience a false pleasure. Similarly, those who believe they are experiencing pain, simply because they are not experiencing pleasure, experience a false pain (see also the *Republic* 584e–585a). The discussion of the third type of false pleasures makes even more explicit than the earlier ones that the truth and falsity of our pleasures depend on whether the object enjoyed is in fact worthy of being enjoyed, that is, whether the object in question does bring about the corresponding replenishment of a lack.

It has been sometimes argued that Plato's conception of pleasure as return to the natural state is inadequate as far as the actual phenomenology of our experiences of pleasure is concerned. Experience shows us that we do, in fact, enjoy being in a state of freedom from distress in its own right and not only the process of transition toward that state. Once I have recovered from an illness, for instance, I take genuine delight in my present state of health. Thus, scholars have argued that

> Plato overlooks the fact that it is possible to be pleased that one is no longer suffering distress, and even to enjoy freedom from distress. . . . It is indeed a mistake to describe as pleasant a state which is neither pleasant or unpleasant, but the invalids and others whom Plato describes do not make that mistake; they expect to find, and do find, a certain state enjoyable just because it is a state of freedom from distress. There is no misidentification involved here, any more than there is a mistake involved in finding a cool shady room pleasant just by contrast with the heat and glare outside. This account of the invalid's enjoyments is indeed inconsistent with any general account of pleasure as consisting in the perceived filling up of deficiencies. For what the invalids enjoy is not any (perceived) process of restoration, but the state of having been restored, of not having some deficiencies any longer. Thus they provide further evidence of the inadequacy of the general account, to add to the others (pleasures of anticipation, pleasure in colours, smells, etc.) which Plato cites in this dialogue. (cf. 7.3)[4]

While it is true that a state of being replenished or satiety, and not just the process toward it, can be enjoyed in its own right, the above criticism misses the point of Socrates's objection to people's misidentification of pleasure with a neutral state. Socrates could reply that a state of health or satiety will be enjoyed in its own right precisely insofar as, while it lasts, it contributes to the restoration of the overall balance of our organisms and not simply because it is a state free of distress. Socrates's notion of lack is very broad, covering not only the obvious cases of deficiency but also the less obvious cases of inactivity. Inability to exercise some of the functions of our organism while we are sick is already a lack; a state of health, on the other hand, allows us to exercise those functions properly and is thus an experience of replenishment. If this is correct, then Plato's conception is consistent with Aristotle's characterization of pleasure as unimpeded activity of a disposition in its natural state (NE 1153a12–15). Health is only a necessary, not also a sufficient, condition for our overall balance, and in this sense, what we enjoy when we are pleased by our health is actually only a stage in a complex process aimed at our overall, physical and spiritual, balance.

Plato's main objective with the discussion of the third type of false pleasures is not to deny the genuine enjoyment that a formerly sick individual can experience once he has recovered, but rather, to reject the generalization of the idea that pleasure is reducible to freedom from pain. For, if pleasure is reduced to absence of pain, it becomes impossible to account for any of the more elevated pleasures that do not rest on a previous experience of pain, such as some of our pleasures of learning or artistic contemplation and, in general, all the pure pleasures defined as replenishments of unperceived lacks (51b ff.). Socrates's main intent here is to rebuke the mediocrity of lives content with a general feeling of bodily satiety and well-being and no conscious drive to experience any of the higher pleasures available. This reading is supported by Socrates's repeated point that he is rejecting people's prospect of guiding *their whole life* by the identification of pleasure with absence of pain (43c8, 43c13, 43d7–9, 43e8), and by his rejection of the natural scientists' position, which reduces *all* pleasures to freedom from pain (44c1–2). Socrates is absolutely entitled to reject this position since, as we are well aware, attainment of more elevated pleasures in life often requires us to endure pain. Socrates does not deny, then, that one can genuinely enjoy a state of health; he merely disagrees with those who make physical satisfaction the ultimate object of desire, while remaining insensitive to the more elevated noncorporeal desires and their corresponding pleasures. The danger of the position that Socrates here rejects is that it encourages us to pursue pleasures for their intensity, regardless of the intrinsic worth or worthlessness of the object enjoyed (44d–46a).

It is of crucial importance to recognize that Plato's Socrates does not identify what is here called the neutral condition (absence of pleasure and pain) with what he called earlier the most godlike life in which neither pain, nor pleasure are experienced, *because* it is a life entirely dedicated to rational thought (21d–22c, 32d–33c)—Frede, however, equates the two (Frede 1992, 448). The former state is compatible with the mediocrity of the many, who are content with bodily satisfactions and are completely insensitive to higher pursuits of desire and pleasure precisely because their engagement with reason is limited. The latter characterizes the life of the gods who, liberated from corporeal demands, enjoy a blissful state of contemplation. For us this is the standard that we can only aim at, but which is never fully realizable while embodied. The difference between the two kinds of life is that the former is often devoid of the activity of thinking, whereas the latter is entirely dedicated to it.[5]

The types of false pleasures examined so far have been illustrated with cases of mixed pleasures—the experienced replenishment being preceded each time by a felt lack. Let us now approach more directly the first difficulty mentioned above and see whether Plato can account for the existence of an unperceived lack that is filled when we experience pure pleasures. Of the pure pleasures, Socrates mentions the pleasures we take in the beauty of geometrical shapes constructed with a ruler or a compass (51c–d), of pure colors (51b–d, 53a–c), of smooth and bright sounds that produce one single note (51d), the pleasures associated with smells (51e), and those of learning (51e–52a). These pleasures are hierarchically ordered in direct proportion to the degree of reality of their corresponding objects. Highest of all are the pleasures of learning, with "learning" understood here as restricted to the study of dialectic and restricted to the very few (52b), and lowest are the pure pleasures of smell, described as "less divine" than the other ones mentioned. Pursuit of the ultimate truth through dialectic is also intrinsically related to the pursuit of virtue. The dialectician is envisioned as someone who "understands what justice itself is and can give the appropriate definitions and possesses the same kind of comprehension about all the rest of what there is" (62a).

What, then, must have been lacking prior to our experience of filling in all these cases? To answer this question, we need to refer to the wider horizon of Plato's metaphysical conception about human nature and the rational structure of reality. According to Plato, while embodied, our soul is never completely detached from our corporeal determinations, which constantly obstruct a complete exercise of our reason. In other words, as long as it is embodied, the human soul is essentially defined by lack. Pleasure is a phenomenon that pertains to us precisely insofar as we are also part of the world of becoming. Our very predisposition to feelings of pleasure and pain is by itself a mark of our finitude. The gods, on the other hand, are not subject to passions, pleasure, and pain, and their natural condition is defined as full and exclusive exercise of reason (22c, 33a–b).[6] The metaphysical view disclosed through these assumptions explains that Plato is fully able to account for pleasures of smell, sight, knowledge, or health, not preceded by painful awareness of the corresponding lacks, as nonetheless replenishments of lacks. On this view, pure pleasures fill in us an ontological lack, namely, our ineluctable finitude by gradually bringing us closer in touch with true realities. Our experiences of pure pleasures always get us closer to our natural balance. Thus, the filling at stake has a metaphysical, rather than a physiological sense. Pure pleasures are both inherently valuable and desirable for the sake of our normative state of balance. The fact that they are described as becoming (*genesis*) and as such aiming toward that ultimate normative state does not mean that they lack inherent worth and that they are not also desired for their own sake. Implicit throughout this account is the view that there are objective and universal standards in relation to which the kinds of experiences we have can be assessed, in the sense that we can measure the degree of filling or depletion they bring about.

Absolute Standards of Replenishment and Due Measure

While the reflections developed so far explain how Plato can account for pure pleasures as filling some lack in us, they also open up the gates for the next apparent difficulty, namely the problem regarding the legitimate variety of our tastes to be accommodated to the quasi-objective standards of enjoyment. Even if we may agree that human motivation generally can be objectively assessed, we are reluctant to accept that two people experience the fulfillment of their desires or the replenishment of a corresponding lack in exactly the same way and as originating in the same source. Thus, if we can accept, for instance, that human nature is equipped and predisposed to having aesthetic experiences, we would not want to go as far as to say that we should all experience exactly the same internal state when contemplating the same work of art. People have different natures, and this is why some prefer, for instance, literature over painting, or Euripides over Aeschylus. All these are pertinent remarks, and Plato must have been aware of them, since the whole project of the *Republic* relies on the assumption that people have different natures and are naturally suited for different things (*Republic* 415a–c). The *Phaedrus* continues the same idea, suggesting that people are by nature inclined to follow the temperaments of one or another of the twelve gods (*Phaedrus* 252c–253c). In the *Philebus*, Socrates reiterates the view regarding natural differences when recognizing that "the pleasures of learning are unmixed with pain and belong not to the masses, but only to a very few" (52b). The interesting issue at stake now is not simply to recognize that we have different natures but to see whether and, if so, how Plato's conception of pleasure, based on absolute standards, can account for the fact that different individuals rightly find different things pleasant and often rightly enjoy an impure pleasure more than a pure one.

Pleasure has been defined as perceived return to the natural state of an organism (31d, 33d), but the natural state or balance of one organism does not coincide with that of another. The natural state of an appetitive person will often feel very unbalanced to the rational type, just as the natural state of the spirited type would often be found excessive to both the appetitive and the rational type. To put it in terms of specific vocations, the true pleasure that the skilled businessman takes in his affairs would feel like depletion to a philosopher undergoing the same experience, and yet it would seem odd if the former were to be encouraged to replace right away the delight that he takes in his craft with the practice of philosophy. Socrates himself does not seem to be directly preoccupied with this issue in the *Philebus*. But we legitimately find ourselves wondering whether what Socrates does say leaves room for an account of the fact that, for instance, although the pleasures of dialectic are intrinsically superior to those of music, it might yet be better for some specific individuals, in the specific contexts of their lives, to pursue the pleasures of music instead of those of dialectic, or that the experience of a true mixed pleasure is at least sometimes more valuable than the experience of a false pure pleasure, in the sense that the former is in a particular context more restorative of balance than the latter. Since Socrates himself does not deal with these cases explicitly in the *Philebus*, our account requires a reconstruction of details. In what follows, I suggest that the dialogue incorporates the seeds for such a reconstruction in the notion of measure (*metriotēs*).

The notion of measure (*metriotēs*) needs to be understood as part of the complex ontology elaborated throughout the dialogue. The ultimate standard of self-sufficiency and completeness is the Good (60c). The Good, however, does not lend itself easily to comprehension, and for this reason, instead of attempting an account of the Good in itself, while standing on the "threshold of the good and of the house of every member of its family" (64c), Socrates will approach it only in outline (61a4) through its threefold manifestation as Beauty (*to kalon*), Proportion (*hē symmetria*), and Truth (*hē alētheia*), 65a2.[7] Measure (*metriotēs*) is one of the necessary ingredients of every particular sharing in beauty or virtue ("measure and proportion manifest themselves in all areas as beauty and virtue," 64e6–7) and, in general, in any worthwhile mixture:

It is certainly not difficult at all to see the cause on account of which any mixture whatsoever possesses the highest value or no value at all. —What do you mean? —There is no human being that would not know it. —What exactly? —That any kind of mixture that does not in some way or other possess measure (*metrou*) or the nature of proportion (*tēs symmetrou physeōs*) will necessarily ruin its ingredients and most of all itself. For there would be no combination in such cases at all but really an uncombined mess, the ruin of whatever happens to be contained in it. (64d3–e3)

Since measure is necessary for Beauty, and Beauty is an immediate manifestation of the Good, it clearly follows that measure is a faithful reflection of the Good, inherently valuable and responsible, along with proportion, for the worth imparted to things. Measure (*metriotēs*) is operative both at the cosmic level, regulated by the cosmic *noūs*, and in our own individual lives, where its activity both regulates and is regulated by our human reason (66a–c). Whether used with reference to the order of the cosmos or to the ordering of an individual's life, while it is a normative standard of goodness in a mixture, whether that of an individual human's life or of the cosmos, the measure here at stake must also be changing relative to the way concrete circumstances change. This is why, I believe, measure is listed first in rank among the factors responsible for the goodness of a human life along with *the timely* (*to kairon*), which clearly takes into account the shifting circumstances in an individual's life (66a6–8). In fact, in both cases, of the cosmic order or the order of an individual's life, measure acts as the norm that is intentionally sought and pursued by an intellect or a mind, be it the cosmic *noūs* or the human reason, that acts as cause for the combination of limit with the unlimitedness in the mixture (26e–30e). All this is to say that the notion of measure in the *Philebus* is, as I argue below, synonymous with or at least very closely related to that of due measure or the mean, which Plato has also involved in dialogues such as the *Statesman*, the *Republic*, or the *Phaedrus*.

The Good itself transcends every mixture and, for this reason, is not mentioned as an ingredient of the human life. Nevertheless, the Good will show up through its reflection as measure (*to metrion*) in such a life. Of highest value among the ingredients of a good human life is what is connected with measure (*to peri metron*), the measured (*to metrion*), and the timely (*kairion*), and whatever else is similar to these (66a6–8). Second come the well-proportioned (*to symmetron*), the beautiful (*to kalon*), the perfect (*to teleon*), the self-sufficient (*to hikanon*), and whatever else is akin to them. Third come reason and wisdom (*noūs te kai phronēsis*), fourth the sciences, the crafts, and right opinions, and finally the pure pleasures of the soul. Guthrie and Wood suggest that Socrates's enigmatic ending with a quotation from an Orphic Theogony—"With the sixth generation the well-ordered song may find its end"—may well mean that Socrates, just like the Orphic poet, did include a sixth, namely, the necessary and temperate pleasures, as part of a good life (Guthrie 1978, 236; Wood 2016, 280). The reason why, in the final ranking of these constituents, wisdom (*phronēsis*) comes only third, while the first and second rank are given over to measure and beauty, proportion and symmetry, respectively, is that the wisdom here ranked third is humanly attainable wisdom, which remains weaker than the universal reason (*noūs*) that governs the universe as a whole (28d–30c). Reason (*noūs*) in its purity remains the "king of heaven and earth" (30d), while the measure, beauty, symmetry, and proportion, which rank highest in human life, are our points of contact with the supreme cosmic *noūs*.

The measure here at stake covers, as I argue below, the sense of an absolute moral or practical mean, defining the right choice between the extremes of too much or too little in various areas of our lives. The mean or due measure is not identical with the Good, yet it cannot be understood independently of the Good. It is more like a reflection of the Good, a faithful image of it that can be achieved during this life and is, in fact, a necessary ingredient of a fulfilling and self-sufficient human life. Due measure is neither a Form, since Forms, unlike the mean, can exist independently of the realm of human life, nor a specific sensible instance, since the mean functions as an absolute standard of rightness and fittingness by which we evaluate particulars.[8] Due measure is, then, the absolute criterion for judging when an intentional action in a concrete set of circumstances reflects the overall Goodness or rationality of the universe. The peculiar nature of this sort of mean is that it takes into account specific circumstances and explains the way in which the Good can be accommodated to our world of change. Hence, what we are dealing with is a practical measure, not an abstract, theoretical, and strictly mathematical sense thereof.

Articulating the distinction between these two senses of measure is central in the *Statesman*, where we find no fewer than seven passages in which Socrates spells out and clarifies the distinction between two arts of measurement—practical and theoretical—and their corresponding conceptions of measure.[9] The abstract mathematical or theoretical mean is defined by the extremes, and is therefore relative to them, while the practical mean is an absolute measure in relation to which alone extremes can be assessed as extremes.[10] The first characterization, which for the most part remains rather obscure, distinguishes two arts of measurement, insofar as one of them deals with the way in which greatness and smallness relate to one another, whereas the other is concerned with a necessary production or generation of something (283c11–d9). A second passage connects due measure with the moral worth of human action. While relative measure allows us to estimate things only relative to one another, due measure has an absolute normative function in relation to which we can determine the goodness/badness of the characters originating action and is thus intrinsically connected with value (283d11–e6). A third formulation objectifies the features of greatness and smallness into the great and the small and tells us that the two measures are two ways of judging the great and the small, that is, in relation to each other and in relation to due measure respectively (283e8–e11). A fourth passage explains that due measure is necessary for a variety of arts (*technai*) and their products and is responsible for the expert production of good and fine (*agatha kai kala*) things (284a5–b2). Due measure is therefore essential to the coming into being of everything that is designed with a purpose in view, and thus, a necessary component of all the various arts (*technai*), for to be skilled at something means being able to discern the right configuration of a product in view of the function or purpose it has, that is to say, what makes it as it ought to be (284a, 284d). Without measure, we cannot have statesmanship, or dialectic, or any other art, nor would there be a product of divine craftsmanship, the universe (*kosmos*) itself, which is designed to be replete with beauty and purpose: "being a living creature and having had intelligence granted to it by the one who fitted it together from the beginning" (269d); "it (the world) acquired all fine things from the one who put it together" (273b6–7). A fifth passage emphasizes the difficulty of discovering the due measure, a difficulty even greater than that of giving an account of Non-Being (284b7–c7).[11] A sixth passage spells out the mutual dependence of arts and due measure: arts depend for their existence on due measure, just as much as due measure too depends for its own existence on the arts, since both arts and due measure are strictly connected with the production and coming into being of things. Since due measure is strictly dependent on the realm of becoming (*genesis*) in concrete circumstances of life, it is not itself an eternal and unchangeable reality, but rather an absolute norm hovering between Forms and shifting circumstances (284d1–d8). Finally, the seventh passage restates the contrast between the two kinds of measure: relative measure evaluates numbers, lengths, breadths, and speeds of things in relation to one another, while due measure deals with what is fitting (*to prepon*), the right moment (*ton kairon*), what is as it ought to be (*to deon*), everything that removes itself from the extremes to the middle. (284e2–8).¹²

Just as in the *Philebus*, in the *Republic* also due measure or the mean is identified as key to a good life and as essential for knowing how to combine and how to separate the ingredients of such a life. Speaking about the key to happiness, Socrates tells Glaucon that the man preoccupied with happiness and the good life ought to know the effects of beauty, wealth, and poverty upon a soul:

> He will know the effects of high or low birth, private life or ruling office, physical strength or weakness, ease or difficulty in learning, and all the things that are either naturally part of the soul or are acquired, and he will know what they achieve when mixed with one another. And from all this he will be able, by considering the nature of the soul, to reason out which life is better and which worse and to choose accordingly, calling a life worse if it leads the soul to become more unjust, better if it leads the soul to become more just, and ignoring everything else: We have seen that this is the best way to choose, whether in life or death. . . . And we must always know to choose the mean in such lives and how to avoid either of the extremes, as far as possible, both in this life and in all those beyond it. This is the way that a human being becomes happiest. (618 c–619a, trans. G. M. A. Grube and C. D. C. Reeve)

Though the *Philebus* is usually accepted as of a later date of composition than both the *Republic* and the *Statesman*, we need neither assume, nor prove, if at all possible, that Plato had in mind the very same distinction between the theoretical and the practical mean when he was composing the later work. It is nonetheless highly plausible that he might be alluding to something like the latter, as an absolute, practical mean, or due measure in the *Philebus* through his notions of measure (*metriotēs*), the measured (*to metrion*), and the timely (*to kairon*). We have at least two reasons in support of this claim. First, there is the linguistic ground that the term used for the measured in the *Philebus*, *to metrion* (66a6), is the same as that used for "due measure" in the passages of the *Statesman* cited above and also in the *Laws* 691c, where sensitivity to due measure is a defining feature of the good lawgiver. Second, and even more importantly, we have the semantic reason that the meaning assigned to measure in the *Philebus* has strong affinities with the meaning assigned to due measure in the other two dialogues mentioned. For measure (*to metrion*) is grouped on the first rank of the ingredients responsible for a good life alongside of the timely (*to kairon*) (66a6), thus designating the Good insofar as it is manifest in the shifting circumstances of one's life. Thus, if not entirely reducible to the senses of due measure in the *Statesman* or the *Republic*, the measure of the *Philebus* must at least also cover the senses ascribed to due measure or the mean in these other dialogues. In the *Philebus*, measure results from the imposition of Limit upon the Unlimited and is thus the mark of harmony and proportion in the members of the mixed class. Since the Unlimited lacks any limit whatsoever, its imbalance covers at once the more and the less, the great and the small, the hotter and the colder (24a–e). To bring measure to this restless and excessive nature is to approximate the absolute mean between excess and deficiency, between abundance and scarcity. In the *Statesman*, due measure is regarded as necessary for the preservation of every craft (*technē*) and for the production of good and fine things, which closely resonates with the role assigned to measure in the *Philebus* passage quoted above (64d–e).[13]

From all that has been said so far it is quite plausible that the *Philebus*'s notion of measure, whereby imbalances are avoided at once in the direction of what is too much and too little, covers also the sense of the absolute, practical mean, which is explored in the *Statesman* and the *Republic*. A reading of measure in the *Philebus* along these lines offers a plausible and pertinent answer to our question regarding the possibility of reconciling the absolute hierarchy of value with the recognition that the individuals' specific talents, natures, and distinctive circumstances of their lives will sometimes recommend pursuing mixed rather than pure pleasures, and pleasures of the body rather than those of the soul.

If, then, the due measure that Plato ranks highest among the ingredients of a good human life is a practical not a theoretical mean, it will account for the right choices in specific circumstances. The earlier-mentioned hierarchy of pleasures along with the corresponding hierarchy of various types of knowledge (55c–59c) were in that context meant absolutely. But when we assess the pleasure enjoyed by an individual in a specific situation, we must do so by reference to the mean that is relative to particular aspects of that individual's life. Depending on their natural inclinations and talents as well as on the particular circumstances of their lives at certain times, individuals will sometimes rightly find productive knowledge more fulfilling than pure mathematics, or mathematics more fulfilling than dialectic.[14] We can thus also see that, although he recommends the practice of dialectic as intrinsically superior to all the other pursuits and pleasures of life, Plato's Socrates never implies that we should, for the sake of philosophical pleasures, actively neglect bodily pleasures, cutting off, say, the healthy and true pleasures of eating and rest. Extremes such as starvation and chronic fatigue succumb into the unreality of those experiences that come with excess generally and with the lack of all measure. Not only does Socrates's account thus accommodate necessary pleasures into a good human life, but it also explains why, for people lacking an aptitude for philosophy, pursuit of true impure pleasures is at least sometimes more rewarding than a failed attempt to pursue pure pleasures of studying dialectic. A passage in the *Republic*, warning us about the dangers of exposing immature and unprepared students to dialectic, readily illustrates this point:

> And then a questioner comes along and asks someone of this sort, "What is the fine?" And, when he answers what he has heard from the traditional lawgiver, the argument refutes him, and by refuting him often and in many places shakes him from his convictions, and makes him believe that the fine is no more fine than the shameful, and the same with the just, the good, and the things he honored most. What do you think his attitude will be then to honoring and obeying his earlier convictions? —Of necessity he won't honor or obey them in the same way. —Then, when he no longer honors and obeys those convictions and can't discover the true ones, will he be likely to adopt any other way of life than that which flatters him? —No, he won't. —And so, I suppose, from being law-abiding he becomes lawless. (538d–e, trans. G. M. A. Grube and C. D. C. Reeve)

On similar presuppositions about the diversity of our talents, the philosophical rulers of the *Republic* design specific educational curricula for individuals with different natures—appetitive (iron, brass), spirited (silver), or rational (gold) (415a–c). To hit the mean of genuine enjoyment is certainly not the same as to go for the average intensity of feeling, to never experience strong pleasure and to be always content with a moderate amount. The "calculation" of the mean is always a very complex process that takes into account a large variety of factors. The due measure of pleasure that a musical person takes in a powerful musical work is certainly much more intense than the average feeling of musical enjoyment. Similarly, as far as the pure pleasures of mathematical learning are concerned, Plato would want us to become highly sensitive to the joys of such experiences and to cultivate them well beyond the average feeling of contentment that a novice experiences when solving a simple geometrical problem. For those who have the intellectual abilities to cultivate such sensitivity, the mean is the highly intense and not the moderate enjoyment. Since the good human life is understood as the right mixture of knowledge and pleasure, recognition of the mean in an individual's experience of pleasure is always dependent upon the degree of knowledge or general intellectual development that the person has achieved and is still able to achieve. This conception of the mean accounts also for changes in taste experienced by individuals during their lives. These modifications can be explained as functions of one's coming to have a better understanding of one's own nature and/or as depending on significant changes in one's circumstances of life. The model of the good human life that Plato has in mind is one in which knowledge and pleasure are in due harmonious blend (64e) and not at odds with each other, as Philebus assumed at the very beginning (11a–12a). Only this way can pleasures be brought into dialogue with knowledge and speak in unison with reason (62e–64a).

To say, then, that pleasure is the perceived replenishment of a lack and that the Good is the ultimate standard for our evaluation of what we lack does not imply that every individual will take pleasure in the same object and in the same way. Drawing the opposite conclusion would be, according to the *Philebus*, to behave like the clever ones who "make a one, haphazardly, and a many, faster or slower than they should; they go straight from the one to the unlimited and omit the intermediaries" (17a). So, then, while people situated at different levels of sophistication and with correspondingly different natures can experience true pleasures, the dialectician alone will be able to give a complete account of the truth or falsehood of these experiences because he alone can estimate all the intermediary steps in light of the Good.[15]

To conclude, then, the fact that the Good is highest in the absolute order of reality implies that, absolutely speaking, there is a universal objective hierarchy of values. Plato, however, is not a monist, and his rationalism does not deny contingency in the phenomenal world. When Socrates outlined the fourfold ontological model of Limit, the Unlimited, their Mixture, and the

Cause of their mixture, and Protarchus asked whether they should not add a fifth term, the cause of the healthy mixture's separation, Socrates replied that he did not think they need to do so, at least not for the time being, but that they would search for it, if it turns out they need to (23d). As it turns out, a special occasion to search for a fifth term never occurs during their conversation. Yet often throughout the text we are presented with deficient mixtures, such as various forms of disturbance and sickness whether regarding the body or the soul. In all these cases, the cause of disturbance is the lack of measure or Limit in the mixture and the excessive amount of the Unlimited. The implicit suggestion seems to be that the cause for the separation is already part of the fourfold model: its domain is that of the Unlimited, insofar as it resists due imposition of Limit. Furthermore, Socrates's remark that "there is plenty of the unlimited in the universe as well as sufficient limit" (30c) clearly suggests that contingency is part of our phenomenal world. The fact that our lives are permeated by contingency and irrationality alongside of reason explains why hitting the mean is such a difficult task and accounts for the fact that there is just one mean for every specific action or pleasure and yet plenty of ways to go astray from it.

V

Pleasures of Learning and the Role of Due Measure in Experiencing Them

Let us continue the exploration of the role of due measure begun in the previous chapter, this time with specific focus on our pleasures of learning. Since Plato's Socrates says very little explicitly with regard to the pleasures of learning in our dialogue yet allows for several insights to emerge between the lines, and since the topic is at once complex and crucial for our understanding of pleasure, this chapter will undertake its exploration to some extent beyond the letter of the text, while remaining faithful to its spirit.

The text mentions explicitly only a very narrow category of pleasures of learning, those that are pure, and true, and reserved to the very few (52b), which I take to mean in this context pleasures taken in practicing dialectic. The "learning" at issue must, correspondingly, be restricted most likely to the contemplation of intelligible objects, rather than be inclusive of any attempt to study through trial and error, since it is said to occur without any "hunger for learning" or some other pain and since it is said to be available "not to the masses, but to the very few" (52b). Nevertheless, side by side with this restricted sense of learning, there must be implicitly at work throughout the *Philebus* a much broader understanding of "learning" corresponding to the study that we undertake in the various crafts or branches of knowledge that Socrates mentions, from the most imprecise ones based on guesswork to the very precise ones of pure mathematics and, finally, dialectic itself (55c–59d). My focus in this chapter will be primarily on this broader sense of "learning" that is only implicit in the text, and the corresponding pleasures we take in exercising it. I hope to show that when we take learning in this broader sense, Plato's account leaves room for mixed (impure) pleasures of learning in a variety of fields, and perhaps also for outright false ones. The importance of mediation comes to the fore as we realize that Plato's account is complex and flexible enough to allow the use of mixed (impure) pleasures of learning as stepping stones for pure ones, and to regard a genuine experience of a mixed (impure) pleasure of learning as intrinsically valuable. Sensitivity to due measure helps us choose the right pleasures of learning given the level of self-awareness that we have as well as the concrete circumstances in which we find ourselves.

Upon distinguishing pleasures that are intrinsically mixed with pains from pleasures that are free (pure) of any admixture of pain, Socrates places the pleasures of learning (*ta peri ta mathēmata hēdonas*) that he discusses in the latter category (52a–b). A handful of puzzles stem from this situation. To begin with, (1) Can pleasures of learning be pure and unmixed with pain even when they emerge in response to the experience of *aporia*, which seems to be painful? The uneasiness arises here from the fact that at least in the most paradigmatic Socratic situations *aporia* precedes and is instrumental to learning, and genuine experience of *aporia* presupposes awareness of our ignorance, which is a lack, and thus it seems that the experience of *aporia* is always painful. The more painful our experience preceding and leading to acquisition of knowledge, the more intense, it would seem, is the delight we take in the learning that follows upon it and is initiated by it. If this is the case, it seems that our most paradigmatic pleasures of learning, those following on the heels of *aporia*, are mixed (impure).[1] Is this *always* necessarily the case, or can there be *some* cases in which pleasures of learning prompted by *aporia* turn out to be pure, unmixed with pain? (2) Secondly, once we broaden the meaning of "learning" as suggested above, is there room within Plato's framework for false pleasures of learning alongside true ones, and mixed pleasures of learning alongside pure ones? Finally, (3) since due measure and the timely (*to metrion, to kairion* 66a6–8) turn out to be the most important ingredients of a good human life, what role exactly do they play in our experience of the pleasures of learning, broadly construed?

Since none of these issues is explicitly discussed in our text, my present exploration is going to rely on mere hints that the dialogue offers. In reply to the first, I am going to argue that, while pleasures of learning that stem in response to the experience of *aporia* are most of the time mixed with pain, they *might* be experienced sometimes as pure pleasures. What makes all the difference is the disposition of the soul undergoing the experience of *aporia*, and, in particular, the capacity of our souls to experience *aporia* sometimes primarily, if not exclusively, as replenishment, rather than as painful depletion. In reply to the second question, I am going to argue that, while the pleasures of learning specifically illustrated in the *Philebus* are true and pure and reserved to the very few, the theory of pleasure outlined in this dialogue leaves room for a variety of experiences related to "learning" understood in a broad sense: false pleasures of learning alongside true ones, mixed pleasures of learning alongside pure ones. Finally, in reply to the third question, we are going to see that and how self-knowledge and sensitivity to due measure (*to metrion*) and the timely (*to kairon*) are essential to the way in which we experience pleasures of learning. Self-knowledge predisposes us to experience frequently true pleasures of learning, while self-ignorance predisposes us to take false pleasures in learning. Not recognizing my ignorance is just as dangerous as exaggerating my ignorance, for the former makes learning feel redundant, while the latter makes the situation feel overwhelming and thus impedes learning; in both cases we miss on true pleasures of learning.

Aporia and the Purity of our Pleasures of Learning

Once he defines pleasures as perceived fillings or replenishments of lacks (33d), Socrates distinguishes mixed pleasures, which presuppose that the lack they replenish was felt as painful, from pure pleasures, which presuppose that the lack filled was imperceptible and, therefore, painless (51b). The examples of pure pleasures that Socrates mentions are the delight we take in the beauty of geometrical shapes (51c), in pure colors (51b–d, 53a–c), in smooth and bright sounds which produce a pure note (51d), in smells (51e), and, finally, the pleasures of learning reserved to the very few (52b), when these experiences are not preceded by perceptible lacks. In the very next step, Socrates clarifies that pleasures of learning that he is concerned with are pure although they often emerge after forgetting, since the process of forgetting takes place unconsciously and thus the depletion we suffer as we forget is not painful. Consequently, he argues, perceiving the replenishment of this unperceived lack through the acquisition of knowledge produces pure pleasure (52a–b).

> Let us then add to these the pleasures of learning, if indeed we believe that there is no hunger for learning, nor any pains originating in a hunger for learning. —I agree with you. —What about this: if once they are filled with knowledge, people later on lose it due to forgetting, do you see any pains in such

experiences? —Not by their nature, but there is pain in reflecting upon the experience, whenever someone deprived is in pain due to recognizing the need. —But, my dear, we are now concerned only with the natural affections independently from our reflections on them. —Then you are speaking the truth when you say that forgetfulness of things learnt occurs without pain. —We have to say then that the pleasures of learning are unmixed with pains and they never pertain to the many, but only to the very few. —How could one disagree? (51e7–b8)

The passage explains that perceiving the replenishment of the unperceived lack that comes through forgetting will give us a pure pleasure of learning. This is useful to know, though it does not address our initial concern regarding learning after *aporia*. For *aporia,* unlike forgetting, presupposes awareness of one's state of mind. It seems, indeed, that the more aware we are of our own ignorance, the more we are going to enjoy acquiring knowledge, and thus pain is inextricably mixed with pleasure. Are there *any* situations in which our pleasures of learning, with learning understood in the broad sense specified above, can nonetheless be pure even when they are preceded by *aporia*?

It is worth emphasizing that the pure pleasures of learning that Socrates explicitly mentions are restricted to the very few, and not accessible to the masses (52b), and thus cannot be expected to accompany every one of the kinds of intellectual pursuits considered (55c–58e). Earlier in the text, dialectic was said to be concerned with the serious One-Many puzzles (15b–c), and the divine method of collections and divisions was introduced as its main strategy of investigation (16c–19b). In the later part of the dialogue, dialectic is characterized primarily as the most precise kind of knowledge, given the absolute stability, immutability, and eternity of its objects. It is thus said to be "the discipline concerned with being and with what is really and forever in every way eternally the same, by far the truest kind of knowledge" (58a2–5) and its objects are characterized as "eternal and self-same" (61e).

The stability of the knowledge achieved by dialectic is responsible for the stability and truth of the pleasures we take in studying these objects: the more stable and unchanging the objects that fill us through learning, the truer the pleasures we feel through replenishment. However, Plato never suggests that this learning is an uninterrupted contemplative act. In fact, he acknowledges that the process of learning is obstructed by forgetfulness (52a).

Like everybody else, dialecticians too are prone to forgetfulness, and like everybody else, they too experience *aporia*. In fact, the One-Many puzzles articulated at 15b are some of the most profound *aporiai* and dialecticians are even more prone to experience *aporia* than other people, since they tend to be especially aware of their own ignorance and the difficulty of these matters. Thus, our earlier question resurfaces: Does the dialectician's *presumed* pain experienced in *aporia* necessarily ruin the purity of the pleasures of learning *in all those cases* in which learning is preceded by *aporia*?

The solution to our puzzle comes through realizing that Plato conceives of the genuine experience of *aporia*, that is, awareness of one's own ignorance, not necessarily as a painful experience of depletion, but rather as a possible experience of perceived replenishment, insofar as *aporia* is regarded as a moment of self-discovery or increased self-awareness, or at least as an experience mixing pleasure with pain, one in which we can choose to focus on the pleasure of self-discovery rather than on the pain produced by recognizing our lack. For the philosophically minded, ignorance of one's own ignorance characterizes the experience of unconscious lack, while turning from ignorance of ignorance to awareness of one's ignorance through the experience of *aporia* is some sort of replenishment, which *can* be felt as such, since it is a moment of *self-discovery* in the process of *self-knowledge*. For those who can appreciate the awareness of their own ignorance positively as an opportunity to grow, this experience is either one of perceived filling, or at least one that mixes this perceived filling with the perceived pain of ignorance.[2] In support of this, let us remind ourselves how the slave boy's state of *aporia* is depicted in the *Meno*:

> Do you understand, Meno, what stage he has already reached in his recollection? For at first he did not know which was the side of the eight-foot square, just as he does not know that now, but then he thought he knew and answered confidently as if he knew and did not think that he was at a loss. However, now he thinks that he is at a loss, and while he does not know, neither does he think that he knows. —That is true. —So is he not doing better now in regard to the things he did not know? — That too seems to me to be the case. —And so have we then harmed him in any way by making him perplexed and numb just as the torpedo fish does? —I do not think so. . . . —So has he then been benefited by being numbed? —I think so. (*Meno* 84a–c, trans. G. M. A. Grube)

According to this passage, experience of *aporia* might be beneficial, and thus some sort of fulfillment or replenishment. Pleasure, however, does not arise automatically whenever replenishment happens, but rather occurs only on those occasions in which the replenishment is *perceived* as such. For *aporia* to be truly appreciated, one must have developed a sensitivity to the kind of beneficial effects it brings about. The slave in the *Meno*, though benefited by *aporia*, does not yet perceive his experience as a replenishment. Consequently, he is not taking pure pleasure in his discovery of the diagonal as the side of the double-sized square. Finding that solution is to him at best a relief from his earlier pain of *aporia*, generating at best a mixed pleasure. Nevertheless, we can imagine Socrates himself, as normative character, or someone like him, experiencing *aporia* as simply pleasant or at least as a mixture of pleasure with pain that would nonetheless allow him to experience as *pure* the pleasures associated with the learning following upon and initiated by *aporia*.[3] As normative character, Socrates would experience *aporia* as pleasant insofar as he would be perceiving as replenishment his turn from being previously unaware of his ignorance to his current awareness of ignorance. Alternatively, he would experience *aporia* as a mixture of the pain of recognizing his ignorance with the pleasure of self-discovery.[4] In either case, whether *aporia* is experienced as simply pleasant or as a mixture of pleasure and pain, an individual sharing Socrates's disposition toward philosophy can experience the learning following upon solving the *aporia* as pure pleasure, in the former case, because *aporia* itself is not painful at all to him, in the latter one, because he, unlike most of Socrates's interlocutors, can and will choose to focus on the pleasure of self-discovery while ignoring the pain of his ignorance. Recognition of his cognitive state as part of the process of self-knowledge or self-discovery is for Socrates a restoration of his natural harmony, a harmony or balance of knowledge and ignorance that characterizes not humanity as such, but the specific person that Socrates is. Many of Socrates's interlocutors reach *aporia*, but hardly any of them experience in it the pleasure of self-discovery or self-awareness that is part of it. Yet, those who, like Socrates, spend their lives not only examining others, but also examining themselves, develop sensitivity for emphasizing in this experience the pleasure of self-discovery more than the pain of a lack, and thus become able to take pure pleasure even in their learning that follows on the heels of *aporia*.

While the *Philebus* does not provide clear textual evidence for this, I believe we are staying within the spirit of Plato's texts by concentrating our attention on the disposition of the various souls undergoing the experience of *aporia* and recognizing the superior achievement that this experience marks in the case of Socrates and others like him, as opposed to Socrates's typical self-assured interlocutors. And while there is no direct evidence for this, our text provides us with at least indirect evidence based on the way each character is sketched, so that we can imagine the kind of experience that Philebus, Protarchus, and Socrates, respectively, have with *aporia*. Clearly, Philebus, who drops out of the conversation within the first few exchanges with the dogmatic and unexamined declaration that "to my mind pleasure wins and will always win, no matter what" (12a), experiences *aporia* as something extremely painful, *if* he ever experiences it. Trouble is, Philebus's extreme sensualist hedonism might prevent him from ever experiencing *aporia* in any way, since he is so unwilling to engage in dialogue and to recognize his own limitations. Protarchus, on the other hand, while being refuted a few times during the conversation, must have been enjoying learning throughout, since the conversation ends with him reminding Socrates of "a little that is still missing," and urging Socrates to continue their joint search: "Surely you will not give up before we do; rather, I will remind you of what is left" (67b). Also, during the conversation, Protarchus openly declares his enjoyment of it, as he says that he is rather pleased (*areskei*) by the fact that his own thesis (*logos*) and Socrates's are on the same footing (14a). Socrates, for his part, clearly embraces every opportunity to converse about the good life and takes delight in every experience that leads to increased self-awareness, even when such experiences come at the expense of *aporia*. Hence, for Socrates, pleasures of learning whenever they deal with learning about virtue, happiness, and the good life are often, though not always, pure. *If* awareness of one's own ignorance *can* be perceived *primarily* as replenishment or restoration of balance insofar as it is a moment *of self-discovery*, as it seems to be for Socrates, then the experience of learning following it *can* generate pure pleasure. Having this kind of experience requires a humble character that appreciates awareness of ignorance as an opportunity to learn, not as painful lack.

False and Impure Pleasures of Learning Alongside True and Pure Ones

The reflections we are about to launch into take us again *beyond what the Philebus says explicitly* about the specific pleasures of learning he mentions, yet they remain within a domain of speculation that is allowed and created by what the dialogue does say about pleasures. The pleasures of learning that Socrates explicitly refers to in *Philebus* 52a–b are restricted to the very few, hence, most likely related to learning that has intelligible realities as objects; and since they occur without a prior "hunger for learning" (51e7), they are always pure. Nevertheless, since Socrates goes next to classify different types of knowledge, ranging from the most imprecise to the most precise one of dialectic (55c–59d), and since we do often learn upon having experienced some "hunger for learning," it is worth stepping beyond the letter of the text to explore the pleasures we could take in learning that corresponds to these other fields, as pleasures of learning worth investigating in their own right. How would these other pleasures of learning, possibly mixed ones and perhaps even false ones, fit within the conception of pleasure sketched in the *Philebus*?

Before turning our attention to the pleasures that we might take in learning in various fields, let us remind ourselves of an aspect already discussed in more detail in chapter III, namely, that "purity" is used equivocally in the *Philebus*, sometimes to refer simply to the absence of admixture of pain in our pleasures and other times to mean more broadly "reality" and "truth" as an ontological characteristic that belongs not only to pleasure, but also to the structure of the universe (29b6–c4, 30a3–c1) and to the various kinds of knowledge and their corresponding objects (55c–d, 57c, 58d, 58d, 59c). When "purity" is used in the ontological sense of dignity pertaining to the noblest of realities it admits *degrees*, whereas when applied to pleasures insofar as they are simply unmixed with pains, it does not admit degrees, pleasures are either pure or mixed with pain.

The transition from using "purity" in the strict sense of absence of admixture of pains in our pleasures to the ontological sense of purity as being most fully what a thing is to be is made through the discussion of the sensible pleasure we take in the sight of pure white. For in that illustration "purity" designates both our pleasure's unmixedness with pain and the unmixed nature of the object we delight in:

> Then let us go and see whether all those that we say belong in the pure kind can be thought of as follows: let us first pick out one of them and examine it. —Which one shall we choose? —Let us take whiteness first, if you agree. —Indeed, let's do so. —How can there be purity in the case of whiteness? Is it the greatest quantity or amount, or is it rather the lack of any admixture, such that there is not even the slightest part of any

other kind contained in this color? —It will obviously be the perfectly unmixed color. —Right. And shall we not also say that this is the truest and the most beautiful of all instances of white, rather than what is greatest in quantity or amount? —Certainly. —So we are perfectly justified if we say that a small portion of pure white is to be regarded as whiter than a larger quantity of an impure whiteness, and at the same time more beautiful and possessed of more truth. —Most rightly said. —What then? I think we don't need to run through many more examples to justify our account of pleasure, but this example suffices to prove that in the case of pleasure, too, every small and insignificant pleasure that is unmixed with pain will turn out to be pleasanter, truer, and more beautiful than a larger quantity and amount of the impure kind. (52e7–c2)

As Harvey insightfully explains, Socrates uses the pleasure taken in the sensible contemplation of pure white as symbolic image for the purity of dialectic itself, a purity it has on account of the "truly real" nature of its pure intelligible objects: the arresting sensible pure pleasure we take in looking at a pure patch of white or in hearing a simple tone is analogical to the intelligible pure pleasure we take in contemplating eternal intelligible realities by means of dialectic. Thus, he argues, the discussion of the pleasure we take in pure whiteness guides our understanding of the ways in which dialectic differs from other types of knowledge: for one thing, unlike the other types of knowledge, in the case of dialectic just like in that of whiteness, purity pertains to both its objects and the psychic states that it generates in us; furthermore, just as the beauty of a patch of white is due to its purity, so too intelligible objects of dialectic owe the manifestation of their inherent natures to their purity; finally, just as pure white has a distinctive pleasure-producing capacity in virtue of its inherent beauty, so too the objects of dialectic have such a capacity on account of their inherent natures (Harvey 2012, 292).

Why does Plato choose to use "purity" in this double way, to cover both the psychological sense of pleasure's unmixedness with pain and the ontological sense of dignity and reality associated with the objects of our cognitive grasp? A careful reading shows that the two senses are related to one another. The more likely we are to attain higher degrees of purity in cognition, the more we delight in pleasures that are pure rather than mixed with pain; and also, the more likely we are to delight in pure pleasures, the readier we are to progress in our knowledge toward eternal and stable objects, which are the purest realities. It is only when "purity" is used to mean strictly no admixture of pain that pure pleasures can also be false. When, on the other hand, "purity" is used in the ontological sense to mean "reality," pure pleasures cannot be false, for they occur as a result of a learning that has intelligible, eternal, and unchanging objects. This explains why the pleasures of learning that Socrates explicitly mentions at 51e–52a, which are reserved for the very few who practice dialectic, are always pure *and true*. The reality (purity) of the intelligible objects accessed through dialectic determines and is responsible for the truthfulness of the pleasures we take in such learning. Having the sensitivity required for taking pleasure in intelligible, stable objects presupposes that one knows or at least has some cognitive grasp of these objects, since taking pleasure is not just filling or replenishment, but *perceived* filling. Thus, in order to be capable of perceiving filling or replenishment we must have a cognitive grasp of the object filling us. The stability and reality of intelligible objects responsible for our replenishment rule out the possibility that we might be misestimating the replenishment we are experiencing, and this is why the pure pleasures of learning that Socrates explicitly mentions admit no falsity whatsoever. With these clarifications in mind, let us now turn to see how our experience of mixed and false pleasures of learning, with "learning" here understood in the broad senses specified in the opening of this chapter, might look like.

Mixed Pleasures of Learning

Many of the pleasures we take in learning various crafts are pleasures mixed with pain and triggered by some sort of "hunger for learning" (51e7). Most of the time we acquire knowledge and skills in the more imprecise branches of knowledge—whether they are the ones guided by lucky guesses (music, medicine, agriculture, navigation, strategy), or the more precise productive arts (shipbuilding, house building) which make use of the applied vulgar branch of mathematics (55c–56a, 56c, 57b–d, 58a–c, 59c)—through experiences that combine pleasure with pain: the frustration at not knowing something is followed by the subsequent elimination of that frustration through the assimilation of relevant information. This is *not* to say that experiences of learning in the various applied crafts are *always* mixed or impure, for it is certainly possible to be pleased at learning things in any of these fields even when there is no previously perceived experience of lack. Learning any new skill or information can feel intrinsically fulfilling in cases in which such learning was not preceded by some sort of "hunger for learning." In such cases our pure pleasures of learning in the productive or applied arts would be pure yet "less divine," just as the pure pleasures of smell are (51e), by comparison with the pleasures of learning that we experience while engaged in dialectic, since their object is sensible, and thus unstable, while the object of dialectical learning is eternal and stable.

Furthermore, even the pursuit of dialectic is often fraught with mixed pleasures of learning, as we have seen in the earlier part of this chapter, where we realized that for most of us pleasures of learning in response to *aporia* generate most of the time pleasures mixed with pain. It is essential to realize that "dialectic" designates throughout the *Philebus* not only the highest *technē* of full precision and accuracy in contemplation, but also a tentative progress in thinking along the lines of collection and division. These two conceptions of dialectic are in somewhat of a tension with one another, for one regards dialectic as a journey, the other one as destination.[5] Clearly, when Socrates declares as pure the pleasures of learning reserved to the very few (52b), he has in mind dialectic as the highest and most precise type of knowledge envisioned as destination, and not merely as a journey toward that. When viewed as engagement in search along the lines of collection and division, dialectic can easily give rise to mixed pleasures of learning. Watch, for instance, the way in which Socrates moves from his initial equation of pleasure with replenishment or restoration (31d, 32b) to the refined definition of pleasure as *perceived* replenishment of a lack or restoration (33d): though he does not say so explicitly, we must imagine that Socrates is experiencing pleasure as he advances from an initial rough and tentative conception to a more adequate understanding of pleasure. Even Protarchus, when engaged in dialectical search side by side with Socrates, declares himself pleased (*areskei*) by the equal standing of their respective theses at some point in the conversation (14a). Throughout the conversation in the *Sophist*, the Eleatic Stranger takes up anew seven times the attempt to define the sophist, while in the early stages of the *Statesman* the Stranger develops his thought first along a longer way, then along a shorter way (*Statesman* 259d–266e), thereby suggesting the tentativeness of the dialectical method of division, the frequency of detours, the dialectician's openness to challenge. These and numerous similar instances invite us to view overcoming impediments as occasions to experience replenishments mixed with disruptions of natural balance along the paths of our intellectual journeys.

Continuing to extend for a moment our reflections outside the *Philebus*, the *Phaedrus*, the *Symposium*, the *Republic*, and even *Laches* 187e–188b provide clear accounts of the way in which pain is integral to the pleasure of doing philosophy. Far from rejecting mixed pleasures from the philosopher's life, in the *Phaedrus* and the *Symposium*, Plato's Socrates develops insightful accounts that show the relative value and force of mixed pleasures of learning in our lives.[6] Thus, in the *Phaedrus* learning is depicted as a process of the soul growing its wings which it had lost at the moment of embodiment. The loss of wings is depicted as a dramatic experience that mixes pleasure with pain, and the erotic encounter between lover and beloved can serve as a catalyst for starting to grow wings once again:

> [L]ong ago, you see, the entire soul had wings. Now the whole soul seethes and throbs in this condition. Like a child whose teeth are just starting to grow in, and its gums are all aching and itching—that is exactly how the soul feels when it begins to grow wings. It swells up and aches and tingles as it grows them. But when it looks upon the beauty of the boy and takes in the stream of particles flowing into it from his beauty (that is why it is called "desire"), when it is watered and warmed by this, then all its pain subsides and is replaced by joy. . . . From the outlandish mix of these two feelings—pain and joy—comes anguish and helpless raving; in its madness the lover's soul cannot sleep at night or stay put by day; it rushes, yearning, wherever it expects to see the person who has that beauty. (*Phaedrus* 251c–e, trans. Nehamas and Woodruff)

Pain is mixed with pleasure also in the lover's ascent to Beauty as depicted throughout the *Symposium*. Remember the pangs of labor that the lover experiences as he gives birth to the beauty he carries inside himself:

> That's why, whenever pregnant animals or persons draw near to beauty, they become gentle and joyfully disposed and give birth and reproduce; but near ugliness they are foul faced and draw back in pain; they turn away and shrink back and do not reproduce, and because they hold on to what they carry inside them, the labor is painful. This is the source of the great excitement about beauty that comes to anyone who is pregnant and already teeming with life: beauty releases them from their great pain. (*Symposium* 206d–e, trans. Nehamas)

> What do you think causes love and desire, Socrates? Don't you see what an awful state a wild animal is in when it wants to reproduce? Footed and winged animals alike, all are plagued by the disease of Love. First they are sick for intercourse with each other, then for nurturing their young—for their sake the weakest animals stand ready to do battle against the strongest and even to die for them, and they may be racked with famine in order to feed their young. They would do anything for their sake. (*Symposium* 207a–b, trans. Nehamas)

The philosopher's struggle to adjust his eyes to light as he exits the cave in the *Republic*, or again, as he reenters the darkness of the cave speaks to the same experience:[7]

> When one of them was freed and suddenly compelled to stand up, turn his head, walk, and look up toward the light, he'd be pained and dazzled and unable to see the things whose shadows he'd seen before. (*Republic* 515c–d, trans. Grube, rev. Reeve)

> And if someone compelled him to look at the light itself, wouldn't his eyes hurt, and wouldn't he turn around and flee towards the things he's able to see, believing that they're really clearer than the ones he's being shown? —He would. —And if someone dragged him away from there by force, up the rough and steep path, and didn't let him go until he had dragged him into the sunlight, wouldn't he be pained and irritated at being treated that way? (*Republic* 515e, trans. Grube, rev. Reeve)

In short then, the philosopher's pleasures of learning are very often mixed with pains. None of this contradicts what Plato's Socrates says in the *Philebus*. For while he singles out specifically the always pure and true pleasures of learning experienced by those engaged in dialectic, Socrates does not mean to restrict our pleasures of learning to these. Pure along with mixed and sometimes even false pleasures of learning are part and parcel of everyone's life, including the good life of a philosopher. Not even the most accomplished of philosophers are exempt of experiencing the less than perfect pleasures of learning. Learning is at times a painful experience even for the most talented among us.

Implicit in all this discussion is a distinction between the narrow sense of "learning" as contemplation, and the broad sense of "learning" as study in general. It might well be that the pleasures we take in studying in general in various branches of knowledge are sometimes pure and sometimes mixed with pain, while the highest and most satisfying pleasures of contemplation reserved for the accomplished dialectician are always pure and true. Socrates's account in the *Philebus* is restricted to the latter even though he calls them "pleasures of learning," and not of contemplation. Nevertheless, being able to enjoy such elevated pure pleasures as the most accomplished philosophers do is in no way a guarantee that those enjoying them will never be tempted and at times corrupted by lower pleasures.

This reading helps us avoid what seems to me a misguided issue concerning the pleasures that are left for the philosopher to enjoy "once he has acquired the knowledge that he lacked": if pleasure ceases once the replenishing ends, then as soon as one becomes a successful mature philosopher, his experience of pleasure ceases.[8] It seems to me that this is a false problem. For one thing, the difficulty so formulated assumes that one can become philosopher once and for all, and that once one turns out to be successful at thinking philosophically, he cannot be corrupted, an assumption that Plato clearly would never endorse, especially since he has Socrates depict even the most accomplished philosopher rulers as capable of mistakes since they too, like everybody else, use also sense perception alongside reason (*Republic* 546a–b). Hence, the philosopher needs to be constantly on his watch to fight potential sources of corruption, and to maintain himself attuned to the intelligible realities that feed his soul. Thus, in an essential sense, one is never done learning. For learning covers a broad array of phenomena, which include, among others, reviewing and testing past associations, making new connections among things we learned by constantly shifting the angle from which we view things. Furthermore, philosophers, just like everybody else, enjoy a great variety of pleasures alongside those of learning or contemplation and they are always going to continue to enjoy these. The superiority of the philosopher's life resides not in the fact that he enjoys exclusively pleasures of learning, but rather in the much more wholesome and truer way in which philosophers enjoy along with learning also the necessary and mixed pleasures of eating, drinking, comedy, health, etc., a more wholesome and truer way than the way in which everybody else enjoys these (cf. *Republic* 586e4–587a2).[9]

False Pleasures of Learning

Once we take "learning" in the broadest sense specified, we come to see several types of falsehoods that can infect our pleasures of learning. Thus, for instance, we could take pleasure in the study of facts or theories that appear to be true, yet turn out to be false; consequently, the pleasures themselves we take in such studying will be touched to a certain degree by falsity. Furthermore, our pleasures of learning could be false insofar as we misestimate the degree of replenishment we perceive while learning. Or, in another sense, sophists and eristic debaters take false pleasure in learning argumentative tricks and winning debates. The text of the *Philebus* offers sufficient hints for us to reconstruct a way in which Plato's Socrates could likely have explored these situations.

Before we proceed to investigate these types of false pleasures, let us first address a potential objection. It might be objected that, since Socrates introduces the discussion of pleasures of learning in response to Protarchus's question about the pleasures that can be "rightly regarded as true" (51b), Socrates takes all the pleasures of learning to be necessarily true. Notice, however, that Socrates himself regards the present discussion to be moving from the mixed pleasures to the unmixed, pure pleasures, which he, unlike Protarchus, doesn't automatically call true (50e). It is only after he introduces the pleasures of learning that Socrates says he will next move to address the question about the relation between purity and truth as applied to pleasures (52d). Indeed, a close look at the text shows that once he finishes the examination of mixed pleasures, Socrates declares that they will next proceed to the discussion of unmixed, pure pleasures (50e). It is Protarchus who, in response, asks Socrates to specify the kinds of pleasure that could rightly be regarded as true (51b), thus presumably assuming that pure pleasures must also be true. Socrates replies by listing the perceived replenishments related to pure colors, shapes, smells, and sounds, insofar as they are based on imperceptible and painless lacks (51b), but it is not at all immediately clear whether Socrates's list is to be taken as an unqualified reply to Protarchus's question about pleasures that are *true* or is rather only the follow-up of his own plan to discuss *pure* pleasures. I believe that the latter is the case, and the main textual support for this is that it is only *after* this exchange and *after* a more extended list of pure pleasures has been produced that Socrates addresses explicitly the question about the relation between purity/impurity and truth as applied to pleasures (52d3–8). And the text makes explicit this sequence in the examination of these pleasures:

> After these there is still another thing to examine about them.
> —What is it? —What is more closely related to truth: the pure and the unmixed, or the intense, abundant, and great? (52d)

Since, as argued in chapter III, truth and purity are not overlapping criteria, not all pure pleasures must also be true. Socrates proceeds by elucidating the nature of purity in the case of whiteness: purity resides not in quantity or amount, but in the absence of any admixture of something foreign, and as such it makes something *truer* than impurity by preserving the thing's genuine nature (53b4–6). At the end of this stretch of reasoning, Socrates concludes that pure pleasures are always more pleasant, truer, and more beautiful than their impure counterparts (53b–c), but not also that pure (unmixed) pleasures are always true and cannot be false.

Let us now turn to the types of false pleasures of learning mentioned above and look at each of them in turn. A first type refers to the experience we all sometimes have of enjoying learning something that eventually turns out to have been false, thus what we basically enjoy is the merely apparent discovery of something. Imagine enjoying learning about the discovery of a powerful medicine that could cure cancer, only to discover a few days later that the data on that research were incorrect and a cure is yet to be found. One might say that the falsity in this case affects only the content that is learned, not also the pleasure taken in learning it, but it is possible that, at least sometimes, it affects both. Pleasure was taken in a false object. What has been perceived to replenish a lack would in fact not replenish that lack. This situation resembles very closely a surface reading of the falsehood of the pleasures of anticipation (38c–40b). On a surface reading, pleasures of anticipation would be false because they rely on factual mistakes about the object expected to occur in the future. The object anticipated to occur, for instance, winning the lottery, does in fact not occur. Similarly, the object supposed to cause the perceived replenishment in the case of these false pleasures of learning simply turns out to have been misidentified, just as when seen in the distance a man could have been taken for a statue (38c–d). As explained in detail in chapters II and IV, it is not this surface sense of falsehood marring these pleasures that worries Plato the most.

Another type of false pleasures of learning occurs frequently on account of our exaggerations or underestimations of the actual degree of pleasure we take in a particular episode of learning.[10] I might, for instance, easily exaggerate the pleasure I take in studying music or psychology when I assess the pleasure I take in these studies by contrast to the lack of enthusiasm I have had when studying a subject that I am much less interested in. Conversely, I might underestimate on occasion the replenishment I feel in studying a subject I am typically less interested in, simply because my earlier attempts to study in that field have not been enjoyable. Viewing my current experience in the lights and shadows of previous ones distorts my perception of the replenishment that is taking place. This sort of falsity can affect both our mixed and our pure pleasures of learning, and, in general, any pleasure we experience.

A more intriguing and complex type of the false pleasures of learning is to be found in the sophists' and eristic debaters' experience of "learning." Being ignorant of their own ignorance, sophists and eristic debaters do not experience their intellectual lack as painful. Does that mean that their assimilation of verbal tricks, catchy argumentative strategies, rhetorical devices, etc., gives them pure pleasures of learning? Not at all. Although they do not feel their intellectual lack to be painful, sophists constantly experience pain related to what in the *Republic* Plato's Socrates calls the lower parts of the soul, namely spiritedness and appetite, as they are in constant hunger for fame and financial success, and it is *these* perceived lacks that they hope to replenish through learning catchy phrases and argumentative strategies. Hence, sophists misperceive their acquisition of knowledge and take it to be replenishing in them the painful lack of not being as famous, honored, and wealthy as they might wish. And since their pain tends to be excessive, so too is their pleasure, which thus ends up being false. So, then, the falsity of these pleasures of learning stems from the fact that, while learning is supposed to replenish our rational needs and desires, it is being erroneously regarded as replenishing spirited and/or appetitive desires.

Sophists or eristic debaters are mentioned a few times throughout the *Philebus*, whether directly through the way they are pleased by their endeavors or as proceeding in opposition with Socrates's philosophical approach. Let us look at a number of passages along these lines:

> [1] Are we to behave and speak in just the same way as those who are most incompetent and at the same time newcomers in such discussions? —What way do you mean? —This: suppose I imitate you and dare to say, in defense of my thesis, that the most unlike thing is of all things most *like* the most unlike; then I could say the same thing as you did. But this would make us look quite childish, and our discussion would have an unstable foundation. (13c9–d6)

Childishness is here associated with the eristic debaters' preoccupation with contradiction when their involvement with arguments is done strictly for amusement's sake and not for figuring out the way things are. The next paragraph emphasizes the eristic debaters' concern for victory and draws a sharp contrast between their love of victory and the philosophers' rightful search and love for truth:

> [2] Let us not cover up the difference between your good and mine, Protarchus, but put it right in the middle and confront the challenge to see, when scrutinizing it, whether pleasure should be called the good, or wisdom, or yet a third thing. For we are not competing here out of love of victory (*philonikoūmen*) for my thesis to win or for yours. Rather, we have to fight together side by side as allies in support of the truest one. (14b1–7)

A third passage connects the exaggerated pleasures that eristic debaters get from randomly maneuvering arguments in every direction and jumping from the One to the Many, thus using *aporia* not as an opportunity for self-awareness, but as a strategy for confusing themselves and others, including presumably also even nonhuman living beings:

> [3] When any one of the young is having for the first time a taste of this [the condition of discourse of becoming one and many] he is as pleased (*hēstheis*) as he would be if he discovered a treasure of wisdom, he is enthused by pleasure, and enjoys moving every statement, now turning it to one side and rolling it into one, and then again unrolling it and dividing it into parts. Thus, first and foremost he throws himself into confusion and secondly anyone else who happens to be around, be they younger or older or of the same age, sparing neither father, nor mother, nor anyone else who may be listening. And he would almost apply this treatment to other living beings, not only to humans, and would show no mercy to foreigners either, if only he could find an interpreter somewhere. (15d8–16a3)

A fourth passage goes deeper than the previous one to spell out the cause responsible for the sophists' and eristic debaters' random jumps from the One to the Many forgetting the intermediaries, namely, missing the insight for due measure and therefore going either too slowly or too quickly from one extreme to the other:

> [4] The gods, as I said, have left us this legacy of how to search, and learn, and teach one another. But nowadays the clever ones

among us make a one, haphazardly, and a many, faster or slower than they should; they go immediately from the one to the unlimited and omit the intermediaries, while it is exactly these, that make all the difference as to whether we are engaged with one another in dialectical or only in eristic discourse. (16e3–17a5)

Finally, Socrates concludes by spelling out the ultimate contrast between philosophy and eristic debaters in terms of the former's clarity, precision, and highest degree of truth and the latters' pragmatic usefulness and grandeur:

[5] But, my dear Philebus, I was not searching for the art or science that surpasses all the others by its greatness, nobility, and great usefulness to us, but for the one that keeps watch over clarity, precision, and the highest degree of truth, even if it is a minor discipline and our benefit small—this is what we have been searching for. But look: you don't need to set Gorgias as your enemy if you give primacy to his art as far as usefulness to human beings is concerned, while the discipline I was concerned with receives primacy with regard to the highest degree of truth, just as I said earlier about the white, that even if in a small amount, if it is pure, it surpasses the great but impure amount as far as the highest degree of truth is concerned. (58b9–d1)

Not only the pleasures of learning experienced by sophists are most of the time false, but their corresponding pains are also false. Pain is perceived depletion or perceived disruption of the natural balance (31d, 32b). What the sophists take to be pain, namely, their perceived lack of riches, honor, and prestige, is not depletion when measured by an absolute standard of goodness. Plato's Socrates never talks explicitly about "false pain" in the *Philebus*. It is conceivable, nonetheless, that he would envision the experience of false pains in close correspondence to that of false pleasure. I have in mind the case of sophists or tyrants, for instance, imagining themselves in pain while in reality not suffering true depletions or disruptions of their natural balance, or, better, thinking that they suffer one type of depletion while in fact they suffer some other type thereof. The tyrant suffers pain due to his *pleonexia*, whereby he constantly thinks he needs to have more in terms of riches and fame. He mistakenly thinks that having more of these would restore his balance, while in fact that would only enhance the imbalance. While he thinks that the depletion caused by material lacks causes his disruptions of balance, it is in fact his excessive desires for material riches that cause that imbalance. But, of course, he does not perceive his misdirected desires to be disruptive, and hence does not experience pain on account of those. Similarly, sophists too experience their perceived lack of riches, honor, and prestige as painful, but this is not a true experience of depletion measured by an absolute standard of goodness and harmony. What they should be pained at is the fact that they care so much about prestige and honor, for it is this depletion that causes disharmony in them. It is in this vein that Socrates declares the lack, rather than the possession, of riches and political offices more virtuous and more truly an acquisition in cases when such possessions presuppose unjust acquisition (*Meno* 78e). The analysis of comic malice in a previous chapter has shown us already that taking pleasure in the misfortune and ignorance of another, the way sophists or eristic debaters do, is equivalent to taking depletion for replenishment. The sophists' experience of pleasure is thoroughly permeated with falsehood.

While in the *Philebus* Socrates does not explicitly mention the tripartition of the soul that we know from the *Republic*, he does, nevertheless, implicitly acknowledge distinct desires of the soul by distinguishing (1) pleasures satisfying our bodily needs for food, drink, and sex (31d–32c, 46c–47d) from (2) pleasures of the victory lovers (*philonikoûmen*, 14b, 15d–16a), who take delight in manipulating the inherent ambiguities of discourse in order to assert their presumed superiority over others (15d–16a) or from the pleasures associated with our emotions of fear, longing, lamentation, anger, love, jealousy, malice (47d–50e), and from (3) an innate love of truth and corresponding pure pleasures of learning (51b–52c, 58d4–5). There are true and false pleasures corresponding to each type of desire pertaining to the soul. Pleasures of food, drink, sex are true when their degree and object are properly assessed, and false, for instance, when exaggerated or undervalued. So too, pleasures related to honor can be true whenever we take the right amount of delight in the honor shown to us by good people, and false whenever we take too much delight in honor and fame for inadequate reasons. Pleasures of reason are true when seen in their proper light as replenishments of our soul's craving for understanding (the inborn love for truth, 58d), and false, for instance, when we regard learning as a means of satisfying our desire for honor and victory in arguments. Additional support for the view that Socrates recognizes distinct types of desires stems from the fact that each of the three characters is representative for one or another of the three aspects of the soul: the hedonist and sensualist Philebus is clearly appetitive, Protarchus is spirited, and Socrates is primarily rational. Philebus's association with appetite is obvious from the start, as he abandons completely the arena of reason and argumentation refusing even to defend his own hedonistic position in *logos* (11b–12a). Protarchus's spirited nature is evident both in his positive emotions, being pleased (*areskei* 14a) about the status of his and Socrates's arguments, and also in his negative ones, such as his inclination toward anger, when he threatens Socrates and when he feels insulted by Socrates's critique of schemes and stratagems practiced by young eristic debaters (16a–b). And, as it befits a spirited nature, Protarchus lets himself be ruled by reason and positively acts in support of reason, as he admits throughout the cosmological argument that it would be downright impious to believe that anything other than reason rules the universe (28e–30e). Finally, Socrates's rational tendencies are evident and clear throughout.

In the first section I argued that pleasures of learning occurring on the heels of *aporia can at times* be pure, namely when enjoyed by the most apt among the philosophically minded. In this section we saw that the *Philebus* provides us hints to reconstruct an account of mixed and false pleasures of learning, with "learning" here understood in the broadest sense, alongside the pure and the true pleasures mentioned explicitly at 52b.

The Role of Due Measure in Experiencing Pleasures of Learning

It is time now to look at the role of self-knowledge and sensitivity to due measure in our experience of the pleasures of learning. Most relevant for this will be a close examination of the final list of ingredients responsible for a good life provided toward the end of the dialogue (66a–c). The first rank goes to what is connected with measure (*metriotēs*), the measured (*to metrion*), and the timely (*to kairon*), and everything else similar; next come the well-proportioned, and beautiful, the perfect, the self-sufficient and everything else that belongs to this kind; the third place goes to reason and intelligence; the fourth to sciences, to arts, and to right opinions; finally, the fifth rank goes to pure pleasures (66a–c). The placement of pure pleasures as fifth in this ranking might at first look like disparagement and has been taken by scholars as indication of Plato's anti-hedonistic leanings. I, on the contrary, take as a sign that Plato thereby recognizes the value of these pleasures. As Vogt points out, gaining fifth rank in a hierarchy with such illustrious members as measure, the beautiful and the proportionate, reason and intelligence, *elevates* pleasures, rather than demoting them (Vogt

2010, 251–52). Once the five ranks have been explicitly assigned, Socrates ends with an enigmatic remark borrowed from Orpheus: "with the sixth generation the well-ordered song may find its end" (66c), which leaves us wondering whether Socrates is thereby including necessary mixed true pleasures as sixth in this ranking or not. The reference to Orpheus seems indicative of an implicit, even if perhaps qualified, inclusion of a sixth rank as the final "generation," parallel to the ranking of generations in Hesiod's *Theogony*, which concludes with the sixth rank listing the indefinitely many children of Zeus and Hera. For many mixed true pleasures associated with health, temperance, and virtue generally deserve to be included in a good life, just as they were included a bit earlier and described as akin to reason and to the various types of knowledge and were therefore welcomed in a good life (63e). Yet, it makes perfect sense that Socrates chooses not to list them explicitly, and only alludes to them in this veiled and ambiguous way, for these true necessary pleasures are not unconditionally good and don't function unconditionally as factors responsible for the goodness of a good life. The earlier list included simply types of knowledge and pleasure, that is, elements that are simply allowed in a good life (62c–64b), whereas the present ranking is restricted to factors that are responsible for the goodness of our lives (64c5–d2).[11]

That the order of ranking is not at all arbitrary is clear, but what exact sense to make of this specific ranking is not an easy task.[12] To name only a few puzzles that the list gives rise to, especially as far as the specific items listed in the first and second rank and the relation between them are concerned: *Kairos* has not made any earlier appearance in our dialogue prior to this moment and it is thus stunning to see it take pride of place on the first rank! What are we to make of this? Furthermore, in what sense is the beautiful ranked on the same footing with the perfect and the self-sufficient, when we seem to recall that it is, rather, the Good itself that was called self-sufficient and perfect in the earlier pages of the *Philebus* (20d) and the Good is clearly superior to the beautiful (64c–e)? Thirdly, what is the difference between measure and the measured listed first in rank, on the one hand, and proportion, which comes second in rank, on the other?[13]

While some of these questions are likely to continue to puzzle us, we can at least recognize some of the principles that guide the sequence in which the goods are listed. For one thing, as Wood notes, the first two ranks are dedicated to inherent aspects of the Good itself (measure, symmetry, beauty, proportion, self-sufficiency); the following two are reserved for the higher and lower order intellectual faculties respectively, placing intellect and reason first, while various lower types of knowledge, true opinion, and arts follow after, and finally the last two ranks are reserved for higher and lower order pleasures, with pure pleasures being higher, and true necessary pleasures lower (Wood 2016, 280). Furthermore, each subsequent ingredient depends on the one(s) above (Lang 2010, 155). Thus, pure pleasures depend on judgments and true opinions, and true opinions and judgments depend on reason or intelligence as main source. In turn, to the extent that reason or intelligence is to act as cause of good mixtures it must be guided by the well-proportioned and the beautiful. Finally, as long as these ingredients are seen to be responsible for shaping the concrete individual lives of human beings, and not just as abstract principles of order, measure and the timely are necessary for generating proportion and beauty in such a mixture. This turns out to be most relevant for our concern with the role of measure in a good life, and more specifically to its role in calibrating our pleasures of learning. For, as argued toward the end of the previous chapter, this "measure" means due measure, in the sense of a normative standard that takes into account fluctuating circumstances in one's life. Listed as first in rank along with the timely (*to kairon*), measure too must be referring here to a standard that is shifting depending on the concrete circumstances in an individual's life, and not an absolute sense as a metaphysical abstract principle.

It is likely, then, that measure is placed at the top of the list of ingredients of a good life, higher than even reason and intelligence, to suggest that the right combination of pleasure and knowledge differs for distinct individuals, given the varied backgrounds, talents, and natures that we all have, and also that it will shift depending on the concrete changing circumstances of life. Measure is indicative of the proportion of ingredients that best reflects the presence of the Good in a concrete set of circumstances in an individual's life, such that, for instance, in the good life of an individual who is by nature very intellectual, the due amount and intensity of pure pleasures of learning theoretical subjects will be much higher than that of pure pleasures of smell or sight, while in the life of a very intuitive artistic type, the due amount of pure aesthetic pleasures necessary for a good life might be greater than that of pleasures taken in abstract theoretical studies. Depending on their natural inclinations and talents, as well as on the particular circumstances of their lives at certain times, individuals will sometimes *rightly* find learning practical crafts more fulfilling than studying pure mathematics, or mathematics more fulfilling than dialectic, even while the pleasures of dialectical study are by their very nature, absolutely speaking, more valuable than all the other pleasures of learning. If this is correct, it makes sense to place the beautiful and the proportionate on the second rank, for due measure will be responsible for what constitutes beauty and what is proportional in each individual case.[14]

When it comes to our pure pleasures of learning we see that they depend on knowledge in a triple sense: first, like any other members of the class of Mixtures, these pleasures depend on reason or knowledge as their productive Cause, as shown in chapter II; second, as pleasures *of learning*, they depend also on the type of knowledge that the learning is about, such that the more precise the field in which the learning is undertaken, the purer and truer the pleasures of learning accompanying it; and third, they depend on self-knowledge, insofar as the individual experiencing the learning must be able to estimate correctly his/her lack and perceived replenishment. Correspondingly, then, due measure is needed to adjust the right proportions of the matching sorts of knowledge for the various pleasures of learning that we have.

Depending on our distinct natural inclinations, different ratios of limit will specify the range of intensity characteristic to our respective pleasure of learning in one field of knowledge or another, from the most imprecise types guided by lucky guesses (music, medicine, agriculture, navigation, strategy), going through the more precise productive types (shipbuilding, house building), which make use of vulgar or applied mathematics (56d9–e1), and then continuing with pure mathematics (56e–57a), and finally ending with dialectic, which has highest degree of certainty and precision (58a1–5).[15] The due measure for the pleasure that a musical person takes in studying a powerful musical work is much more intense than the average feeling of musical enjoyment. Similarly, for those who have high intellectual abilities, the due measure of pleasure taken in abstract mathematical study is the highly intense and not the moderate enjoyment. I do not mean at all to suggest that the motivation for pursuing, say, abstract mathematical studies is the intense pleasure one takes in doing it, for that would commit one to a very instrumentalist understanding of learning, which is far removed from Plato's view. My claim is only that the pleasure that a competent mathematician takes in solving mathematical problems is more intense than the pleasure that a less skilled student of mathematics would achieve while doing the same thing.

We can in no way conclude, though, that any person with inclination for intellectual speculative thought will *always* prefer learning highly abstract subjects over concrete ones, nor that it would be good for them to do so! The self-knowledge that an individual possesses in this context is highly relevant for the pleasures of learning they will experience. Imagine, for instance, a person with limited cognitive capacities yet totally self-ignorant of his/her limitations hoping to enjoy learning a very complex theory in astrophysics—a total *fiasco*! Imagine, on the other hand, a person of high intellectual competencies, self-aware of his/her intellectual strengths and limitations, discovering the solution to a complex mathematical problem: pure delight! Imagine next an intellectually competent person who doesn't give himself credit for his capacities, but rather distrusts himself—this person would not dare approach a more complex and abstract challenge for fear of being defeated in the process of sorting it out! Similarly, too, someone who has limited cognitive capacities and is, nevertheless, overly confident in his intellectual skills will fail just as much at enjoying appropriate pleasures of learning when he ventures in theoretical landscapes far too challenging for their limited dispositions and abilities! The individual who knows him/herself, is aware of his/her ignorance, is much more prone to experience most of the time true pleasure in learning. Conversely, lacking due measure in assessing our condition with respect to knowledge distorts the pleasure we take in learning and thus predisposes us to take false pleasure in learning. Being ignorant of my ignorance is just as bad as exaggerating my ignorance: both attitudes compromise our learning and the pleasures that could be attendant upon it. The former makes learning feel redundant, while the latter makes the situation feel overwhelming.

Self-knowledge is, then, perhaps the most important cognitive aspect that enables us to enjoy the pleasures of learning, for just having cognitive abilities that we are unaware of impairs us at least as much as not having those abilities in the first place.[16] The *Philebus* constantly encourages our efforts toward self-knowledge and brings to the fore the humble attitude of the philosopher by showing us Socrates poking fun at himself, with a healthy dosage of self-irony, for attempting with his modest means to disclose the ultimate articulation of all there is. Socrates recognizes that the practice of philosophy makes us look ridiculous sometimes (23d1–3). For practicing philosophy invites us to acknowledge in an instant the discrepancy between the loftiest ideals we aspire to and the limited resources we possess for that task. The philosopher's natural tendency to dwell in the medium of eternal truth while neglecting the obvious, the immediate, the simple is also treated with delicate irony (62a7–b9).

On this view, then, philosophers should be able to enjoy the highest and most intense true pure pleasures, since their learning always has stable and eternal objects. Given, however, the understanding of pleasure as a process, and specifically as replenishment of a lack, how can the philosopher continue to live most pleasantly once he acquires the knowledge he has been seeking? What pleasures are left for the philosopher once he attains the understanding and knowledge he has been striving for? Puzzled by these questions, scholars such as Frede argue that in the *Philebus* Plato renounces the view that the philosopher outdoes everyone in the amount of pleasure he gains, a view that he defended in *Republic* IX. On Frede's interpretation, the reason for this turn must have been Socrates's realization that the view of pleasure defended in the *Republic* is incompatible with the generic definition of pleasure as a process (Frede 1993, 61 n3). I doubt that this is a satisfactory answer. A better solution resides, I believe, in realizing, on the one hand, that there is always more knowledge to acquire and more connections to make among things understood, and, on the other, that revisiting in thought things understood is itself a pleasant process of learning, hence there is no such thing as a philosopher ever acquiring all the knowledge he has been striving for.

That a philosopher's cognitive task is never truly at an end, but rather constantly something still to be pursued does not deny its intrinsic value and its worth of being pursued. Once we realize this, we should have no difficulty in recognizing that pleasures, too, even though described as becoming (*genesis*) can have inherent value and are not to be seen merely as remedial goods.[17]

Enjoyment of reestablished balance is intrinsically worth pursuing, as essential manifestation of the good for us humans. Mere intellectual grasp of goodness is worth much less than an intellectual grasp of goodness echoed emotionally as replenishment. Without the experience of our pleasures of learning, for instance, we would not fully appreciate the goodness that is inherent in the fact that, as human beings, we are rational and thus can have cognitive grasp, and thus we would not be able to fully appreciate the kind of beings that we are. Furthermore, in addition to being valuable insofar as it makes us realize what replenishment means and furthers our progression toward our natural balance, pleasures are also beneficial in furthering our intellectual pursuits. Not only are they not obstacles to learning, but they are in fact actively prompting our *desire* to learn more.[18]

To conclude, then, this chapter explored several issues related to pleasures of learning that are not explicitly addressed in the text, yet for whose treatment the text offers sufficient support to encourage a reconstruction of details that, while stepping beyond the letter of the text, remains nonetheless faithful to its spirit. It is in this vein that I hope to have shown that even pleasures of learning that emerge in response to *aporia* can in certain circumstances be experienced as pure pleasures; that, while Plato's text does not address those explicitly, it leaves room for mixed as well as false pleasures of learning alongside their pure and the true counterparts; and that due measure plays an essential role in our experience of the pleasures of learning.

VI

Plato's Conception of Pleasure Confronting Three Aristotelian Critiques

If the previous chapters uncovered ways in which we are encouraged to think about mediation within the *Philebus*, this time we turn our attention to a possible test of the strength and robustness of Plato's conception of pleasure in light of a number of challenges launched from an Aristotelian perspective. Much has been made of Aristotle's refutation of the understanding of pleasure as process or becoming (*genesis*) and his replacement of this with an understanding of pleasure as activity that is complete at every moment.[1] Aristotle directs at least three major criticisms against an understanding of pleasure that is akin to Plato's own account, whether Aristotle had Plato's specific account in mind or not: (1) that the definition of pleasure as perceived replenishment is too narrow, as it seems to account only for mixed pleasures and not also for pure ones, and is especially suited for mixed pleasures of the body, and little, if at all, for those of the soul; (2) that pleasure cannot be unlimited since it is not excessive per se; and (3) that we need to reconsider the understanding of "purity" when talking about "pure pleasures," and instead of taking it to mean mere lack of any admixture of pain we should envision it to be determined by the ontological status of the object of pleasure.[2] Three requirements for a viable conception of pleasure transpire through these challenges: (1) that we need a generic definition of pleasure that can account for all pleasures, (2) that pleasures need to be conceived as definite and determined rather than excessive or unlimited, and (3) that the "purity" of pleasures needs to be assessed in relation to the objects of pleasure. In what follows, I want to see whether Plato's conception of pleasure developed in the *Philebus* can meet these requirements or is, rather, in need of some profound revisions. I hope to show that his view is solid and complex enough to withstand this threefold test.

My present concern then is not to elucidate and assess Aristotle's view in its own right, but simply to see whether Plato's conception can survive the critical points mentioned above. Even though I am not interested in undertaking a thorough examination of Aristotle's own view of pleasure, I will nonetheless start with an outline of its main moments delineated in the *Nicomachean Ethics*. I want to suggest, if only tentatively, that the Aristotelian account developed here could be accepted by Plato *as a phenomenological description of the experience of pleasure*, while preserving intact Plato's own account as far as *the nature of pleasure and its metaphysical placement* as *genesis* in the fourfold articulation of reality are concerned.

Aristotle's View of Pleasure in the *Nicomachean Ethics*

Aristotle's discussion of pleasure consists of a forceful critique of the view that pleasure is not intrinsically good and a development of his own view that pleasure is inseparable from the good life. It is in this context that Aristotle criticizes the idea that pleasure is replenishment of a lack, which would make it, he argues, a merely remedial good, a process of getting rid of an imperfect and undesirable state. If pleasures are perceived replenishments of lacks, then in order to experience pleasure one would almost seek an itch, so that they could scratch it. It makes you want to have the imperfection, so that you might enjoy getting rid of it.

The *Nicomachean Ethics* dedicates several sections to an account of pleasure, first, in the concluding sections of book VII, and then in the opening sections of book X. The topic of pleasure in the last few sections of book VII (VII.11–14) fits in naturally at the end of a discussion of continence and incontinence and their respective relations to virtue and vice (VII.1–10), for it is, after all, the presence or absence of pleasure in our activities that marks the difference between a virtuous (temperate) and a merely continent character. The temperate person's refraining from indulging their appetites is echoed in the pleasure they take in their virtue, whereas the continent person only reluctantly refrains from indulging their appetites, and thus takes no pleasure in refraining. Similarly, dedicating the first five sections of book X to pleasure fits organically within a context in which the final culminating topic of the *Nicomachean Ethics* is happiness: Is pleasure also part of a happy life? Can we classify pleasures as higher or lower depending on the extent to which they are conducive to or reflective of our happiness?

While there are clear overlaps and a great deal of continuity between the accounts offered in books VII and X respectively, there is also at least one significant inconsistency that has been puzzling scholars. In both accounts, Aristotle argues against the view that pleasure is a movement or a change (*kinēsis*), a process or a becoming (*genesis*), and, instead, connects pleasure closely with activity, though he does this in different ways. Book VII of the NE does it by equating pleasure with an unimpeded activation of our faculties in accord with their nature (1153a14–15), while book X does so by conceiving of pleasure as something that completes or perfects activity, as a supervening end (1174b23, b33). The main difference is that book VII identifies pleasure with an activity, while book X identifies it with something *supervenient upon an activity,* like "the bloom of youth" on a young person. Since the discussion developed in Book X is more complex, scholars have typically considered it as of later composition and have often accounted for the difference between the accounts in terms of a later and more mature refinement of an earlier view.[3] G. E. L. Owen, however, explains the difference between them as due to the fact that the two passages address distinct questions. Book VII, he argues, attempts to elucidate what are the objects of pleasure, asking, "What is it that we are pleased about?" whereas book X explores the essence of pleasure: "What is pleasure and being pleased?"[4] Correspondingly, then, when in book VII Aristotle writes that pleasure is unimpeded activity of a faculty in its natural state, what he means is that, what we enjoy, for instance in regaining health, is not convalescing, but rather the activity of the healthy part of our body. Thus, the question addressed in book VII concerns the object of pleasure, or under what description we enjoy our state. Book X, on the other hand, attempts to explain what it means to enjoy something. Aristotle argues that enjoying something means to have an experience that completes or perfects the activity we are engaged in. Owen is probably right to argue that the two discussions address somewhat different questions about pleasure, yet this does not exclude the possibility that the two are stages in the articulation of a single inquiry. "What is the object of pleasure?" and "What is enjoyment?" can be two stages in the attempt to answer a complex question about the nature of pleasure, a view consistent also with Harte's proposal that book X takes a step farther beyond what was argued in book VII:

[I]n NE vii 11–14, Aristotle makes only one of the two points he makes about pleasure in NE x 4–5. In both he identifies as source or location of pleasure certain perfect/unimpeded activities. In NE x4, but not in NE vii11–14, he goes on to characterize the enjoyment component of such a pleasure as something that itself perfects an activity in a distinct, though apparently inevitable manner. (Harte 2016, 312)[5]

Let us consider the major moments of the discussion of pleasure in book VII. Aristotle starts off by considering the following possible answers to the question whether pleasure is good: (1) no pleasure is good, whether in itself or incidentally; (2) some pleasures are good, but most are bad; (3) even if every pleasure is a good, the good cannot be a pleasure (1152b8–12). The reasons typically invoked in support of the view that (1) no pleasure is good are: that pleasure is considered to be a coming into being (*genesis*), and not an end intrinsically desirable for its own sake, the way building is in relation to a house; that the temperate person avoids pleasures; that the prudent person pursues what is painless, not what is pleasant; that pleasures impede prudent thinking; that every good is the product of a craft, but there is no craft of pleasure. In support of the view that (2) most pleasures are bad, people will typically emphasize the numerous pleasures that are shameful and harmful. Finally, in support of (3), people will say again that pleasure is a becoming and not an end in itself.

Aristotle's counterarguments against (1) and (2) are that many pleasures that are good on the whole are bad on occasion and that some so-called bad pleasures are not pleasures at all. Against (1) and (3) Aristotle will argue that pleasure is not essentially *genesis* or restoration, but rather an unimpeded actualization of our faculties:

> Further, it is not necessary for something else to be better than pleasure, as the end, some say, is better than the becoming. For pleasures are not becomings, nor do they all even involve a becoming. They are activities, and an end [in themselves], and arise when we exercise [a capacity] not when we are coming to be [in some state]. And not all pleasures have something else as their end, but only those in people who are being led toward the completion of their nature. That is why it is also a mistake to call pleasure a perceived becoming. It should instead be called not perceived, but unimpeded. (NE 1153a8–13)[6]

The underlying assumption here seems to be that, as long as pleasure is regarded as *genesis,* there will always be something better than it for the sake of which it is pursued and, as such, pleasure ends up being merely instrumental and never something desired for its own sake. To counteract this view, Aristotle declares pleasure to be unimpeded actualization.[7] What he means by this most likely is not that pleasure itself is some special sort of activity, but rather that, whenever we are engaged in some activity, we take pleasure in the very exercise of our faculties involved in that activity.[8]

From identifying pleasures with unimpeded activity, Aristotle moves on to argue not only that at least some pleasures are inherently good, but also that at least some pleasure might be the good itself, that is, the supreme most desirable and most choiceworthy of the things pursued, even though some pleasures might still be bad. He argues for this by pointing out that happiness itself is the most unimpeded activity. If, then, an activity becomes pleasant only insofar as it is unimpeded, and if the most complete and perfect unimpeded activity is happiness, it follows that pleasure and happiness might coincide, although some pleasures might still be bad.

> Besides, just as one science might well be the best good, even though some sciences are bad, some pleasure might well be the best good, even though most pleasures are bad. Indeed, presumably, if each state has its unimpeded activities, and happiness is the activity—if the activity is unimpeded—of all states or of some one of them, it follows that some one unimpeded activity is most choiceworthy. But pleasure is this, [namely, an unimpeded activity]; and so some type of pleasure might be the best good even if most pleasures turn out to be bad without qualification. (NE 1153b8–14)

After explaining that pleasure received a bad reputation due to the bad pleasures of base characters, which are not, properly speaking, pleasures (1154a15–1154b2), Aristotle elucidates why bodily pleasures appear more choiceworthy than other pleasures, namely, that they come as reactions to pain, and excessive pain will make people eager to seek a cure for them in the pursuit of excessive bodily pleasures.

Book VII ends by integrating the discussion of pleasure in an account of the limitations and finitude of human nature, and arguing that the kinds of pleasure that we, human beings, enjoy fall short of those enjoyed by god.[9] God enjoys continuous everlasting activity through contemplation, whereas as humans, as composites of soul and body, or form and matter, we can be engaged in activities only intermittently, and thus the pleasures we derive are also temporary.

In book X, Aristotle intensifies his critique of pleasure as a process or *genesis* (1173a31–b4, 1174b7–9) and as replenishment of a lack (1173b7–13), and proposes instead his own view, that pleasure *completes* the activity (1174b31). The most important new development in understanding pleasure, which goes beyond what has been said in NE VII, occurs in NE X.4 and begins by comparing pleasure to vision. Just as seeing is complete at every moment, so too is pleasure complete at every moment, and not a mere process that takes time and aims at some end beyond itself, the way that building, for instance, does (1174a14–25). Unlike complete activities, such as pleasure and seeing, whose parts are uniform all the way through, processes such as building or walking have stages of completion and are not whole and complete before their end has been achieved. From comparing pleasure with sight, Aristotle makes a subtle shift to talk about the pleasure *of sight*, which he will use as paradigm for all pleasures. Pleasure occurs in an act of awareness, whether of sense perception or thought.

The most pleasant act of vision occurs when our faculty of sight in its best condition is directed upon the most beautiful and most powerful object proper to it. Pleasure arises when the perceptible object and the perceiving faculty are at their best (1174b14–31) and, while pleasure itself is not the activity of perception or sight or any other awareness, it completes or perfects those activities (1174b23, b24, b31–32, 1175a15–16, a21):

> Pleasure completes the activity—not, however, as the state does, by being present [in the activity], but as a sort of consequent end, like the bloom on youths. (NE 1174b31–33)

Figuring out what Aristotle means by characterizing pleasure as perfecting our activities not as an indwelling state (*ouk hōs hē hexis enuparchousa*), *but as a supervening end (alla hōs epigignomenon ti telos), like the bloom on youths in their prime* (1174b31–33) has been a heated subject of debate among scholars, and I cannot possibly even begin to do it justice here. Some scholars have been debating whether we are to take pleasure as formal or as final cause in relation to the activity it "perfects" (Gauthier and Jolif 2002, II.2, 838–41; Gosling and Taylor 1982, 241–54; Harte 2016, 304–305), while others have suggested that pleasure might be better understood neither as formal nor as final cause, but rather as some sort of fusion of the two.[10] The image of the "bloom of youth" that Aristotle uses to illustrate that relation suggests that, just as youth is a necessary, yet not sufficient condition for the bloom of youth to be manifest, so too completion of activities is a necessary, yet not sufficient, condition for pleasures. Just as the bloom of youth is an indication of perfection that becomes manifest in special circumstances, so too pleasure is manifest in cases of ideal performance of the activity.

In a synoptic overview, we can summarize Aristotle's view of pleasure developed in books VII and X in the following ten ideas:

1. Pleasure is complete at any time, while processes are never complete but becoming so.

2. Every process, such as building, walking, etc. takes time, aims at some end beyond the activity itself, is complete only when it has produced the product it seeks or in the whole of time that it takes, and consists of dissimilar subprocesses.

3. Pleasure differs from processes in all the above features. Hence, pleasure is not a process.

4. Pleasure is an activity (from 1,2,3).

5. For each faculty the best activity is the activity of the subject in the best condition in relation to the best object of the faculty.

6. The best activity is the most pleasant. Every faculty of perception and every sort of thought and study has its pleasure; the most pleasant activity is the most complete; and the most complete is the activity of the subject in good condition in relation to the most excellent object of the faculty.

7. Pleasure completes an activity, not, however, as a state does, by being present in the activity, but as a sort of consequent end, like the bloom on youths (1174b31–33). Hence, as long as the objects of understanding or perception and the subject that judges or attends are in the right condition, there will be pleasure in the activity.

8. We cannot sustain an activity continuously without any interruption whatsoever, nor can we be pleased continuously without interruption (115422–32, 1175a5–11).

9. Pleasure completes all of our activities, and therefore it also completes life, for living too is an activity (1175a12–17).

10. Different activities have different pleasures to complete them. An activity is always promoted by its proper pleasure and impeded by an alien pleasure. E.g., for the pleasure that flute players take in playing the flute, conversation can be disruptive; for the pleasure of watching good performance at the theater, eating popcorn can be disruptive.

A Platonic Response to Aristotle's Critique of Pleasure as *Genesis* and as Replenishment of a Lack

We are looking, then, at a threefold requirement for a viable conception of pleasure: (1) that the definition of pleasure ought to account for all pleasures, mixed as well as pure; (2) that pleasures need to be conceived as definite and determined, rather than unlimited; and (3) that the purity of pleasures must be regarded as determined by the ontological status of the object of pleasure. In what follows, we are going to explore whether Plato's understanding of pleasure satisfies these requirements. In addition, we are going to consider a possible Platonic reply to the other worry articulated above, that by regarding pleasure as *genesis* we reduce it to a purely instrumental good.

To begin with, Aristotle is concerned that defining pleasures as perceptible replenishments is restrictive and cannot account for the more refined pleasures that are not based upon a previous depletion or emptying. For how could that characterization of pleasure account for the pleasures of artistic contemplation or for those related to study for its own sake, when they don't seem to be preceded by any previous lack? As he puts it:

> This belief [that pleasure is refilling] seems to have arisen from pains and pleasures in connection with food; for first we are empty and suffer pain, and then take pleasure in the refilling. The same is not true, however, of all pleasures; for pleasures in mathematics, and among pleasures in perception those through the sense of smell, and many sounds, sights, memories, and

expectations as well, all arise without [previous] pain. In that case what will they be comings-to-be of? For since no emptiness of anything has come to be, there is nothing whose refilling might come to be. (NE 1173b14–22)

How could Plato respond? Plato's understanding of pleasure is ultimately anchored in his metaphysical account, whereby, upon embodiment, our souls' powers have been reduced compared with what they used to be before. As I tried to argue already in chapter I, aside from the physiological and psycho-physical senses of filling or replenishment, the conception of pleasure developed in the *Philebus* relies heavily also on a *metaphysical sense of "filling"* (*plērōsis*). As finite beings our lives are permeated by lack through and through, and our desire to live a good life is nothing other than an expression of our eagerness to get ever closer to a normative state of well-being, a state in which the ratios of all the various pairs of opposites that enter our makeup reach their highest degree of balance and harmony and, as such, constitute the closest reflection of the Good that we are ever able to instantiate. The "normative state of balance" or "natural state" that we try to achieve is not, however, something readily given, but rather something that we keep establishing and reestablishing again and again as we move forward through life. The ratios that represent our respective normative states, defined in relation to the project of our life as a whole, differ from one person to another, and even the ratios defining an individual's normative state of balance shift over time depending on that individual's intellectual maturation and development, or change of circumstances, etc. The more attuned our own reason is to the divine cosmic *noūs*, the closer it comes to bringing about the ideal instantiation of the Good in our life (26e–27b, 28c–30e). For as cause of the mixture that we are, our own reason is responsible for bringing about the right combination of limit with the unlimited in the huge variety of aspects that make up the conglomerate of ratios that we are.

Our experiences are fulfilling to the extent that they bring us closer to that ideal normative state that instantiates the Good as perfectly as possible, and are depleting, to the extent that they take us farther away from it. What is at stake, then, with this metaphysical sense of filling or replenishment is our constant effort to approximate as best as we can the project of a good life. That Socrates's concern is for the good life as a whole, and not merely for momentary states independent of or apart from the rest of one's life, is evident throughout (11d6, 20b–23b, 43c8, c13, d7–9, e8, 66a–c).

Again, as pointed out already in achapter I, the more literal translation of *plērōsis* as "filling" is more adequate than the usually adopted one of "replenishment." This normative state that we establish and want to achieve is *not* something that we, as embodied souls, used to have, then lost, and now want to recover! Hence, it is not a *re-turn* to something specific we once had. Rather, it is a motion forward, a constant attempt to approximate more and more the parameters of a fulfilling good life for each of us. Since our existence is permeated by lack, there is always need for ever more filling to get us closer to the fulfillment of our potential.

Nevertheless, in this story of our attempt to progress through more and more filling, our *soul* does indeed aim to get *re*-plenished. As I indicated in chapter IV, I take seriously a few hints at recollection in our text. First, the earlier distinction between empirical and a priori memory (remembering a perception and remembering a piece of knowledge, a *mathema*, respectively [34b–c]), and then the reference to our soul's innate love of truth (*tis pephuke tēs psuchēs hēmōn dunamis erān te toū alēthoūs* [58d4–5]), coupled with the argument that we can only *desire* an object that we had before and that has been preserved in our memory (35a–c). If, then, there is in us an innate desire for truth (58d), and if all desires require memory's contact with the object that satisfies that desire (35a–c), it follows that our memory must have been in touch a priori with the truth that we now desire to learn, and, hence, our soul must have been in touch with the Forms prior to being embodied. The trauma of embodiment which Plato's Socrates renders through the metaphor of forgetfulness is the source of great loss. Throughout our lives we try to recover some of the a priori memory that was lost at embodiment.

With this metaphysical backdrop in mind, accounting for the way pure pleasures can count as fillings of unfelt lacks is not all that problematic any more. As finite beings we are always in a condition of lack on account of our finitude. In experiencing pure pleasures we experience awareness of gradual advancements toward our natural balance, transitions toward ever closer approximations of our normative state of well-being, and thus gradual fillings of the lack that is ontologically constitutive to us.[11] While in the cases of hunger, thirst, and perhaps most of our bodily needs the lacks are *felt* and thus are painful, in the cases of many of our psychic needs our lacks are oftentimes not felt as painful. Thus, when we enjoy for instance, learning something for its own sake or contemplating art, we experience these as pure pleasures insofar as the preexistent lack of our finitude was not felt as painful and there had been no prior "hunger" or pain of some sort for learning or art. Pure pleasures then replenish in us an ontological lack, part of our ineluctable finitude. Since this lack is inscribed in our makeup, we need not fear that one would almost need to create a lack or an imperfection to have something to fill or something to get rid of, or that we'd almost seek an itch, so we could scratch it, as Aristotle worried. Whether we want to or not, our existence is shot through with a sense of lack, and thus imperfection or ontological precarity is already inscribed in our constitution.

It is legitimate, nevertheless, to ask: If Plato's understanding of "replenishment" is so wide, *why* doesn't he have Socrates say so explicitly in the *Philebus*? The main reason for this has to do, I believe, with Plato's pedagogical strategy and his understanding of dialectic. He has Socrates basically define pleasure as perceived filling or replenishment of a lack (33d) and illustrate at an early stage what he means by this simply and solely by appeal to physical pleasures, and only in later stages of the conversation do we come to see illustrations of pure pleasures and of pleasures of the soul all by itself that can be accounted for by means of the same definition, yet by implicitly enlarging the meaning of the filling or replenishment at stake. As argued in detail in chapter II, we witness, throughout the dialogue, a dialectical development of the understanding of pleasure, from its simple equation with thoughtless thrill or sensation to recognizing its complex cognitive structure anchored in the general beliefs we have about the value of things and life generally. I believe that we also witness a dialectical development of the notion of "replenishment" (*plērōsis*), which goes hand in hand with the development of the understanding of pleasure. While in the early stages "replenishment" is understood primarily in a physiological sense, as we advance it comes to acquire a pronounced metaphysical meaning, whereby as fundamentally finite creatures we constantly aspire to be filled with what we lack and thus to reestablish a balance of our organism that represents the best instantiation of the Good we are capable of. This strategy is adopted primarily for pedagogical reasons. At the beginning of the conversation, when Protarchus was just starting to defend Philebus's hedonist position privileging bodily pleasures, he would have been reluctant to accept a metaphysically complex understanding of replenishment.

This dialectical development of the notion of pleasure mirrors what Plato's Socrates does with the notion of knowledge, which he uses in the *Philebus* loosely as synonymous with *technē*, and sometimes also interchangeably with *phronēsis*. In the passage dedicated specifically to the classification of knowledge, Socrates calls *epistēmē* and *technē* everything ranging from guesswork to the heights of dialectical contemplation (55c–59c). He rates as lowest the knowledge associated with the arts guided by lucky guesses (music, medicine, agriculture, navigation, strategy), followed by the more precise productive arts (shipbuilding, house building). Next he places the knowledge associated with educational arts, first mathematics (56d–57a), and then dialectic (57e–59c). Educational arts are superior to the productive sort due to their greater share of Measure and Proportion, and thus implicitly of certainty and precision. Most valuable of all is the knowledge of dialectic, since it is the discipline "concerned with being and with what is really and forever in every way eternally the same . . . by far the truest kind of knowledge" (58a1–5). Even though he uses *epistēmē* and *technē* interchangeably for all these pursuits, Socrates doesn't collapse the differences among the various arts. They remain differentiated on account of the distinct objects each of them takes, just as pleasures, while all included under the common umbrella of perceived replenishments, differ widely among themselves by virtue of the distinct objects doing the filling in each case.

The reply sketched so far does a lot to mitigate Aristotle's criticism. It shows that there is a coherent way within Plato's metaphysical horizon to make his definition of pleasure as perceived filling of a lack cover not only mixed, but also pure, pleasures and not merely of a physiological, but also of a purely psychic nature. Aristotle could still insist, nevertheless, on the superiority of defining pleasure as *activity* rather than perceived filling, pointing out that replenishment is pleasant only incidentally: we do not enjoy the replenishment as such, but rather the natural functioning of the faculties that provide that replenishment. So, pleasure is possible during recovery because we are not entirely deficient, and thus we owe the pleasure to the healthy functioning part of us. The activity of the healthy part is truly what is enjoyed as such, and not the replenishment itself, which is only enjoyed *per accidens*. Aristotle points out that what we enjoy during our recovery is not the restoration of the deficiency, but the fact that the healthy part of our organism is active and engaged in its proper activities (1152b34–1153a1).

In light of the broad metaphysical conception of "replenishment" sketched above, Plato could probably place the Aristotelian understanding of perfect performance of an activity under the comprehensive umbrella of fillings and restorations of balance that we undergo. Thus, for instance, when I actualize my intellectual faculty by being engaged in artistic or theoretical contemplation, I am thereby actively engaged in reestablishing my natural balance and replenishing lacks that, as a finite human being, I clearly have. There is no contradiction between the unimpeded actualization and the perceived filling or restoration of balance. Each episode in which I actively contemplate and take delight in doing so—which we could describe in Aristotelian language as actualization of our natural faculties—would constitute for Plato yet one more stage in the overall project of approaching my natural state of balance and harmony according to my normative standards. The natural balance of an organism is that organism's optimal state, a state defined normatively by ratios of well-being that expresses its livelihood, which presuppose that person's active stimulation and vibrant feeling of wellness and harmony. If so, then Plato can accept Aristotle's understanding of pleasure as a phenomenological description of *what it feels like* to enjoy something, namely, to be fully engaged in an activity that feels complete at every moment, while still maintaining his own account of what enjoyment *means* metaphysically speaking.

It seems to me that calling pleasure a *genesis* is for Plato primarily, if not exclusively, a way of qualifying it ontologically, as a Mixture, and not a way of describing phenomenologically the experience of pleasure and what that feels like. Envisioning pleasure as a process that takes time and has stages, the aspect that Aristotle is critical of, does not seem essential, if at all important for Plato. Of course, like everything that is included in the class of Mixtures, pleasures too pertain to the world of change and are themselves experienced in time. But Plato seems unconcerned with the phenomenological aspect of what it feels like for us to experience pleasure, the very aspect that seems primordial for Aristotle. If anything, Plato can learn about that from Aristotle and incorporate his student's account into his own view in the way suggested above.

Recall our distinction in chapter IV between the neutral condition, absence of pleasure and pain, and the natural condition, which Socrates called earlier the most godlike life in which neither pain nor pleasure are experienced precisely because it is a state entirely dedicated to rational thought (21d–22c, 32d–33c). The former state is compatible with the mediocrity of the many, who are content with bodily satisfactions and are completely insensitive to higher pursuits of desire and pleasure, precisely because they do not engage in rational thought. The latter state characterizes the life of the gods, who, liberated from corporeal demands are entirely dedicated to contemplation, and it is thus a standard we aspire to achieve, but which we can never fully realize while embodied. The difference between the two kinds of life is that the former is often devoid of the activity of thinking, or it keeps thinking at a very minimal level, whereas the latter is entirely dedicated to it. What I describe now as the state of reestablished natural balance of an organism is not reducible to either, though it is much closer to the godlike life than to the neutral state. It is the closest that we can come in this life, as a soul-body conglomerate, to live the godlike life. In light of this, the actualization of our healthy faculties in activities directed to their proper objects is itself for Plato a stage in our ontological filling, and it is part and parcel of our reestablishment of natural balance. Whether we define the pleasure as a perceived reestablishment of our natural balance or an awareness of our perfect activation of a faculty in relation to its proper object, is a difference of perspective, not of substance.

At the end of the day, the major source for the differences between Plato's and Aristotle's understandings of pleasure resides in the fact that they emphasize distinct aspects of the complex reality of human nature. In particular, for Plato the inclusion of pleasures even in the best of human lives is primarily a mark of our finitude and an indication of the way in which the animal side of human nature falls short of the divine, whereas for Aristotle the most valuable pleasures that we can experience are primarily indicators of our capacity to transcend human nature and have a share of the divine life, while we remain nevertheless forever finite and by nature fall short of the divine (see also Harte 2016, 291). Their distinct takes on pleasure in the good human life correspond to whether or not they conceive of pleasure as an experience that the god(s) also have: Plato denies it, while Aristotle eagerly accepts it. For Plato, our very predisposition to feelings of pleasure and pain is by itself a mark of finitude. The gods, on the other hand, are not subject to passions, pleasure, and pain, and their natural condition is defined as full and exclusive exercise of reason (22c, 33a–b). While Aristotle also recognizes our natural finitude, he does not believe that the experience of pleasure is by itself indicative of limitation. In fact, for Aristotle, God himself experiences pleasure through his perfect and self-sufficient activity, his perpetual self-contemplation (NE X.7–8, *Met.* XII. 7–10).

The second requirement formulated above is that pleasures ought not to be regarded as unlimited since they are not excessive per se. As Aristotle puts it:

> They say that the good is definite, whereas pleasure is indefinite because it admits of more and less. If their judgment rests on the actual condition of being pleased, it must also hold for justice and the other virtues where evidently we are said to have a certain character more and less, and to act more and less in accord with the virtues, for we may be [more and less] just or brave,

and may do just or temperate actions more and less. If, on the other hand, their judgment rests on the [variety of] pleasures, then surely they fail to state the reason [why pleasures admit of more and less], namely that some are unmixed [with pain] and others are mixed. (NE 1173a17–24)

A close examination of the *Philebus* reveals that Plato agrees fully with this point, since he has Socrates place all true pleasures, whether mixed with pain or pure, in the class of Mixtures, and not in the Unlimited. In effect, Aristotle's point does not reject, but rather confirms Plato's view.

We have seen in detail in chapter II that Socrates only *seems* to consider all pleasures unlimited, but in fact he places them in the class of Mixtures. Whenever he associates pleasures with the unlimited he does so while expressing Philebus's extreme hedonistic position and not while speaking in his own voice or while talking about false and excessive pleasures. As argued in that earlier context, the three passages that seem to support the placement of pleasures in the Unlimited (27e–28b, 31a, and 65c–d) refer only to sybaritic pleasures, while several other passages unambiguously and explicitly place true pleasures in the class of Mixtures (26b7–c1, 31c2–d1, 52c4–d1).

Hence, Plato and Aristotle agree on the fact that pleasures are not intrinsically excessive, and Plato's Socrates is clear also on recognizing that the fact that pleasures come in degrees and thus admit of the more or less does not commit them to the class of the Unlimited. For Plato, not everything that can have degrees or the "more or less" is a member of the Unlimited class. As articulations in the fourfold scheme, Mixtures and the Unlimited include distinct members in their respective classes, given the distinct roles that the more and less play in each of them. The excessiveness of the members of the Unlimited is not simply a reflection of the fact that those members have degrees, but a reflection of the lack of measure and determination upon any degree they have. Members of the Unlimited are too indefinite to be specific instances, with natures of their own, and thus neither instances of pleasure nor of virtue can fit in here. Mixtures, by definition, comprise limit, too, in addition to indefiniteness. Change characterizes both the members of Mixture and those of the Unlimited, yet the change that characterizes mixtures allows nonetheless for a relative permanence and preservation of their nature, for the presence of Limit in them ensures that their becoming is a coming-into-being (*genesin eis ousian* 26d8), and not a random, indefinite, indistinct fluctuation, unlike the turbulence that characterizes the members of the Unlimited.

If this is correct, then the pleasures we experience and the virtues we acquire are Mixtures and not instances of the Unlimited class, in spite of the presence of degrees in each of them. For they are orderly enough to have limit in them as well. As members of the Mixtures, though, virtue comes closer than pleasure to approaching Limit, and instances of virtue carry within themselves the normative mark of the ideal Courage, Justice, Wisdom, etc. expressed through ratios. The courage I might manifest on one occasion or another is an expression of the ratios that define the right intensity on the continuum that goes between shyness and boldness. If this is correct, then Aristotle's next comment simply makes explicit Plato's view that instances of health along with those of virtue and of pleasure all belong to the class of Mixtures and not to the Unlimited:

> Moreover, just as health admits of more and less, though it is definite, why should pleasure not be the same? For not every [healthy person] has the same proportion [of bodily elements], nor does the same person always have the same, but it may be relaxed and still remain up to a certain limit, and may differ in more and less. The same is quite possible, then, for pleasure also. (NE 1173a25–29)

Along the same lines, Aristotle's view that the vicious person is vicious insofar as he pursues excess, not insofar as he pursues necessary and true pleasures, again only confirms what Plato also believes.[12] For Plato's Socrates included among the ingredients of a good life all the true and pure pleasures, and his veiled silence about a possible sixth rank can be read as a reference to the presence of necessary pleasures, as witnessed in the previous chapter.

Furthermore, for Plato also, again, just like for Aristotle, vice goes hand in hand with false pleasures and these are often characterized by excess. We only need to remind ourselves of the characterization that Plato's Socrates gives to some of our mixed pleasures experienced with overwhelming intensity and in a vicious state of the soul:

> The moderate people somehow always follow the proverbial maxim "nothing too much" and obey it. But as to foolish people and those given to debauchery, the excess of their pleasures drive them near madness. —Good. But if this is the case, then it is obvious that the greatest pleasures as well as the greatest pains have their origins in some vicious state of the soul and body, and not in virtue. —Obviously. (45d7–e4)

Now in all those cases in which the mixture contains a surplus of pleasure, the small admixture of pain gives rise only to a tickle and a mild irritation, while the influx of pleasure, which is much stronger, causes the body to leap and kick, produces color changes of all sorts, distortions of shapes, and wild palpitations; it drives the person totally out of his mind, so that he shouts aloud like a madman. —Very much so. —And what is more, my friend, this state causes him and others to say of him that he is almost dying of these pleasures. And I would add to this that the more profligate and foolish he is, the more will he pursue them by any means possible, and he calls them supreme and considers as the happiest of all living beings whoever lives in continuous enjoyment of them. (47a3–b7)

While members of Mixture are never to be identified with *the good*, nothing prevents them from being inherently good, and from having a positive contribution to increasing the good in our lives. After all, a good life itself is, ontologically speaking, as member of the class of Mixtures, a *genesis*, yet very much desirable as such. As a *genesis*, a good life is not something achieved in any given moment, but rather a process of continuous change and transformation while living well unfolds. Once we recognize that pleasures too are Mixtures, we can recognize their inherent worth and contribution to improving the quality of our lives and vice versa.[13] The quality of the pleasures that we experience depends greatly on the quality of our lives. Pleasures reflect the way we feel the harmonization of our being, the increased balance in our organism, and our growth in goodness. Hence, it makes perfect sense to say that, as such indicators of our progression in goodness, pleasures themselves are inherently valuable, both insofar as they are manifestations of worth already achieved and insofar as, psychologically, they help motivate our continued improvement of our lives. The fact that pleasure is dependent upon the good life and thus desirable primarily for the sake of a good life rather than desirable for its own sake alone does not annul the inherent goodness of pleasure.

A third requirement concerns the understanding of "purity" when talking about "pure pleasures": instead of taking "purity" to mean mere painlessness, the purity of pleasures is to be determined ultimately by the ontological status of the object of pleasure.[14] As Gerd van Riel puts it:

> According to him [Aristotle], there is a difference in purity between different activities, and thus also between the pleasures

that accompany those activities. Seeing, he maintains, is purer than touching, and hearing and smelling are purer than tasting (1175b36–1176a3). The norm for this distinction seems to be the degree to which an activity is able to grasp the form and to detach from matter. Pure pleasure is, then, the pleasure that is detached from material things. It reaches its highest realization in the pleasure of God, completely devoid of the instability of matter (NE 1154b26–28; see also *Meta*. XII 107224–25). This also has consequences for a human, who is the bearer of a divine element: a human must strive to achieve immortality (at least as far as possible) by living in accordance with the highest part of him. And the highest, divine element in human being is intellect (NE 1177b30–34; cf. *Meta* xii 1072b22–24). (Gerd van Riel 2000, 134–35)

As argued in chapters III and V, Plato has Socrates use "purity" in a double sense, sometimes to designate the lack of admixture of pain in an experience of pleasure, other times, just like Aristotle, to designate the ontological status of the object of pleasure or of knowledge (55c–59c) and in general the metaphysical power and dignity that characterizes everything, including the structure of the universe as such (29b, 30b). Branches of knowledge and crafts are ordered hierarchically in relation to the purity of their objects, and thus they go from the most uncertain and imprecise ones based on guesswork and conjecture to the most precise and pure art of dialectic, whose objects possess certainty, purity, and truth in an eternal and unchanging way (59c).[15] Similarly, when dealing with pure pleasures, Plato's Socrates alludes to the dual sense in which these are pure: first, insofar as there is no admixture of pain in them, and secondly, insofar as their objects are strictly themselves—pure colors, sounds, smells, intelligible objects of learning, with no extrinsic admixture in them.[16] Moreover, the very activities that Aristotle mentions in NE 1175b36–1176a3 and the hierarchical order of their purity mirror the order in which Plato's Socrates arranged the pure pleasures attendant upon the same activities: the pleasures of smell are "less divine" than those we take in pure colors and sounds, the pleasures we take in pure geometrical shapes that are built with the ruler and compass are superior to those we take in colors and sounds, since the former rely more heavily on mathematics and measures, and finally, the pleasures we take in learning that is reserved to the very few are higher than all the others mentioned (51b–52b).

The two senses of "purity" are also related to one another. The more likely we are to attain higher degrees of purity in cognition, the more we tend to delight in pleasures that are pure, rather than mixed with pain. Also, the more likely we are to delight in pleasures that are pure in the sense of being unmixed with pain, the readier we are to progress in our knowledge toward eternal and stable objects, which are the purest realities ontologically speaking. Since Plato already extended the discussion of the purity of pleasures in the direction in which Aristotle develops it, Aristotle's discussion of purity is not a rejection of Plato's account thereof, but only an elaboration of a direction already delineated by Plato.

We started off by saying that the main target of Aristotle's criticism is the idea that pleasure is merely a remedial good, a process of getting rid of an imperfect and undesirable state, since in this negative light, pleasure does not present itself as a good that characterizes and contributes positively to the ideal life. Throughout this chapter, I have argued that, on the contrary, the fact that Plato calls pleasure *genesis* and regards it as perceived replenishment of a lack, does not mean that he cannot recognize the intrinsic worth of some pleasures. I tried to show that for Plato "replenishment" is not merely a physiological process, but rather a metaphysical one as well, and this allows Plato to conceive of pleasure as a valuable contributor to a good human life. In support of this claim we have (1) the explicit inclusion of pure pleasures in the list of ingredients responsible for the goodness of a good life (66c); (2) the implicit inclusion of necessary pleasures as sixth in rank among the ingredients of a good life (66c–d); (3) the realization that, without pleasure, a human life, however accomplished in all the other respects, would not be *desirable,* since pleasure just is the sensible manifestation of the increased balance of our organism.[17]

Pleasure, then, even as *genesis,* is not detached from the Good for Plato, but is rather itself experienced as manifestation of the goodness of a human life. Included, as we have seen, in the class of Mixtures, pleasure too is a "coming into being" (*genesis eis ousian* 26d8), thus an expression of goodness through limits imposed on the Unlimited and, as such, an essential part of a desirable good human life. Even so, the worry might still linger that for Plato pleasure remains forever an instrumental good, a means toward an end.

The text seems to suggest, however, that the "for the sake of" (*heneka tou*) relationship that connects pleasure as *genesis* with *ousia* does not necessarily describe an instrumental, means-ends type of relationship. When Socrates tries to explain to Protarchus what he means by calling pleasure a *genesis*, Socrates proceeds by following the guidance of certain "subtle thinkers" (53c6), according to whom pleasure, because it is a *genesis*, is always "for the sake of something" (*to heneka tou* [54c9]) and not "that for the sake of which" (*to hoū heneka* [54c9]) something is, and therefore cannot be placed in the same category as the good aimed at. Protarchus asks three times for clarifications in the course of Socrates's exposition of that view, and Socrates appeals to several illustrations to make his point understood:

> There are two kinds of things, one kind sufficient to itself, the other in need of something else. —How so, and what sorts of things do you mean? —The one kind possesses by nature supreme dignity; the other falls short of it. —Say this more clearly please. —We must have met some handsome and noble youths, together with their courageous lovers. —Certainly. —Now try to search for another pair that corresponds to this pair in all the relevant features that we just mentioned. —Do I have to ask you for the third time? Please say more clearly what you want to say, Socrates! —Nothing complicated, Protarchus; this is just a playful manner of speaking. What is really meant is that all things are either for the sake of something else, or they are that for whose sake the other kind comes to be in each case. —I finally managed to understand it, thanks to your numerous repetitions. (53d3–e8)

In this passage, Socrates is trying to convey the way in which pleasure, as *genesis*, falls short of *ousia*. The "for the sake of" relationship is explained here by appeal to four consecutive illustrations: (1) needy, not self-sufficient in relation to the self-sufficient; (2) lacking dignity in relation to the supremely dignified; (3) a lover in relation to his beloved; and (4) shipbuilding in relation to the ship (54b). Commenting on this passage, Carpenter insightfully suggests that the relationship at stake is one of "normative-metaphysical dependency" and that "*genesis*" here cannot possibly refer strictly to physical generation. For mere physical generation would hardly need so much explaining, and a single illustration would have sufficed for Protarchus to understand. Besides, of the four illustrations of the "for the sake of" relationship, only the ship illustration refers to strictly physical generation, and that was offered by Protarchus, not by Socrates, hence it is meant to work most likely as a physical image of a metaphysical sense of *genesis* that Socrates intends (Carpenter 2011, 76).[18]

The passage shows also that, even though it is a *genesis*, pleasure does not have a strictly instrumental value for Plato. The illustrations that Socrates provides to clarify for Protarchus the "for the sake of" relationship show that this clearly is not reducible to a relationship of means-ends. The way in which a lover, for instance, is "for the sake of" his beloved cannot mean that the lover is instrumentally necessary for the beloved in the same way in which, say, shipbuilding is necessary for a ship. Rather, the lover's worth *as a lover* is all the more confirmed on account of his beloved. Similarly, pleasure's worth is not denied, but rather confirmed and emphasized on account of the *ousia* of the Good and its reflection in Limit. Pleasure is not more of a means toward the end of balance than the lover could be a means toward his beloved. In both cases, pleasure and the lover, we talk about something other than merely instrumental goods! Similarly, with the first two illustrations, the deficient is not an instrument for attaining the self-sufficient, and what lacks dignity is not a means toward the supremely dignified either.

It is worth wondering whether the close association between pleasure and the goodness of a human life that we find in Plato is not analogous with the association between pleasure and activity for Aristotle, when Aristotle calls pleasure supervenient upon activity the way the bloom of youth is to the young, which basically means that the bloom is not something added upon and separable from the youth, but rather a glowing manifestation of it. While the full meaning of that image of the bloom and its relation to youth remains hard to decipher, it is worth listening to some of Warren's remarks regarding Aristotle's choice for that image. Warren argues that this image of the bloom of youths is inspired by Socrates's reference to lovers and their young beloveds that he uses in the *Philebus* to explain pleasure as *genesis*. According to him, Aristotle's main reason for choosing this image is to emphasize the disparity between his own and Plato's accounts of pleasure and the direction in which he hopes to improve his teacher's account. To make his point about pleasure as *genesis* comprehensible to Protarchus, one of the analogies that Socrates used was that of the relation between lover and beloved, whereby, just as pleasure is a coming into being for the sake of something, so is the lover for the sake of the beloved. Thus, for Plato's Socrates, the nature of pleasure is analogous to the sense of lack and sought replenishment that the lover experiences and puts himself in service to. Aristotle, on the other hand, when accounting for pleasure, shifts the focus from the lover to the beloved, and from an emphasis on what is missing and requires filling to something that expresses completion, the glow or bloom of youth that the beloved manifests and that is itself responsible for the lover's feelings.[19] This gives us at least some hints for the direction in which the relation between pleasure and activity is to be elucidated: (1) just as the condition of youth is necessary for the bloom of youth, so too is the activity prior to the pleasure that can occur as supervenient on it; (2) while dependent upon the condition of youth, the bloom is not identical with the biological stage of development, but is rather the manifestation that confirms the value of biological youth. Similarly, pleasure is a manifestation that confirms the value of the activity that produced it. Aristotle thus makes clever use of the same image that Plato's Socrates used, of youths in their prime, in order to make ever more obvious the divergence between his and Plato's account: while for Plato pleasure is associated primarily with process, motion, and change, for Aristotle it is associated primarily with something complete and perfect.

Aristotle preserves part of the normative framework that Plato uses, but relocates pleasure in it. For Aristotle accepts the idea of a normative standard, in his case revealed by the virtuous person, and he too might accept that pleasure and pain have something to do with disruptions of the normative standard. But what he clearly objects to is *the specific way* in which pleasure is related to such restorations in the Platonic framework. He rejects the idea of viewing restorative pleasures as paradigmatic for all pleasures, for he fears that this understanding would take away the possibility of recognizing the inherent goodness of pleasures. Once we see that, as argued above, the understanding of pleasure as *genesis* does not commit Plato to reject the inherent goodness of pleasures, and, in fact, even helps us regard pleasures as inseparable from the goodness of a good life, we can also conclude that Plato could import and incorporate Aristotle's dense and phenomenologically accurate account of the experience of pleasure as something complete at every moment, while still maintaining that, ontologically speaking, pleasure is *genesis* and belongs to the class of Mixtures. As argued above, Plato's main interest in calling pleasure a *genesis* is not to say that its manifestation unfolds over time and, as such a process, it has stages and is not complete at every moment, but rather to place them in the class of Mixtures, at once rescuing them from the flux of the unlimited and preventing our rash assimilation of pleasures with the *ousiai* of Limit.

Despite incontestable differences, Plato's and Aristotle's accounts of pleasure have also a lot in common. The presence/absence of pleasure is for both a significant indicator of genuine virtue: the presence of pleasure helps Aristotle distinguish between the virtuous and the continent (NE VII), and it helps Plato distinguish between the truly virtuous and the person having only civic virtue (*Phaedo* 69a–d). Both thinkers recognize the importance of due measure and this helps them account for the differences in the objects that people with distinct natural inclinations and talents would find enjoyable. Furthermore, both Plato and Aristotle recognize the tight connection between happiness and pleasure, yet neither one equates the two. For both of them true pleasures do not impede, but rather enhance the activities that produce them. Aristotle defends this by showing how pleasures enhance the activities they complete, while only alien pleasures impede an activity or another by distracting our attention and interrupting the activity (1153a22–24, 1175a30–1176a15). For his part, Plato imagines a dialogue between pleasures and knowledge and has pleasures asking for support from knowledge, while knowledge admits to being intensified by the experience of true and pure pleasures which are of the same kind (63b–e). Finally, both thinkers recognize our inherent limitation and finitude as human beings, and both discuss ways in which pleasure is interwoven with our ontological limitation and lack. While Aristotle regards our experience of pleasure as something that we share with the divine, whereas Plato regards pleasure as something characteristically human that we specifically do not share with the gods, nevertheless, both thinkers agree on the real distance between us and the gods. For Plato the divine, unlike us humans, is already full and complete and hence leaves no room to experience more filling or replenishment, whereas for Aristotle humans and the divine have *distinctive ways* of experiencing pleasures. Since our natures are not simple and, hence, we cannot engage in any activity without interruptions, we cannot experience pleasure continuously, whereas the god's uninterrupted activity of thinking is an uninterrupted experience of delight (1154b21–32).

In closing, then, the reflections here developed show that Plato's account can pass the test of at least some of the challenges formulated through the lens of an Aristotelian account. Aside from strengthening our trust in the complexity and internal consistency of Plato's understanding of pleasure and the human condition, our present discussion has also shown us something about the value of a constructive dialogue between thinkers and about the pleasure that accompanies such an undertaking.

Appendix

The *Philebus*'s Response to the *Aporiai* of Participation from the *Parmenides*

As indicated already in chapter I, there is some overlap between the concerns raised in the three puzzles of the *Philebus* 15b–c and the *aporiai* of participation spelled out in the first part of the *Parmenides*. Just as I suggested in the closing of that chapter that the *Philebus* implicitly addresses the three puzzles regarding the intelligible monads, I want now to suggest that the *Philebus* addresses also implicitly the *aporiai* regarding participation that are mentioned in *Parmenides* 128e–130a. A comprehensive treatment of either the *aporiai* of participation themselves or of the ways in which the *Philebus* implicitly addresses them is beyond the boundaries of this Appendix. I only aim to sketch here some hints for the direction that a study dedicated to these issues could take. In what follows, I discuss briefly each one of the six *aporiai* and then suggest what I envision to be the direction of a response based on the *Philebus*.

The *Parmenides* is set up as an encounter between the young and promising metaphysician Socrates and Parmenides, the versed thinker who presses Socrates on several issues that concern his understanding of intelligible realities and their relation to perceptible things around us. Whatever we might think about the order of composition of the *Philebus* relative to the *Parmenides*, the dramatic setting at least, whereby Socrates is young in the *Parmenides*, while being seasoned and experienced in the *Philebus*, encourages us to view the elaborations of the *Philebus* as a subsequent, more mature return to the same questions that troubled his youth. The six *aporiai* in the opening of the *Parmenides* concern difficulties that arise from trying to understand the "participation" of sensible things in intelligible Forms.

"Participation" in this context works as a metaphor and, if anything, is the name of a cluster of problems, not of a solution. In fact, most of the problems arise from wanting to treat "participation" in this context on a par with what "participation" means literally when talking about sensible things partaking of other sensible things. What is at play with "participation," then, is the right way to envision a mediation between the absolute universal eternal and unchanging Forms and their changing precarious instances.

That Plato takes these *aporiai* seriously and that he actually believes that it is worth searching for a solution to them emerges clearly from the way Parmenides concludes his conversation with Socrates about these. Once the challenges are formulated, Parmenides offers some sort of an overall assessment of their force and value. The objections ask serious questions that need to be taken into account if we want to make sense of Plato's Forms. The puzzles reveal real tensions intrinsic to Plato's theory concerning the scope of intelligible realities, the relation between the transcendence and immanence of Forms, and the nature of participation. Nevertheless, the existence of these tensions and difficulties is not fatal to Plato's theory, and, in fact, at the end of the day, Parmenides unwaveringly recognizes that we must accept the existence of Forms if we are to have meaningful discourse and rational activity at all:

> Yet, on the other hand, Socrates, said Parmenides, if someone, having an eye on all the difficulties we have just brought up and others of the same sort, won't allow that there are forms for things and won't mark off a form for each one, he won't have anywhere to turn his thought, since he doesn't allow that for each thing there is a character that is always the same. In this way he will destroy the power of dialectic entirely. But I think you are only too well aware of that. —What you say is true, Socrates said. (135b5–c2)[1]

The fact that Plato himself is the one to point out through his character Parmenides the weak spots of his theory shows once again how nondogmatic a thinker he is, allowing for a certain open-endedness to be built into his theories and be operative throughout his vision. Let us then turn to the difficulties themselves and see how they can be addressed with the instruments provided in the *Philebus*.

Aporia I: The first *aporia* concerns the scope of the Forms, and comes down to asking whether, since Forms are supposed to explain all the things around us, we need to postulate Forms even for such ignoble things as hair, dirt, or mud (130b–e). The reasons why the existence of Forms for these instances poses a challenge is that throughout the middle dialogues we typically witnessed examples of Forms for values, and also because the Forms themselves, characterized as perfect exemplars of the qualities they impart, are said to possess those features absolutely. Thus, it would be strange to say that there are noble archetypes for rather ignoble and undignified things, such as a Form of Mud or of Dirt, for instance. Yet those sensible things too need to be somehow accounted for. To get a full sense of the meaning of this challenge, it is important to take a closer look at the progression and sequence of the actual formulation of this puzzle. Here is how the conversation between Parmenides and Socrates unfolds:

—Socrates, he said, you are much to be admired for your keenness for argument! Tell me, have you yourself distinguished as separate, in the way you mention, certain forms themselves, and also as separate the things that partake of them? And do you think that likeness itself is something, separate from the likeness we have? And one and many and all the things you heard Zeno read about a while ago? —I do indeed, Socrates answered. —And what about these? asked Parmenides. Is there a form itself by itself, of just, and beautiful, and good, and everything of that sort? —Yes, he said.

—What about a form of human being, separate from us and all those like us? Is there a form itself of human being, separate from us and all those like us? Is there a form itself of human being, or fire, or water? —Socrates said, Parmenides, I'd often found myself in doubt whether I should talk about those in the same way as the others or differently.

—And what about these, Socrates? Things that might seem absurd, like hair, and mud, and dirt, or anything else, totally undignified and worthless? Are you doubtful whether or not you should say that a form is separate for each of these, too, which in turn is other than anything we touch with our hands? —Not at all, Socrates answered. On the contrary, these things are in fact just what we see. Surely, it's too outlandish to think there is a form for them. Not that the thought that the same thing

might hold in all cases hasn't troubled me from time to time. Then, when I get bogged down in that, I hurry away, afraid that I might fall into a pit of nonsense and come to harm; but when I arrive back in the vicinity of things we agreed a moment ago have forms, I linger there and occupy myself with them.
—That's because you are still young, Socrates, said Parmenides, and philosophy hasn't yet gripped you as, in my opinion, it will in the future. (128e–130a)

Notice the gradations in Socrates's replies. His answers move from absolute certainty when he declares that there are Forms for abstract realities like Likeness, Unity, or Plurality, and also for values such as Justice, Beauty, and Goodness, to hesitating endorsement of Forms for natural kinds, such as human being, water, or fire, and end in an open rejection of Forms for undignified instances like mud, dirt, or hair. Socrates rejects the possibility of Forms for such entities, but he doesn't come up with an alternative account to explain the existence of such things around us. He is uneasy about that, since those instances, too, however ignoble, need to be accounted for in some way. Whenever troubled by the thought of how then to account for such undignified existents, he rushes away, fearing that he "might fall into a pit of nonsense and come to harm," and thus flees from the indefinitely many undignified sensible instances to the safety of Forms, troubled nevertheless by his own leap that ignores the intermediaries between. Socrates's reaction here illustrates *to some extent* the kind of attitude that the more mature Socrates of the *Philebus* guards us against, namely, running too quickly from the many to the one and forgetting the intermediaries (16e–17a). The fact that Socrates in his youth feels somewhat uncomfortable, rather than carefree and assured as do "the clever ones," about his flight to the haven of Forms makes it likely that he will one day return to figure out the intermediaries in an attempt to give an account to these lower and less dignified existents. And this is exactly the oracular prediction that Parmenides makes in the dialogue named after him, as he puts Socrates's fear and flight on account of his youth, yet expresses his confidence that Socrates will return to these later, when philosophy would have "gripped him" (130a).

The *Philebus*'s response. The clue that can help us solve this puzzle comes through the introduction of the Unlimited and, in general, through the explanation of Mixtures as results of Limits imposed on the Unlimited. Characterized essentially by flux and indetermination, the Unlimited is the source of disequilibrium and disorder in things. More specifically, it is the overbearing presence of the Unlimited that is mainly responsible for missing the right proportions in the mixture whenever that phenomenon occurs. Let's take, for instance, mud. When integrated in the fourfold structure developed in the *Philebus*, an instance of mud is to be accounted for as follows: intelligible Forms of Earth and Water combine with one another in certain proportions; Earth and Water have certain ratios corresponding to each of them, and these ratios are Limits that structure the Unlimited. In each case, the proper ratio (limit) will pick places on the indefinite continuum that stretches between wet and dry. A good combination of Water and Earth would have a ratio that corresponds to fertile soil. When the respective proportions of water and earth are disturbed, and their combination lacks harmony, the resulting mixture is no longer soil, but mud. And the occurring disturbance is due to the resistance manifested by the Unlimited, its opposition to the imposition of strict limits and determinations.

Thus, we do not need to postulate a specific Form of Mud in order to account for specific instances of mud. It suffices to postulate the Forms of Water and Earth and propose an account that explains why their combination is sometimes more proportionate and measured than at other times. It is here that the Unlimited comes to our aid. Recall Socrates's response to Protarchus's question as to whether they need to postulate also a fifth, as cause for destruction:

> Don't we also need a fifth kind to provide for their separation? —Maybe, but I do not think so, at least for the moment. But if it turns out that we need it, I suppose you will forgive me if I should search for a fifth kind. —Yes, for sure. (23d–e)

The need to search for a fifth kind never occurs in this dialogue. And this, I think, is not arbitrary. For we must avoid an unnecessary multiplication of the explanatory principles, and since the Unlimited already accounts for destruction and disarticulation, thus doing exactly what the projected fifth cause would do, we simply do not need a fifth; the model is complete as it is, in four terms.

As long as the underlying metaphysics is articulated simply in terms of copies participating in Forms, as it was in Plato's middle dialogues, it remains impossible to account for such ignoble and undignified occurrences as hair, mud, dirt, and, with them also, of ugliness and disarray. Once we understand that the Cause responsible for the combinations of Limit with the Unlimited is manifested in degrees of rationality and that a lower level of rationality in the Cause is correlated with an unbalanced proportion of Limit and the Unlimited in the mixture, we can envision a way to account for such instances.

***Aporia* II** arises from the need to clarify what is meant by "participation": What does it mean to say that things participate in or have a share of the Forms? Does each sensible thing partake of the whole Form or only of some part of it? [a] If the Form is present as a whole in each thing that partakes of it, then the Form becomes plural and is in separation from itself, losing its self-identity. [b] If the Form is present partly in each thing, at least two difficulties follow: (1) it loses its universality, since it is no longer a one over many, and (2) we end up having to explain whether a part of Largeness would still be large (130–131e).

In his immediate response to Parmenides, Socrates takes up the first alternative and argues that the absurd consequence just mentioned need not arise. Take, for instance, the case of a single day and notice how it exists simultaneously as a whole in many places (131b). In response, Parmenides surreptitiously replaces the image of the day present in many places with the image of a sail distributed over many people and asks whether this image of the sail is analogous to the relation that Socrates envisions between the Form and its instances. But notice that the two examples are not alike in a relevant respect. The day is wholly present simultaneously in all the places that it covers, whereas a sail is spatially partitioned or divided over the people it covers. Even the analogy with the day is only a partial analogy, since the day is temporally divided, while Forms, being neither spatial nor temporal, are simply indivisible. Nevertheless, the image of the day is still closer to the relation that Socrates envisions between Forms and instances than that of a sail covering many people.

This *aporia* emerges on account of an assimilation of Forms to physical entities, whereby we are applying to the former the same kinds of features and logic of relations that are suitable only for the latter. What this puzzle shows is that, if we apply the same logic that characterizes relations among particular things to relations between Forms and their instances, we fall into insurmountable difficulties.

Our tendency to assimilate the kinds of relations at stake is rooted in at least two sources. One of them is that fact that our default, most comfortable way of looking at things, is through the lenses of what is immediately given and known through direct perceptual experience. The other has to do with our use of language. The language that Plato's Socrates uses when speaking about Forms is much the same as the language he uses for physical things. And indeed, this is not only the way Plato's Socrates speaks of Forms, but the way we all do. The situation reveals, among others, the intrinsic limitations of language. We are constrained to use the same words when talking about sensible as we use when talking about nonsensible realities, though we mean different things by them.

The *Philebus*'s response: If, then, this *aporia* relies on a misguided assimilation of relations between physical things to relations between an intelligible reality and its physical instances, we are prompted to ask whether the *Philebus* provides us tools by means of which to addresses this worry. I believe that it does this in two major ways: (1) through the dialectical method of collection and division, and (2) by replacing talk of "participation" with talk about the way the rational Cause brings Limit to the Unlimited in such a way that Limit structures the Unlimited by imposing ratios upon the fluctuating pairs of opposites.

To begin with the first, Socrates's use of collections and divisions shows that, while collections and divisions are sometimes applied to sensible features and other times to intelligible realities, it is essential to know each time what kind of objects we collect and divide. Even flute playing based on mere guesswork makes use of collections and divisions, but while in flute playing classifications are done based on the *perceived* sounds, the classifications that the musicologist makes when writing music theory are precise, since they are based on *mathematical ratios,* describing the *intelligible structure of* sounds of different intensities. As long as each of the classifications is correctly seen for what it is, its objects rightly identified as sensible or intelligible, respectively, both classifications are useful and help us understand a lot about the world.

Secondly, Socrates's unfolding of the basic structure of reality, with Forms as sources of Limit and sensible things pertaining to the class of Mixture, has important consequences in suggesting that the properties of the Forms should not be assimilated to or assessed with the same measuring unit as those of the mixtures. We should therefore be cautious not to equate the way in which Forms can be present in sensible things with the way in which sensible things or properties can be present in other instances of the same rank. This explanation dissolves the initial paradox, since it opens up the possibility that Forms can be wholly present in each sensible thing partaking of them yet without losing their unity and self-identity, since, as intelligible, and not sensible, Forms give themselves over to others without diminution or partition of any sort. As sources of Limit, Forms would then be fully present in mixtures the way the sources of ratios are present in a thing embodying those ratios.

Aporia III: The third *aporia* concerns the universality of the Forms. If Forms have the same quality as their instances, Forms and instances have something in common and therefore must be subsumed together under a higher Form that accounts for their common feature, and so on, which leads to an infinite regress. The challenge is basically that, if we require a Form to explain the largeness of individual large objects, then we also require a Form to explain the largeness of Largeness itself and so on to infinity. Hence, we end up multiplying indefinitely the Forms of each character they impart (132a–b).

Notice that, just as in the previous case, here too the challenge emerges from assuming that Forms are just like sensible things, and thus, if a certain feature is true of sensible things or of relations among them, it must be true of Forms too or of relations between Forms and sensible things. Both this and the previous challenge are built on the same assumption that imports the logic of sensible realities and applies it to Forms on the hasty assumption that the same rules apply to both. Correspondingly then, here, just as in the previous case, the response we can gather from the *Philebus* would stress the distinctive logic of relations by placing sensible things and Forms in clearly distinct categories governed by distinct sets of rules.

The *Philebus*'s response. According to the *Philebus*, Forms are sources of Limit, and as such admit within themselves no indetermination, whereas sensible things are members of Mixture, combining limit with indetermination. Hence, it is just natural that different rules apply to relations between mixtures, on the one hand, and to relations between a Form and an instance of mixture, on the other. The Form of Health, for instance, and the health of a specific person share something in common: they both express certain ratios of normal range in terms of blood pressure, heartbeat rate, proportion between muscles and bone structure, between height and weight, etc. But that still leaves plenty of room for the health of a specific person and Health itself to remain clearly distinct entities. The spatiotemporal conditions that concretize and individualize the health of an individual clearly do not apply to the generic and atemporal nature of the Form.

Aporia IV: The fourth *aporia* reminds us of the first of the three puzzles concerning monads articulated in the opening of the *Philebus*: Are Forms real or are they only thoughts in our minds, thus having a merely subjective existence as conceptual entities? (132b–d). In an important way, the fourth *aporia* stems from an attempt to avoid the difficulties revealed in the previous two challenges. If those challenges rested upon a misconceived assimilation of Forms to sensible things, one way to avoid this trap is to envision the Forms as radically different from physical things, and thus to conceive of them as thoughts in someone's mind rather than realities on their own (132b–d). If Forms are thoughts, thoughts must be *of* an independently real universal: (1) a thought must be of something; (2) it must be of something that is; and (3) it must be common to all of its instances. As Dorter explains, the point seems to be that conceptualism is self-refuting, since it implies its opposite, realism, because thoughts are of independently real existents (Dorter 1994, 35).

The *Philebus*'s response: The worldview developed in the *Philebus* is built on the assumption that Forms are real and not just conceptual, if we intend the classifications and hierarchical orderings of pleasure and knowledge to have objective and universal value. While not offering a demonstration for the existence of Forms, the *Philebus* presents us with an architectonic account that is coherent and meaningful only on the assumption that Forms are real as sources of Limit, and not mere thoughts.

***Aporia* V:** The fifth *aporia* confronts us with a new infinite regress, this time generated by the understanding of Forms as paradigms and by, once again, illegitimately assimilating Forms to sensible things, this time in view of their "likeness." The challenge is directed at the view that Forms are paradigms for the particulars that participate in them. If something is "like" the Form, then the Form in turn must be "like" the thing. But then they are alike by partaking in a third. The Form and its image, as similar things, must participate in the same Form. This way we will always need yet another Form to explain the likeness of the initial Form with its like (132d–133a). The challenge brings to the forefront the notion of "likeness" or resemblance. As long as the "likeness" at stake is treated as a symmetrical relationship, and we assume that the Form is "like" its copy in exactly the same way that the copy is "like" its corresponding Form, we run into the difficulty of an infinite regress.

The *Philebus*'s response. With the resources of the *Philebus*, Plato's Socrates could counteract this misunderstanding by showing that the relation of "resemblance" between Forms and sensible things is not symmetrical. The Form is more like a pattern, the way a recipe is a pattern for a cake, while the recipe does not look like the cake. If Forms are patterns, after which particulars are made, we avoid that infinite regress: the pattern of a house is not another house, but a plan or a sketch of it; the pattern of a dress is not itself a dress, but a sketch with some very specific ratios for proportions and size. The relation between a Form and its instances is not symmetrical, the way that Parmenides assumes in his challenge: there is likeness between Form and instance, and it may even be true that both the instance is "like" the Form and the Form is "like" the instance, yet *the way in which the Form is "like" the instance is not the same as that in which the instance is "like" the Form*. The Form is "like" the instance the way an original or an equation is in relation to a copy or a product designed in accordance with it; the way an instance is "like" the Form is the way a copy is in relation to its original! If we deny that the resemblance relation is reciprocal and symmetrical, the regress no longer arises. The resemblance relation that holds between Forms and phenomena is nonreciprocal or asymmetrical: sensible things resemble the Forms in a defective way, but not also the other way around, for Forms do not resemble sensible things in a defective way. It is legitimate to ask of a copy from where it had derived its properties, that is, from the original, but it is not legitimate to ask the same question of the original since, by definition, it did not derive its own properties from anywhere else, being an original. In the *Philebus*, the asymmetry of the relationship is clearly expressed by making Forms sources of the ratios that structure the Unlimited to obtain sensible things. The direction from where the ratios are imposed is unmistakably clear. Forms are the sources of these ratios. The way, then, in which the ratio is a manifestation of a Form and the way in which that ratio is incorporated in a sensible thing are remarkably different from one another. Forms can exist without sensible instances, whereas the latter cannot exist without their corresponding Forms.

Aporia VI: The sixth *aporia* is born from a renewed attempt to avoid the earlier difficulties, an attempt that, again, carries things to an extreme, skipping the intermediaries. More specifically, if earlier difficulties emerged because Forms were too quickly and unreflectively assimilated to sensible things, and in an attempt to avoid their assimilation, this last *aporia* emerges due to too wide a gap created through a presumed separation between Forms and sensible things (133a–134e). Forms are what they are due to relations among themselves; sensible things are what they are due to relations among themselves. The Form Master is what it is in relation to the Form Slave, whereas human masters are what they are in relation to human slaves. Similarly, the Form of Knowledge will be Knowledge in relation to Truth itself, whereas our knowledge will be knowledge of the things among us. If so, there is no way for us to have access to the Forms, and nor can there be an account of efficacy that the gods, or the Demiurge, or Forms themselves can have in the realm of change and becoming. This is also the most dramatic of the *aporiai* in the sense that, if left unsolved, it leads to the most devastating results for both the possibility of knowledge and for metaphysics. While earlier criticisms raised questions about the nature of participation, this one questions the very possibility of participation. In short, the challenge is to see how Plato can distinguish Forms from physical things, yet not create an unsurpassable gap between them.

The *Philebus*'s response. The *Philebus* provides several clues as to how this challenge can be addressed, in such a way as (1) to affirm the separation of Forms, yet continue to maintain the causal role that Forms have on sensible instances; (2) to uphold the independence of Forms from sensible things, while recognizing the dependence of sensible things on Forms; and (3) to distinguish Being from becoming, while maintaining a certain continuity between them in the sense that our knowledge can move from dealing with becoming to dealing with Being.

To begin with the first point regarding the need to keep Forms apart from their instances, yet to regard them as causally responsible for the latter, remember that, as sources of Limit, Forms are at once referred to as "what is really and forever in every way eternally self-same" (58a), "things eternal" (*ta onta aei* [59a]), and "things that are forever in the same state, without anything mixed in it" (59c), in clear contrast with "things that come to be and perish" (15a), "things that come to be" (*ta gegonta* [59a]), and yet Forms are also at the same time envisioned as limiting causes upon the indefinite fluctuations of the Unlimited. How can something so radically different—eternal and unchanging—act and have impact upon something that is temporal and subject to change? The *Philebus* helps us understand this by means of the rational Cause, which plays a mediating role between Forms and the instances of Mixture. For the Cause of Mixtures is responsible for the proportions of Limit and the Unlimited that are combined in sensible things. Most importantly, the Cause is not depicted as static, but as amenable to degrees of power and rationality. According to the cosmological argument, reason or wisdom can operate in various degrees at the divine and human levels respectively, which helps us understand that the degree of rightness and harmony in mixtures depends on the degree to which reason presides over the combination of Limit and the Unlimited in each case (28e–30e). The Cause mediates between the Forms and the Mixtures, yet it is clearly more akin to the former than to the latter.

Furthermore, it follows from what has already been said that Forms are ontologically prior to sensible things, such that the latter depend on

Forms, while Forms do not depend on sensible things. Forms would *be* even if sensible things did not exist, but the converse does not hold.

Finally, while Being and becoming remain completely distinct from one another, Plato's Socrates develops an understanding according to which knowledge comes in degrees and as such covers among its objects everything between the most fluctuating and changing ones dealt with in the imprecise arts of flute playing, medicine, navigation, up to the most stable and eternal ones contemplated by dialectic (55a–59b). That Plato's Socrates uses here *epistēmē* and *technē* interchangeably for all these arts, should not be taken as a deviation from classical middle period dialogues, since clearly the registers of intelligible versus sensible objects are kept as distinct from one another as ever. If anything, with its clear echoing of the segments on the *Republic*'s Divided Line, *Philebus* 55a–59b confirms the same need to keep the objects distinct, while it also brings to light new ways in which transitions from one cognitive level to the next are possible. The dialectical method of collection and division, with its widespread application in all the various arts (16c), encourages us to do just that, transitioning from collecting and dividing sensible instances to collecting and dividing their intelligible counterparts.

Notes

Introduction

1. For exceptions from this view see Waterfield and Ryle, both of whom argue that the *Philebus* is a middle dialogue written most likely right after the *Republic* (Waterfield 1980, 270–305; Ryle 1966, 251f.). Striker and Gosling have also raised doubts about the placement of the *Philebus* among late dialogues (Striker 1970, 56–57; Gosling 1975, 110).

2. Kahn 2010, 56.

Chapter I. The Unity of the *Philebus*

1. For a summary of the various positions adopted vis-à-vis this issue, see Desjardins 2004, 13n5, 14n6, 16n10. For a commendable recent attempt to reveal the unity of the *Philebus*, see Garner 2017.

2. Nails writes that "nothing is known about this Protarchus," and goes on to consider and reject various possible identifications (Nails 2002, 257). As for Philebus, she writes that his name "is not known in Greece in ancient times, except for a fictional instance in the 4th c. C.E. in the epistolographer Alciphro (3.50)." (ibid., 238) The fact that Plato chooses as Socrates's interlocutors a fictional character and one whose biography is irrelevant could be taken, I believe, as indication that the emphasis is truly on the topic at issue, the good life, and that Plato wants to make it easier for us, readers, to identify at the start with Protarchus and see whether we can make real progress throughout the conversation.

3. Similar puzzles are dismissed as uninteresting also in the *Parmenides* 129c–d.

4. With some modifications throughout, the translations from the *Philebus* are largely in following with Frede 1993.

5. For further discussion, see Benitez 1989, 21, 24–31.

6. For scholars who believe there are only two serious puzzles see Waterfield 1980, 289; Hackforth 1945, 18, 20; Frede 1993, xx–xxii. For scholars arguing that

there are three questions, see Friedländer 1969, 534–536n27; Hahn 1978, 159–72; Casper 1977, 20–26; Benitez 1989, 24–31; Hampton 1990, 13–21; Carpenter 2009, 103–29; Gill 2010, 39–41; Scolnicov 1974, 3–13; Scolnicov 2010, 326–35; Garner 2017, 18–19. Not all scholars pertaining to the latter group interpret the three questions the way I do.

7. For discussion, see Hampton 1990, 18–19; Benitez 1989, 58. It is worthwhile noticing that the interrelation of Forms was alluded to already in the *Phaedo* 102d–105a and the *Republic* 497a.

8. The first and the third puzzles of the *Philebus* have direct correspondents among the *aporiai* of participation voiced in the *Parmenides* (130b–e, 132b–d, 131a–c). In the Appendix I sketch an account of how the *Philebus* implicitly addresses the *aporiai* of participation raised in the *Parmenides*.

9. The dialectical method of the *Philebus* closely resembles the method of division introduced in the *Phaedrus* 265d–266c, 273d–274a; *Sophist* 218c–236c, 253a–e; and *Statesman* 258b–263a, 279b–283e, 284e–285d. Some emphases are different in each of these dialogues: (1) the *Philebus* emphasizes determinant-determinate relations between a Form and its subdivided types, the other works emphasize genus-species relations; (2) the *Sophist* and the *Statesman* use the dialectical method in search for definitions, whereas the *Philebus* and the *Phaedrus* use it in order to map out ramifications and interrelations of a particular reality under consideration; (3) divisions tend to be predominantly bisective in the *Sophist* and the *Statesman*, and non-bisective cuts, drawn at natural joints in the *Philebus* and the *Phaedrus*. Even so, the core of the method remains the same. For a strong defense of this view, see Benitez 1989, 43–51; Moravcsik 1979, 81–104, esp. 87–88; Benson 2010, 19–24. For discussion that emphasizes differences between the "divine method" introduced in the *Philebus* and the method of collection and division that we find in the *Phaedrus, Sophist*, and *Statesman* respectively, see Gill 2010, 31–46. My own view is akin to that of the former group of scholars. I take the differences mentioned by Gill to be accounted for by the distinctive overall intentions of the dialogues and the distinctive angles that each of them takes in uncovering and analyzing the metaphysical horizon within which this method is being employed.

10. Since the discovery of musical intervals and of the system of letters making up the alphabet have taken place a while before Socrates is exhibiting them here, scholars have sometimes argued that the "method" of collection and division serves more as a dogmatic exhibition of readily given results than as real method of discovery that proceeds heuristically. Thus, Fossheim, for instance, voices this view when he writes: "The musical intervals are simply presented dogmatically by Socrates, who knows them already. They have been handed down from earlier generations, just as letters are presented as handed over from Theuth. . . . My highly tentative suggestion is that collection and division does not appear to offer any substantial method for intellectual development because what happens in collection and division is the reporting of results" (Fossheim 2010, 33–34). On the view I defend,

on the contrary, Socrates's point is that Theuth and those who were first to figure out musical intervals have done their work of discovery by means of collection and division, just as Socrates himself is about to proceed in his search to discover classes of pleasure and knowledge.

11. Although Plato has Socrates talk explicitly about collection of the *infimae species* into a genus complementing the division of a genus into its subspecies, Hackforth complains that the process of collection is chimerical and that all that is done is division. Hackforth's rationale is that, in order to gather the species under one genus, we must have already had the generic concept in mind. As he puts it: "You must start with the conjoint apprehension of a Genus and an indefinite Many, and proceed by division until you reach *infimae species*, where your task ends" (Hackforth 1945, 26). Menn is right to respond to this objection by pointing out that "the generic concept that Theuth ends by discovering is not *phonē* but *stoicheīon* (18c6); these terms are definitely not equivalent, and, while Hackforth is certainly right that Theuth must have had a concept of *phonē* as a unity from the beginning, he need not have had the concept of *stoicheīon*" (Menn 1998, 293). *Phonē* is the continuum of sound, whereas *stoicheīon* refers to the elemental letters that correspond to distinct sounds. So, between envisioning the *phonē* and discovering *stoicheīon*, one needs to have also gone through discerning and identifying all the particular letters corresponding to various sounds. And the way Theuth must have come to discern letters within the continuum of sound is by comparing distinct segments of speech or syllables and noticing which elements they have in common and which they don't, in a manner that is similar to what Plato has the Stranger describe in the *Statesman* 277e–278a. As Menn puts it: "Theuth was thus doing for the first time what the children learning their letters repeat under the guidance of their tutors in discerning the different phonemes in spoken language. A *prōtos heuretēs* like Theuth was needed to compare the different syllables of spoken language, and to collect the particular letters or phonemes within them, in order to establish the writing system that the children are now learning. For Theuth to do this, without a guide, would of course be much more difficult than for a child to do it now, and Plato has chosen in Theuth an excellent example of the difficulty and importance of collection" (Menn 1998, 298).

12. For an excellent analysis of systematic relations of parts and wholes as illustrated in Socrates's examples with linguistic and musical sounds, see Harte 2002, 199–208.

13. As Frede explains, "Socrates can explain rhythm by reference to body movements because music was intimately connected with dance. So the division into long and short measures ('feet') had quite a literal sense; the lengths and shortness's were not abstract time units" (Frede 1993, n2 *ad hoc* at *Philebus* 17d).

14. The need for a repeated application of divisions and collection in the *Philebus* reminds us of Socrates's allusions to repeated applications of the hypothetical method in the *Phaedo* 101d–e and in the *Republic* 510b–511d.

15. It is worth noting that this may be the only time within the Platonic corpus when Truth itself seems to be treated as one of the Forms (*Philebus* 65a). In the *Republic* 508d–e and the *Phaedrus* 248b–c Socrates talks about truth as the horizon of intelligibility, the "plain" where Forms are manifest.

16. I am indebted to Jessica Deal for this observation.

17. The temporal adverb *now* (*nūn*) in "all the things that are *now* in the all" (23c4) suggests that the phrase refers to temporal, particular things, and implies that all particular things are to be analyzed by reference to the four articulations of reality here introduced. In light of this, some scholars have declared that the present assertion at 23c4 is inconsistent with the earlier reference to "the things that are always said to be" being composed of limit and unlimitedness (16c9–10), where, according to at least some translations, the composition from limit and unlimitedness seems to be attributed to intelligible Forms, not to particular things. Thus, see for instance Dancy, who translates the phrase at 16c9 as "the things spoken of as always being," where the adverbial "always" modifies the verb to be (*einai*), and not the way things are said (*legomenai*). The Greek is there, admittedly, ambiguous. Dancy, in fact, also provides two alternative translations, yet he interprets each of them, (1) "the things that are always said to be" and (2) "the things that are said to exist always" to refer either to Forms alone or to Forms alongside of particular things. For an elegant and persuasive defense of the view that the subject of 16c9–10 are "the things that are always spoken of as being," that is, only temporal particular entities that people throughout the ages, past and present, have agreed exist, and not (also) intelligible realities, see Reshotko 2010, 92–97, esp. 93–97.

18. Note that the characterization of the Unlimited as pairs of opposites framing continua governed by more and less reflects only Socrates's understanding of it, not also Philebus's view. For Philebus, the Unlimited designates only the indefinite increase, not also the fluctuations and indefiniteness between more and less. See also Sanday 2016, 367 n10.

19. Concerning the ontological status of the members populating the domain of the Unlimited, Miller writes: "Does Socrates intend an actual empirical condition in which whatever actual temperature is reached at one moment is immediately undermined in the next by an increase in one direction or the other? Equally possible—and conceptually more felicitous for what sufficient reason could there be for its being this rather than that temperature that is reached, and for its being an increase in one direction rather than the other that then alters it?—is that Socrates intends to conjure into an image the indeterminateness of the pure potentiality for temperature that is implied by the mutual opposition of the opposites" (Miller 2010, 73). My own reading of the members of the Unlimited converges with Miller's preference for the latter of the two possible interpretations mentioned. It is only through the imposition of limiting ratios upon the continua of this domain that actual empirical instances of weather, health, etc. are obtained. I thus have a hard time understanding the possibility suggested by Moravcsik, that "[w]e have, under

the Indefinite, Forms that admit the more and less, as well as instances of these" (1979, 95). For how can Forms, which are by definition determinate and unchanging, admit of the more or less? Besides, particular, sensible instances come to be through the imposition of Limit on the Unlimited, and are therefore measured and structured, and could not possibly be utterly indefinite.

20. For an inventory of views, see Desjardins 2004, 28–29 n31, 31–33 n33.

21. For elaborations of these and some additional aspects, see also Benitez 1989, 76–80, 87–91; and Kahn 2004, 1–17.

22. I cannot see how, once we get these descriptions of its members as coming into being and being produced, the class of Mixtures could be taken to include also Forms, the way Moravcsik suggests (Moravcsik 1979, 98).

23. For further detailed discussion of whether the class of Mixtures includes only good, harmonious mixtures or also inharmonious ones see Harvey 2009, 11–18; Frede 1993, xxxix–xxxv; Silverman 2002, 232–33; Hackforth 1945, 38; Sayre 1987, 57–58.

24. The fact that divine reason ensures the order and measure at the cosmic level is not inconsistent with the possibility of distortions or perversions of right combinations, e.g., the ones manifest in blizzards or heat waves. For the fact that the universe as a whole is rational or good does not imply that each of its parts must be so as well.

25. Notice, however, that in the passage prefacing the rules for the application of the dialectical method, limit and the unlimited are used in their ontological sense of definite and indefinite degree, respectively (16c9–d2). The function of this passage is to spell out some of the ontological assumptions on which the method operates.

26. For a different view, arguing that there is no intrinsic connection between the senses of *peras* and *apeiron* in the epistemological and ontological passage respectively, see Letwin 1981, 187–206, esp. 188–91. On the basis of the presumably unconnected senses of *peras* and *apeiron*, Letwin argues that the *Philebus* proposes two totally irreconcilable and incompatible models: a purely conceptual one, a theory of universals with no applicability to particulars, and a model that deals with particulars, and cannot account for our knowledge of universals, the former dealing with the question: "What is reason?," the latter with "What is passion?" (199–200).

27. Socrates refers here to the deficient practice of music, as he mentions flute playing and the way in which measure is sought by the perception of the vibrating strings, and not to musicology, which, we have seen, presupposes involvement with mathematical ratios and Forms, such as Harmony and Beauty.

28. Compare *Philebus* 16d–17a with *Statesman* 259d and *Phaedrus* 265e.

29. For a detailed account of the classification of knowledge, see Garner 2017, 103–40.

30. Mixed true and necessary pleasures are most likely inevitable parts of any good life (cf. 62e), but they are not mentioned among the final ingredients at 66a–c because this final list is restricted to those aspects of the good life that are

responsible for its goodness and is not intended to list all the ingredients that ever show up in it. For a detailed account along these lines, see Joachim Aufderheide 2013, 817–37. Guthrie 1978, 236, suggests the possibility that Socrates's enigmatic ending with a quotation from an Orphic theogony ("With the sixth generation the well-ordered song may find its end") might mean that Socrates, just like the Orphic poet, did include a sixth category, the necessary and temperate true mixed pleasures as part of a good life.

31. The instance reminds us of the *Republic*'s depiction of conversion as a turning of the whole soul, comprising the three parts, appetitive, spirited, and rational, from darkness to light (518c). The *Republic*'s metaphor of light and darkness is echoed at the end of the *Philebus*, when indulgence in false pleasures is confined to the domain of night, so that light would not witness it (66a). Like *Republic* 518c–d, the *Philebus* also regards the possibility of such a conversion (the possibility of choosing the mean, cf. *Republic* 619a) as depending ultimately on the vision of the Good (60c, 64d–65a).

Chapter II. The Placement of Pleasure and Knowledge in the Fourfold Articulation of Reality

1. Frede 1993, xxxix; Frede 1992, 439; Frede 2010, 7; Russell 2007, 174; Hackforth 1945, 52n1; A. E. Taylor 1972, 41; Irwin 1995, 326; Isenberg 1940, 154–79, esp. 166; Vogt 2017, 34–49. Some of these scholars admit that knowledge is in the class of Cause, and not in that of Limit, but they all hold that all pleasures are in the Unlimited.

2. Among the voices recently lamenting this lack of unity, Charles Kahn's formulation has dramatic force: "Any reading of the *Philebus* must take account of the extraordinary lack of compositional unity of this dialogue. One of the early modern commentators suggested that the *Philebus* arose 'from a boldly executed junction of two originally separate dialogues.' I think this remark understates the lack of unity. On the one hand, there is a clear central argument; on the other hand, there are a series of poorly integrated discussions of other issues. The central argument concerns the competition between pleasure and knowledge for recognition as the good life, a competition that is settled by the construction of a mixed life combining selected pleasures with all forms of knowledge. But the course of this argument is repeatedly interrupted by problems of dialectic, cosmology and metaphysics that are very loosely tied to the topics of pleasure, knowledge, and the good. Several of these passages can be characterized as intrusions into the main argument" (Kahn 2010, 56).

3. Hence, when Socrates subscribes to the subtle thinkers' position that pleasure is a *genesis* and not an *ousia* at *Philebus* 53d–55a, this need not mean anything more than that pleasures belong to the class of Mixtures, which are indeed

coming into being, and there is no need whatsoever to believe that this argument assigns pleasures to the Unlimited.

4. See also Miller 2010, 79n53.

5. I am indebted for this observation to Marina McCoy. See McCoy 2015, 33–37.

6. As a side note, this distinction between the two accounts helps us also understand what is at stake in Aristotle's criticism of Plato's view of pleasure. Simply put, Aristotle's criticism concerns the way we experience pleasure, as he argues that pleasure is an activity (*energeia*), not a process of replenishment, and thus complete at every moment. Plato could import Aristotle's dense and phenomenologically accurate account of the experience of pleasure, while still maintaining that, ontologically speaking, pleasure is *genesis,* belonging to the class of Mixtures. There will be more on this in chapter VI.

7. To her credit, Bossi recognizes that, alongside passages that include pleasure in the class of the Unlimited, there are also a few that recognize pleasure's being amenable to being limited. However, instead of proceeding the way I do here, by analyzing the dramatic context and recognizing that the association of pleasure with the Unlimited comes always from Philebus/Protarchus, not from Socrates, and is restricted to the sybaritic understanding of pleasure, Bossi tries to reconcile the different passages by simply declaring that, precisely because pleasures are intrinsically unlimited, some of them are amenable to having limits imposed upon them (Bossi 2010, 123–33, esp. 131). I don't find her argument persuasive, as it leaves us in the dark as far as the nature of pleasures is concerned. On Bossi's view, it seems to follow that everything that is intrinsically unlimited is amenable to being limited, but Plato's Socrates never commits himself to this view. Most importantly: If pleasure is intrinsically unlimited, what accounts for the difference between pure pleasures and mixed ones, or between true pleasures and false ones?

8. In a recent article, James Warren endorses the same position, as he writes: "While, strictly speaking, all instances of pleasurable experience, like all instances of any phenomenon, have limit (that is, are mixed), without which they would be nothing at all, when they are relatively lacking in the relevant limits necessary to reflect growth in goodness, they manifest the flux and indeterminacy of the unlimited more than the measure and orderly progression of the mixture. In such cases, Socrates calls pleasure unlimited. In contrast, their possession of the relevant limits to indicate sustained growth in goodness allows them to be more properly designated as mixed and measured." (Warren 2016, 276).

9. Everything perceptible must have a certain measure to it to fit the composition and constitution of our sense organs. Hence, we probably need to acknowledge the presence of limits at several levels: to be experienced and thus given to us in perception any phenomenon is already somewhat structured to fit our sense organs (McCoy 2015, 33–37). What makes true pleasures, ontologically speaking, Mixtures, is not only the limit that makes them suitable for our sense

organs, but also, and most importantly, the limit that makes them genuine fillings of lacks that we have and that helps us acknowledge them as such. Our experience of false pleasures must have some limit at one level to ensure our possibility of experiencing them, yet at another level limit is inoperative on them, insofar as these pleasures only seem to be filling a real lack in us, when in fact they don't, i.e., they either fill an imaginary lack, or else we ourselves misestimate the degree to which they really replenish a lack in us.

10. For detailed interpretations of this argument and of the identification of wisdom as Cause of mixtures see also Carpenter 2003, 100–107 and Garner 2017, 55–66.

11. For Philebus, pleasure is just sensation experienced in the moment with no qualitative difference from one moment to the next, with no necessary qualitative structure determined by the cognitive activity of the subject or by the nature of the intentional object that is expected to bring it about. Frede is quite right to point out that Socrates operates with a much more complex notion of pleasure than Philebus does, one that can only be understood as an intentional state, amenable to having its own species analyzed in relation to the kinds of objects it takes as part of its intentional orientation, while Philebus and, with him, Protarchus take pleasures to be mere feelings or sensations disconnected from the occasions that gave them rise and devoid of content (Frede 1985, 151–80; Frede 1993, xiii–lxvii).

12. For a detailed and insightful discussion of this argument see Harte 2014, 3–20.

13. I am not making here the stronger claim that all of our pleasures presuppose desires, whether conscious or unconscious, but only that many of them do, whether we talk about mixed ones or pure.

14. For a detailed discussion of recollection in the *Philebus*, see Garner 2017, 86–94.

15. For a detailed defense of the view that the painter is meant to symbolize pleasure, not imagination, in the analogy between our soul and a book having a scribe and painter in our soul 38b–40c see Emily Fletcher, "Pleasure, Judgment and the Function of the Painter-Scribe Analogy" (unpublished paper first delivered at the West Coast Plato Workshop, Northern Arizona University, May 2016). For a different view, arguing that the painter stands for the cognitive aspect of imagination, see Thein 2012, 109–49 and Moss 2012, 265–69.

16. Like Gosling, Dybikowski also regards the argument as a failure, but while for Gosling the cause for that failure resides in conflating the picture itself with the act of picturing, for Dybikowski the failure originates in conflating the picture with the object depicted and also in failing to distinguish between the object depicted (a pleasure) and the pleasure taken in depicting that object (Dybikowski 1970, 147–65). For detailed discussion and criticism of both Gosling and Dybikowski, see Muniz 2014, 49–58.

17. Both Frede and Penner acknowledge that belief (*doxa*) is ambiguous because it can refer both to the act of believing (*doxazein*) or to the product of this act, the thing believed (*to doxazomenon*), what one believes. Penner believes that the main limitation on Socrates's argument comes from the fact that he was unaware of this ambiguity and thus that, while Socrates succeeds in defending the view that the object of pleasure (what pleasure is being taken in) can be false, he transfers unawares this falsity upon the very act of taking pleasure in that false object. Frede, on the other hand, argues that Plato is fully aware of this ambiguity and switches on purpose the meaning of *doxa* from the active to the passive sense in order to prove that pleasures, like beliefs, have propositional content. The scribe and painter analogies are introduced precisely to facilitate this switch. The scribe and painter take the active sense of *doxa* and hence the product of their action is the thing believed (*to doxazomenon* 38e). The scribe and painter metaphors bring three new elements into Plato's account of pleasure: (1) the author, (2) the writing or painting, and (3) what is written or painted. Frede identifies the true or false pleasure 'in the primary sense' with (3) what is written or painted, while (2) the activities, writing and painting, are true or false only in a derivative sense.

18. As Harte puts it, "The falsity of the propositional content of a pleasure is falsity of that in which pleasure is taken and not—or not yet—of the pleasure taken therein. Socrates' challenge is to show that the truth-value of a pleasure taken may be called into question and not simply the truth-value of that in which pleasure is taken. He must show that . . . a mistake can be made about that in which pleasure is taken that impacts the evaluation of the pleasure therein, and not just on that of a related belief" (Harte 2004, 118).

19. For further discussion and criticism of the interpretations provided by Frede and Penner, insofar as they reduce pleasures to propositional attitudes, see Muniz 2014, 49–74. Among the more recent defenders of pleasures as propositional attitudes in the *Philebus* see Delcominette 2003, 215–37; Delcomminette 2006; Evans 2008; Thein 2012, 109–49; Warren 2014; Whiting 2014, 21–59.

20. Scholars have oftentimes argued that mixed pleasures as such are representative of yet another type of false pleasures alongside the types considered before (Frede 1993, xlvi; Frede 1992, 443). I believe this is not the case. Rather, mixed pleasures themselves can be either true or false, and when false, their falsity can be of one of the three types just listed. In other words, the intense morbid pleasures that Socrates mentions at 45a–e are false not because they are mixed with pain, but because they are excessive and hence cause all the misperceptions and misapprehensions of filling and emptying that the various types of falsehood are about.

21. For a convincing defense of the view that Protarchus's point is not that truth and falsehood alike apply only to judgments and not to pleasure, but rather that pleasures are always true for the one experiencing them and can never be false, see Mooradin 1996, 93–112.

22. Hampton defends a similar view as she argues that an ontological notion of truth is at stake: "False pleasures result from the inability to grasp what is truly valuable in human life which, in turn, results from a failure to grasp the basic structure of reality" (Hampton 1987, 255; also Hampton 1989, 41–42, 44). "The miser's pleasures are not fulfilling (although they may feel pleasant) because he has a distorted view of what's truly valuable and pleasant. This distortion is not just at the intellectual level for in the miser's soul the desire for wealth rules rather than reason. As a result, insofar as he is dominated by this desire, his actions, motive, emotions, appetites etc. are all false in the sense of being inauthentic. He is not living a proper human life, one that fulfills the human *telos* accurately reflecting the proper ordering of reality, i.e. ontological truth" (1987, 258). Along similar lines, see also Harte 2004, 111–28 and Moes 2000, 140–41.

23. For an insightful detailed analysis of the argument whereby Socrates associates being good men with being loved by the gods and having true hopes and true pleasures, see Carpenter 2006, 5–16.

24. This reminds us of Socrates's metaphorical depiction of the morally corrupt person's soul as a leaky jar in *Gorgias* 493e–494a.

25. As Sanday argues, what is appealing about false pleasures is the appearance of self-sufficiency that unbounded, unlimited experiences of pleasure have. Since self-sufficiency in the mark of the Good, hence the appearance of self-sufficiency that characterizes our false pleasures is deceptively attractive (Sanday 2016, 360, see 347–70).

26. For excellent interpretations along these lines, see Wood 2007, 81 and Tuozzo 1996, 509–13. Tuozzo's account emphasizes the cognitive element involved in all of our emotional pleasures. For alternative interpretations and their inherent limitations see the sources listed in Wood 2007, 80n10.

Chapter III. Hybrid Varieties of Pleasure

1. For this view see De Chiara-Quenzer 1993, 47, 55; Hackforth 1945, 98, 102; and Waterfield 1980, 293, 298. Reidy argues for the first of half of this view, namely, that all the false pleasures are impure (Reidy 1998, 350–55), while Frede attributes to Plato the view that the mixed character (impurity) of pleasures illustrates a fourth type of falsehood affecting our pleasures alongside of the falsehood of our pleasures of anticipation, the falsehood resulting from overestimation and underestimation of the intensity of pleasure, and that resulting from mistaking absence of pain for pleasure (Frede, 1992, 443, 449–52 and Frede's *Introduction* in *Plato: Philebus* 1993 xlv–liii). For scholars arguing for the second half, namely, that all pure pleasures are true, see Cooper 1977, 723; Taylor 1972, 75–77; Van Riel 2000, 126, 134.

2. For an excellent detailed discussion of pure pleasures in the *Philebus*, see Harvey 2012, 279–301, esp. 287–92.

3. Georgia Mouroutsou provides an insightful account of how the difference between the experience of pure and mixed pleasures respectively leads to distinct temporal experiences of the present: "When experiencing pure pleasures, as opposed to impure pleasures, we experience the present in a fundamentally different way: not as a point or part in time following the last and followed by the next event, but as duration and fulfillment. The present emerges and stands out as complete in itself and independent of our past and future" (Mouroutsou 2016, 149, see also 132–33, 146–50).

4. For a comprehensive discussion of this theme, which inspired my treatment here, see Wood 2007, 77–94.

5. Miller provides an insightful analysis of the experience of the malicious person in terms of the disturbed balance and its restoration when witnessing his neighbor's losing his fortune (Miller 2008, esp. 279–80). To cite only a brief passage: "Suppose I see my rich neighbor luxuriating in his wealth. This sight distresses me, for it brings with it the sight of my own painful lack of wealth. Thus, I take my neighbor's riches as normative for myself, as that harmony or balance of the opposites, poverty and wealth, that my own condition falls short of. How may I gain relief from the pain these images cause me? There seem to be several ways. If my phantasy is driven by *phthonos*, I may find myself imagining my neighbor's losing his fortune. And I may combine this with the image of myself as, now, better off than he is. Or, if my fantasy is driven by *zelos*, the zeal that inclines one more towards emulation and competition than resentment, I may find myself imagining my gaining the same wealth or, indeed, even more wealth than my rich neighbor has; that is, achieving the same balance of poverty and wealth, or, again, an even higher proportion of wealth to poverty than my neighbor. These pleasant images free me, if I can lose myself in them, from the initial images of my neighbor and myself that first gave me pain" (280).

6. Wood puts it convincingly: "The danger Philebus poses, then, comes not just from the combativeness of his conversation, but more importantly from the seductiveness of his way of life. For this reason, he must not only be defeated in debate, but also diminished in attractiveness. The ridiculing and humiliation of Philebus, then, is to be explained not by a maliciousness in Socrates' character, or Plato's, but by the commitment to philosophy and the need to overcome an obstacle to philosophy" (Wood 2007, 89).

7. See also Wood 2007, 89; Austin 2012, 130–33.

8. Along these lines, Miller writes: "The 'restoration' that most of us gain pleasure from is only relief from the sting of envy; we are 'restored,' so to speak, only to the uncritical and complacent equanimity that characterizes us in our quite ordinary and unphilosophical self-ignorance. If, laughingly, I put down the text with

the sense of my superiority to Euthyphro or Hippias or Meno, I show myself to have failed to learn from the reflections that Plato tries to generate by portraying Socrates' refutations of them. If, on the other hand, we rise to the challenge of such reflections, if, that is, in turning away from Euthyphro et al., we remain turned toward Socrates and the discovery of our ignorance that Plato aims to occasion for us, then we may join the 'few' for whom the very loss of complacent equanimity is the welcome effect of a 'restoration' of the 'natural harmony' of knowledge and ignorance that, essential to our human being, is genuinely normative for us" (Miller 2008, 288).

9. Aristotle makes this point explicit when he argues that there is no mean for vicious emotions, such as spite, shamelessness, envy, or indeed for actions such as adultery, theft, or murder (*Nicomachean Ethics* 1107a9–26).

10. At 29b and 30b, Plato uses *eilikrines*, not *katharos*, as in the other cases. Nevertheless, the two senses are related. For a similar point in connection to Plato's use of the two terms in the *Republic*, see also Stokes 1990, 23.

11. For the use of "purity" (*eilikrines*) as an expression of reality and truth, see also *Republic* 477a7, where purity is attributed to Being, insofar as it is the object of knowledge.

12. Although throughout *Philebus* 55c–58a Socrates uses the terms for crafts (*technai*) and branches of knowledge (*epistēmai*) interchangeably, the dialogue maintains the epistemological distinction between knowledge proper (restricted to dialectic) and opinion (assigned to the crafts) as drawn in the middle dialogues, and specifies their objects as Being and becoming, respectively (58e–59b). In fact, Socrates starts by distinguishing knowledge itself from disciplines that are more or less closely related to knowledge (55d), and, as it becomes evident, the former is reserved for dialectic, which deals with eternal, immutable Forms.

Chapter IV. The Nature of Pleasure

1. The first one to raise this criticism seems to have been Aristotle (NE 1173b13–20). See, for instance, van Riel 2000, 119–38, and Taylor 2003, 1–20.

2. See A. E. Taylor 1972, 57; Gosling and Taylor 1982, 140; Hampton, 1990, 73; Fletcher 2014, 113–42, and 2017, 195–206.

3. Guthrie 1978, 199.

4. Gosling and Taylor 1982, 450–51.

5. For an excellent account of the difference between the natural and the neutral states, see Arenson 2011, 191–210. According to Arenson, while at first the meaning of two states is pretty much one and the same, signifying absence of pleasure or pain, once Socrates revises the definition of pleasure and switches from identifying pleasure with mere replenishment of a lack (31d) to identifying it with *perceived* replenishment of a lack (33d), the differences between the two states described as

natural and neutral, respectively, become evident. The natural state is impossible to ever achieve though an ideal for us to constantly aspire toward, whereas the neutral state obtains frequently on all occasions when through undergoing replenishment and depletions we do not perceive those (Arenson 2011, 198).

6. Here, we recognize one of the main differences between Plato's and Aristotle's accounts of pleasure. While Aristotle also recognizes human being's natural finitude, he does not believe that the phenomenon of pleasure is by itself indicative of limitation. In fact, for Aristotle, God himself experiences pleasure through his perfect and self-sufficient activity, his perpetual contemplation of himself (NE X.7–8 and *Met*. XII. 7–10). For Aristotle, pleasure is an end in itself, though as final end it has to be the sort of pleasure that God enjoys and that remains only fleetingly achievable for an embodied human soul. For Plato, on the other hand, pleasure is bound to remain part of the world of becoming, itself a generative process, something that is to be desired always as a means and never as an ultimate end, and for this reason not an ingredient of the perfect divine life.

7. The fact that Beauty, Proportion, and Truth rank so high in the order of reality makes them suitable criteria for adjudicating the value of all the lower goods. Thus, the criteria used to assess the superiority of true and pure over false and impure pleasures are purity, beauty, and truth (52d–53c), those used for adjudicating superiority among various kinds of knowledge or crafts (*technē*) are certainty (*saphesteron* 57b), precision (*akribeia*), truth, and the use of measure and number (57d); in addition, when dialectic is declared superior to Gorgias's type of rhetoric, this is done on account of its clarity, precision, and truth, which are explicitly opposed to the alternative criteria of grandeur, nobility, and usefulness to us (58a–c). Finally, the criteria used in establishing the superiority of knowledge over pleasure are measure, beauty, and truth (65c–e).

8. See also Dorter 2001, 349 and Ferber 2003, 121. For the opposite view, namely that Measure is most likely a Form, see Barney 2016, 225.

9. For an insightful analysis of due measure in the *Statesman*, see Harvey 2006, 91–120, esp. 99–118, and Harvey 2009, 1–33.

10. The *Statesman*'s distinction between a theoretical and a practical mean anticipates Aristotle's distinction between what he calls "the intermediate in the object" and "the intermediate relative to us," respectively. Aristotle writes: "By the intermediate in the object I mean what is equidistant from each extremity; this is one and the same for everyone. But relative to us the intermediate is what is neither superfluous nor deficient; this is not one, and is not the same for everyone. If, e.g., ten are many and two are few, we take six as intermediate in the object since it exceeds [two] and is exceeded [by ten] by an equal amount, [four]: this is what is intermediate by numerical proportion. But that is not how we must take the intermediate that is relative to us. For if, e.g. ten pounds [of food] are a lot for someone to eat, and two pounds a little, it does not follow that the trainer will prescribe six, since this might also be either a little or a lot for the person who is to

take it—for Milo [the athlete] a little, but for the beginner in gymnastics a lot; and the same is true for running and wrestling. In this way every scientific expert avoids excess and deficiency and seeks and chooses what is intermediate—but intermediate relative to us not in the object" (NE 1106a30–b7, trans. T. Irwin).

11. In his attempt to reveal how complex this task is, Sayre provides an interpretation of the mean between excess and deficiency in terms of reading the so-called unwritten teachings as implicitly alluded to in the late dialogue, in particular in the *Statesman* and the *Philebus* (Sayre 20006, 191–205). While assessing Sayre's interpretation of due measure in light of Plato's unwritten teachings is beyond the scope of this essay, reference to his work offers an illustration of the complexity of the task at issue in giving an account of due measure.

12. As he explores the connection between the due measure of the *Statesman* and the fourfold ontology developed in the *Philebus*, Harvey argues that the goods produced by the practitioners of various *technai* depicted in the *Statesman* are, from the standpoint of the fourfold division, mixtures of *peras* and *apeiron*: "Mixtures of *peras* and *apeiron* seem to be excellent candidates for being the products of expert practice, and Socrates' remark, that in cases of sickness the right combination of opposites produces health (25e7–8), clearly indicates that the resulting mixture is the healthy state in particular patients. As a mixture, health can be understood as having the right proportions between hot and cold, moist and dry, and heavy and light. Since all practice will seek to establish these proportions in all cases, knowledge of these proportions can therefore constitute an essential component of medical expertise. What this shows is that the generative scheme of the Fourfold Division is directly applicable to the productive activities of the various *technai*. The goods produced by experts are, from the standpoint of the Fourfold Division, mixtures of *peras* and *apeiron*. Thus, the standards constituting the ends of expert activity are here represented as specific ratios or quantities relating to the relevant sets of opposites. The Fourfold Division can be seen as providing at least a partial answer to the question raised by the Visitor's discussion of due measure in the *Statesman*: the *technai* enjoy an 'undisputed existence' to the extent that their products are real goods, where the goodness of these products is grounded in their being mixtures of *peras* and *apeiron*" (Harvey 2009, 12–13).

13. Similarly, in the *Laws*, due measure is responsible for avoiding excess and deficiency in various areas of the practical life: If you neglect the rule of proportion (*to metrion*) and fit excessively large sails to small ships, or give too much food to a small body, or too high authority to a soul that doesn't measure up to it, the result is always disastrous. Body and soul become puffed up: disease breaks out in the one, and in the other arrogance quickly leads to injustice. (691c, trans. Trevor J. Saunders).

14. It is on similar presuppositions that the philosophical rulers of the *Republic* design specific educational curricula for individuals with different natures—appetitive (iron, brass), spirited (silver), or rational (gold) (415a–c).

15. While the *Philebus* emphasizes the importance of the mean for individual lives, the *Statesman* 283c–284e and the *Laws* 691c–d reveal its importance for political life. In the *Republic*, the individual and political aspects are seen in their interrelation throughout, and the search for the mean in our individual lives (618b–619a) is regarded as conducive to the ideal political constitution. For an insightful discussion of the doctrine of the mean in the *Republic*, see Dorter 2001, 346–55.

Chapter V. Pleasures of Learning and the Role of Due Measure in Experiencing Them

1. Indeed, even independently of Plato's texts, the claim that our pleasures of learning are unmixed with pain seems to be running against the phenomenology of our common experiences. Andrew Tallon expresses this worry when he writes: "The 'man in the street' asks, in his most thoughtful (and painful) moments, such 'unpedestrian' questions as whether there is life beyond the grave and whether there is a God. This is a genuine need to know, a heartfelt craving to fill a great emptiness, a tremendous hunger and thirst after understanding" (Tallon 1972, 440). But, of course, Socrates does not mean to say that all the pleasures of learning are pure. He simply chooses to focus here on a very select group of the pleasures of learning, namely, those pertaining to the very few who practice dialectic (52b).

2. Miller accounts for *aporia* as an experience mixing pleasure with pain: "If the discovery of *my ignorance* gives me pain, nonetheless the *discovery* of it, as itself a 'replenishment' of knowledge that counterbalances my ignorance, gives me pleasure. This deeper appreciation of the Socratic sting is, I suggest, a clue to the uncommon serenity with which, in his keen awareness of the limits of understanding, Socrates is always pleased to inquire" (Miller 2008, 288; see also 281–88).

3. In an earlier work I defended the stronger view, namely that the experience of *aporia* is strictly pleasant to an individual such as Socrates, who has the right philosophical disposition to recognize *aporia* as an entirely positive experience insofar as it is an opportunity to learn (see Ionescu 2008a). The position I defend here is more inclusive and accommodating of potential criticisms to my earlier stance. For here I argue that, *even if* we accept only the weaker claim, that *aporia* is experienced as a mixture of pleasure with pain, and not strictly as pleasant, a properly disposed philosophical soul can still enjoy as *pure* the pleasures of learning that follow as a result of that *aporia*. This happens insofar as such a character will choose to focus on the pleasure of self-discovery that comes through *aporia*, and not on his experience of pain at realizing his lack. To him, *aporia* is, then, *primarily* an opportunity to learn both about himself and about the matter at issue, and as such conducive to pure rather than mixed pleasures of learning in the subsequent step of solving the *aporia*. While I thus embrace the view that *aporia* is most often

experienced as a mixture of pleasure with pain, I don't exclude altogether the possibility that at least sometimes *aporia* might not feel painful at all.

4. Mouroursou defends the same view when she writes: "There can be pain preceding the pure pleasures of attaining knowledge, for example, due to *aporia,* or pain following the pure pleasures of knowing, when, for instance, we realize we need a piece of knowledge we have acquired but we have forgotten it. But pleasures of learning will be pure *if and only if* they are not cessation of the opposite pain: that is, *if and only if* the respective pain is not like the pain felt when we feel hunger, which Socrates makes explicit in the above quoted lines: in the pure pleasures of learning there is no hunger for the objects of knowledge someone desires to acquire. There is a desire to attain knowledge, which can sometimes be fervent, but not any accompanying pain as in hunger, whose relief will give rise to the opposite pleasure" (Mouroutsou 2016, 139).

5. Commenting on Gadamer's interpretation of Plato's dialectic, Gonzalez says: "Gadamer ends up with an interpretation of dialectic that is simply incoherent: on the one hand, 'It represents the most certain knowledge because its object is fully revealed in what it is [*voll enthult ist*]' (146; trans. 203), while on the other, it is what Gadamer describes when he writes that, with Plato, knowledge or wisdom (*Wissen*) 'is no longer possible as the wise proclamation of the truth but has to prove itself in dialogical coming to an understanding [*in der dialogischen Verstandigung*]—that is, in an unlimited willingness to justify and supply reasons for everything that is said' (39; trans. 52). Only one of these accounts can be true of dialectic as we actually practice it and the latter is that account. Socrates claims neither for himself nor for anyone else a dialectic that provides an absolutely secure knowledge before which an object is absolutely manifest. The only dialectic he practices is a constant open-ended mediation, and in dialogue, between what is indeterminate and some determinate measure" (Gonzalez 2010, 187). I believe that the tension between the two conceptions of dialectic can be regarded as a fruitful one, insofar as conceiving of dialectic as open-ended mediation does not exclude, but rather presupposes, that this mediation is guided within a horizon of knowledge that, while ultimately desired as final destination, remains for now a mere adumbration and an ideal to aspire toward. I believe that Plato retains under the designation of "dialectic" both the process of search and the result aimed at. Keeping both conceptions together under one name fuels and orients the process of dialectical search toward the most accurate knowledge we aspire to attain eventually.

6. For a detailed account of how much of the philosopher's life is permeated by mixed pleasures of learning in Plato's dialogues, see also Arenson 2016, 30–34.

7. For a detailed discussion of the *Republic*'s depiction of pleasures of learning mixed with pain experienced by the budding philosopher as he ascends and exits the cave, see Warren 2010, 9–11.

8. Gosling and Taylor 1982, 122–23.

9. For a detailed account on how Plato could respond to the difficulty regarding the pleasures experienced by the philosopher, see also Warren 2010, 25–31.

10. It might be objected to this that in this case the falsehood pertains not to the pleasure of learning as such, but to my estimation of that pleasure's truthfulness, intensity, or value. That is correct, at least to some extent. Nevertheless, because these estimations of learning are intertwined with the activity of learning, and our awareness that we learn is intertwined with the awareness of replenishment that we get through learning, it seems to me that the falsity of the estimation can lead to the falsity of the pleasure of learning itself.

11. For the same view, see Hackforth 1945, 139, 140n3; Bossi 2010, 132–33; Vogt 2010, 254; and Wood 2016, 280–82.

12. As evidence for the carefully designed order of the ingredients, Lang rightly notes that (1) while reason (*noūs*), *phronēsis*, and *epistēmē* have been used interchangeably up until this point in the dialogue, especially during the cosmological argument 28c–30e, at this point *noūs* and *phronēsis* are ranked third, while the *epistēmai* receive the fourth rank; similarly (2) while measure, moderation, proportion, and the well-proportioned (*metron, metriotēs, summetria, to summetron*) were used interchangeably at 64d to designate what is responsible for making a mixture good, in the final ranking they are taken to mean different things, since measure is ranked first, while the well-proportioned and beautiful are ranked second (Lang 2010, 155).

13. Hackforth (1972, 138) and Gosling (1975, 224–26) argue that there is no difference except logical perspective between the first and second ranks. In fact, Gosling claims that the same goes also for the third rank, and all the items here listed, they claim, are just different ways of referring to the Good, the same way in which Socrates was glimpsing at the Good through the triune unity of beauty, proportion, and truth. For Hackforth, the goods listed in the first rank name the formal components of the good life taken by themselves, whereas those listed in the second rank are the same components when taken in relation to others. Barney argues that the relation between the first and second ranked goods corresponds to the relation of cause and effect, the higher ranked goods acting as causes for those listed on the second rank (Barney 2016, 222–24). Vogt argues that all the goods listed in this ranking are to be understood as *causes* responsible for a good life (Vogt 2010, 254). I believe that we can hold both that each higher rank acts as cause in relation to the goods listed on the rank immediately following, like Hackforth and Barney, *and* that all the goods listed in the five ranks are causally responsible for the good life, following Vogt.

14. The *Timaeus* also talks about a good life of a virtuous person as generated through the imposition of measure and order on the erratic movements of the circles of the Same and of the Different that make up the soul, see *Timaeus* 42a–d, 43a–c, 88b–90d, 87e–90a.

15. For an insightful discussion of the ranking of knowledge, see Carpenter 2015, 180–205. Carpenter explores the apparent equivocation of knowledge in this passage in which all the cognitive disciplines, from those based on mere guesses to the highest and most elevated ones, receive the designation of knowledge. Carpenter's suggested solution relies on viewing Plato's epistemology as "paradeigmatist." "Like beauty, goodness, justice and so on, knowledge can be instantiated to different degrees, in different ways. Some of these instances may dazzle us with how much more closely they approximate ideal knowledge than any case we usually encounter; but, on the other hand, some of the approximations might be so faint that we are genuinely uncertain whether it is more misleading than otherwise to acknowledge their relationship to knowledge by dignifying them with the name" (199). Carpenter's paradeigmatist reading is built on the assumption that there is a Form of Knowledge, an assumption that is somewhat problematic, insofar as the *Philebus* never talks about a Form of Knowledge. We can nevertheless adapt his reading within an understanding of knowledge as member in the class of Causes, since, as we have seen, reason itself has been described as having degrees and being active as cause in various degrees.

16. For more on the significance of self-knowledge for the truthfulness of all of our pleasures see also Whiting 2014, 21–59.

17. For the view that for Plato pleasures are merely remedial goods, see Gosling 1975, 103; Hampton 1990, 65, 74, 120n28. For the view that pleasures, at least when true and pure, are intrinsically good, see Carone 2000, 283–300; Wood 2016, 272–73; Garner 2017, 71–101. Garner argues that, even though pleasure is a becoming, it is still intrinsically good. He defends this view by rejecting the identification of being with the good, and by insisting on the good's transcendence of being (99). Thus, he shows that pure pleasures are "good becomings," for they do not depend on lack-driven desire (86–101). Hence, Garner concludes, the ontological dependence of pleasures as becoming (*genesis*) on being (*ousia*) is not indicative of a deficiency in goodness.

18. Wood also argues for this view when he writes: "Without pleasure as the sensation of increased harmonization in our nature, we simply could not experience, literally could not *feel* the fulfilment of our nature that proceeds from the activity of learning, and so could not properly appreciate its goodness. Moreover, pleasure as the sensual manifestation of this goodness cannot be construed as an instrument conveying something basically foreign to it, as if pleasure were a mere vehicle for bringing goodness from somewhere outside of us into our possession, or an instrument for producing goodness as an external and independent product. In that case we would perceive goodness as something wholly other than pleasure; but in fact, we experience pleasure as good and good things as pleasant. So, while, it is certainly possible to experience intellectual activity, and other good things, without enjoying them, we cannot do so while fully appreciating their goodness. The reason for this is that pleasure is not merely an external sign of the coming of goodness

to us; rather, pleasure is the sensual aspect of the increasing harmonization of the nature that is our good" (Wood 2016, 272–73).

Chapter VI. Plato's Conception of Pleasure Confronting Three Aristotelian Critiques

1. Scholars debate whether Aristotle has in mind Plato as his opponent, or Speusippus, or some other follower(s) of Plato's view. A. E. Taylor and Gosling and Taylor take Aristotle's attack to be directed against Speusippus (A. E. Taylor 1972, 24–25, Gosling and Taylor 1982, 231–40); Frede and Gerd Van Riel view Aristotle's attack as aimed against Plato (Frede 1993, 63n3; Gerd Van Riel 2000, 123). Elucidating whom exactly Aristotle has here in mind is not essential for my present purposes.

2. These three criticisms are mentioned in Gerd van Riel 2000, 128. While I do not believe that they exhaust the area of criticisms that Aristotle has against the Platonic view, I do, nonetheless, restrict the focus of my attention in this chapter to these points only.

3. A. J. Festugiere 1936, Harte 2016, 292.

4. Owen 1971, 135–52. For criticism of Owen see Gosling and Taylor 1982, 204–24; Gonzalez 1991, 149–50.

5. See also C. C. W. Taylor 2003, 1–20.

6. Unless otherwise specified, all the quotations from the *Nicomachean Ethics* use T. Irwin's translation.

7. What unimpeded exercise is Aristotle talking about? Is it the unimpeded exercise of my capacity for taking in nourishment, or the unimpeded exercise of my perception of my capacity for taking in nourishment? Furthermore, is Aristotle telling us that we can never enjoy a process like building, or that we cannot enjoy it under its description as a process, but can enjoy it under some other description? Gosling and Taylor explain that some capacities such as, for instance, sight, are exercised in acts that are themselves *energeiai*, whereas others, like the capacity to build, are exercised in processes that have stages and are not complete until they are over. However, every stage in the process of building is also an exercise of the building capacity (*energeia*) and it is under the latter description that it is enjoyed. So, then, what is enjoyed in building is the unimpeded exercise of the building capacity. And enjoying building is just enjoying the exercise of the building capacity uninterruptedly (C. C. W. Taylor 2003, 14). Bostock objects to this proposal, arguing that, for Aristotle, building and walking are just processes, *kinēseis*, no matter what one's motive for undertaking them is. Thus, as processes, they are not pleasures (Bostock 1988, 262–63). See also Taylor 2003, 12–20.

8. Harte rightly signals a potential difficulty stemming from the question as to what would Aristotle make of the bad, but apparently unimpeded activities, given

the context of his dispute with his opponent over whether pleasures are (always/ever) good (Harte 2016, 299).

9. "The reason why no one thing is always pleasant is that our nature is not simple, but has more than one constituent, insofar as we are perishable; hence the action of one part is against nature for the other nature in us, and when they are equally balanced, the action seems neither pleasant, nor painful. For if something has a simple nature the same action will always be the most pleasant. That is why the god always enjoys one simple pleasure [without change]. For activity belongs not only to change but also to unchangingness, and indeed there is pleasure in rest more than in change. 'Variation in everything is sweet' (as the poet says) because of some inferiority; for just as it is in the inferior human being who is prone to variation, so also the nature that needs variation is inferior, since it is not simple or decent" (1154b22–32).

10. Arguing for some sort of a fusion between the two kinds of causes, White writes: "The beauty that supervenes on the young is a sort of *finish*, to use a word that suggests a union of both formality and finality, and of both perfection and completion. The finish that a cabinet-maker puts on a piece of work is neither the cabinet's essence-constituting formal cause nor that for the sake of which the cabinet exists, yet it is the cabinet's formal perfection and final completion. Analogously, pleasure is neither the formal cause nor the final cause of an act of awareness. It is rather the finish on an act of awareness in which agent and patient are both at their best, the finish that is repose of appetite. Pleasure is the calm of completion that supervenes on energetic awareness of an object worthy of awareness" (White 2013, 236). White's understanding of the relation between pleasure and activity is inspired by Aquinas's reading of Aristotle: "[T]he beauty of the young and the pleasure taken in an action . . . are properties following from the good disposition of the causes of the essences of youth and of the action, respectively. Pleasure, in short, is a property of an act of awareness in which a cognitive power and a congenial object to which it is directed are both excellent." (White 2013, 235–36) "Distinguishing two senses of end, he [Aquinas] says that pleasure does not perfect action in the manner of an end in the sense in which 'end' means that for the sake of which something is (*id propeter quod alquid est*), but rather in the sense in which every good that supervenes by way of completion (*omne bonum completive superveniens*) can be called an end. Accordingly (*secundum hoc*), Aristotle says that pleasure perfects action as a supervening end, inasmuch as, over and above the good that an action itself is, there supervenes another good, pleasure, which implies repose of appetite in the presupposed good of an action" (White 2013, 236).

11. Mouroutsou seems to me to be gesturing implicitly in the same direction when she addresses the question regarding the specific type of lack that is replenished in our experience of pure pleasures of sensation (Mouroutsou 2016, 142–44).

12. "For though some states and processes allow no excess of the better, and hence no excess of pleasure [in them] either, others do allow excess of the better,

and hence also allow excess of the pleasure in them. Now the bodily goods allow excess. The base person is base because he pursues the excess, but not because he pursues the necessary pleasures; for all enjoy delicacies and wines and sexual relations in some way, though not all in the right way" (NE 1154a14–19).

13. Garner and Wood have recently developed arguments defending the same idea, namely, that pleasure can be intrinsically good in spite of being a *genesis* (Garner 2017, 81–101; Wood 2016, 265–82).

14. For an insightful account of Aristotle's understanding of the "purity" of pleasures, see Gonzalez 1991, 154–57.

15. For more on the various senses of "purity" at play in the *Philebus*, see also Garner 2017, 128–34.

16. For an impressively nuanced and detailed elaboration of this point, see Harvey 2012, 287–99.

17. For the view that pleasure is responsible for making a good life desirable, see Wood, who writes: "Without pleasure as the sensation of increased harmonization of our nature, we simply could not experience, literally could not *feel* the fulfilment of our nature that proceeds from the activity of learning, and so could not properly appreciate its goodness. Moreover, pleasure as the sensual manifestation of this goodness cannot be construed as an instrument conveying something basically foreign to it, as if pleasure were a mere vehicle for bringing goodness from somewhere outside of us into our possession, or an instrument for producing goodness as an external and independent product. In that case we would perceive goodness as something wholly other than pleasure; but in fact we experience pleasure as good and good things as pleasant. So, while it is certainly possible to experience intellectual activity, and other good things, without enjoying them, we cannot do so while fully appreciating their goodness. The reason for this is that pleasure is not a mere external sign of the coming of goodness to us; rather, pleasure is the sensual aspect of the increasing harmonization of the nature that is our good" (Wood 2016, 272–73, 276).

18. "If Socrates had intended to include only physical processes under '*genesis*,' then he would hardly have had to do much to explain it to Protarchus, nor to do so by resuming his questions—and Plato would have given him a most needlessly confusing line of questioning. . . . Only one of the examples offered in the passage involves a physical process of generation, and this example is provided by Protarchus; Socrates' example of lover and beloved clearly does not illustrate a physical process. The definitive formulation—the one Socrates offers when he stops being playful, and the one that Protarchus claims to understand—is in terms of the asymmetrical 'for the sake of' relation, at one or the other end of which all things stand" (Carpenter 2011, 76).

19. As Warren puts it: "Most importantly, by shifting our focus of attention away from the lover towards the beloved, Aristotle will encourage us to think of pleasure not in connection with a deficient or incomplete change, coming-to-be,

or desire but rather towards a something that is complete, an object of desire, and a goal. Aristotle invites us to think that pleasure should be associated not with the incomplete or unsatisfied desire of the lover but rather with the completion and perfection of the young man: the manifest beautiful bloom of youth" (Warren 2015, 343).

Appendix

1. Throughout this section, I use Mary Louise Gill's translation of the *Parmenides*.

Bibliography

Primary Sources

Aristotle. 1999. *Nicomachean Ethics*. Second Ed. Translated with Introduction, Notes, and Glossary by Terence Irwin. Indianapolis: Hackett.
Plato. 1993. *Philebus*. Translated by Dorothea Frede. Indianapolis: Hackett.
Plato. 1901. *Platonis Opera*. Vol. II, Edited by John Burnet. Oxford: Oxford University Press.
Plato. 1997. *Complete Works*. Edited by John Cooper and D. S. Hutchinson, Indianapolis: Hackett.

Secondary Sources

Arenson, Kelly. 2011. "Natural and Neutral States in Plato's *Philebus*." *Apeiron* 44: 191–210.
Aufderheide, Joachim. 2013. "An Inconsistency in the *Philebus*?" *British Journal for the History of Philosophy* 21: 817–37.
Austin, Emily. 2012. "Fools and Malicious Pleasure in Plato's *Philebus*." *History of Philosophy Quarterly* 29: 125–39.
Barney, Rachel. 2016. "Plato on Measure and the Good." In *Proceedings of the Ninth Symposium Platonicum Pragense*, edited by Jakub Jirsa, Filip Karfík, and Štepan Špinka, 208–29. Prague: Oikoymenh.
Bossi, Beatriz. 2010. "How Consistent Is Plato with Regard to the 'Unlimited' Character of Pleasure in the *Philebus*?" In *Plato's Philebus: Selected Papers from the Eight Symposium Platonicum*, edited by John Dillon and Luc Brisson, 123–33 Sankt Augustin: Academia Verlag.
Benitez, Eugenio 1989. *Forms in Plato's* Philebus. Assen/Mastricht: Van Gorcum.
Benson, Hugh. 2010. "Collection and Division in the *Philebus*." In *Plato's Philebus: Selected Papers from the Eight Symposium Platonicum*, edited by John Dillon and Luc Brisson, 19–24. Sankt Augustin: Academia Verlag.

Bostock. David. 1988. "Pleasure and Activity in Aristotle's *Ethics*." *Phronesis* 33: 251–72.
Carone, Gabriela. 2000. "Hedonism and the Pleasureless Life." *Phronesis* 45: 283–300.
Carpenter, Amber. 2003. "Phileban Gods." *Ancient Philosophy* 23: 93–112.
———. 2006. "Hedonistic Persons. The Good Man Argument in Plato's *Philebus*." *British Journal for the History of Philosophy* 14: 5–26.
———. 2009. "Nevertheless: The Philosophical Significance of the Questions Posed at *Philebus* 15b." *Logical Analysis and History of Philosophy* 12: 103–29.
———.2011. "Pleasure as *Genesis* in Plato's *Philebus*." *Ancient Philosophy* 31, 73–94.
———. 2015. "Ranking Knowledge in the *Philebus*." *Phronesis* 60: 180–205.
Casper, Dennis J. 1977. "Is There a Third One and Many Problem in Plato?" *Apeiron* 11: 20–26.
Cooper, John M. 1977. "Plato's Theory of Human Good in the *Philebus*." *Journal of Philosophy* 74: 714–30.
Dancy, Russell. 2007. *Plato on Pleasure and the Good Life*. Oxford: Clarendon Press.
De Chiara-Quenzer, Deborah. 1993. "A Method for Pleasure and Reason: Plato's *Philebus*." *Apeiron* 26: 37–55.
Delcomminette, Sylvain. 2003. "False Pleasures, Appearance and Imagination in the *Philebus*." *Phronesis* 48: 215–37.
———. 2006. *Le Philebe de Platon: introduction à l'agathologie platonicienne*. Leiden/Boston: Brill.
Desjardins, Rosemary. 2004. *Plato and the Good: Illuminating the Darkling Vision*. Leiden: Brill.
Dorter, Kenneth. 1994. *Form and the Good in Plato's Eleatic Dialogues*. Berkeley: University of California Press.
———. 2001. "Philosopher-Rulers: How Contemplation Becomes Action." *Ancient Philosophy* 21: 335–56.
Dybikowski, J. C. 1970. "False Pleasures and the *Philebus*." *Phronesis* 15: 147–65.
Evans, Matthew. 2008. "The Possibility of Hedonic Mistakes." *Oxford Studies in Ancient Philosophy* 35: 89–124.
Ferber, R. 2003. "The Absolute Good and the Human Goods." *Philosophical Inquiry* 25: 117–26.
Festugiere, A. J. 1936. *Aristote, Le Plaisir*. Paris: Libraire Philosophique J. Vrin.
Fletcher, Emily. 2014. "Plato on Pure Pleasures and the Best Life." *Phronesis* 59: 113–42.
———. 2017. "The Divine Method and the Disunity of Pleasure in the *Philebus*." *Journal of the History of Philosophy* 55: 179–208.
———. "Pleasure, Judgment, and the Function of the Painter-Scribe Analogy." Unpublished paper delivered at the West Coast Plato Workshop, Northern Arizona University, May 2016.

Fossheim, Hallvard. 2010. "Method in the *Philebus*." In *Plato's Philebus: Selected Papers from the Eight Symposium Platonicum*, edited by John Dillon and Luc Brisson, 31–35. Sankt Augustin: Academia Verlag.

Frede, Dorothea. 1985. "Rumpelstiltskin's Pleasures: True and False Pleasures in Plato's *Philebus*." *Phronesis* 30: 151–80.

———. 1992. "Disintegration and Restoration: Pleasure and Pain in Plato's *Philebus*." In *The Cambridge Companion to Plato*, edited by R. Kraut, 425–63. New York: Cambridge University Press.

———. 1993. *Plato: Philebus*. Indianapolis: Hackett.

———. 2010. "Life and its Limitations: the Conception of Happiness in the *Philebus*." In *Plato's Philebus: Selected Papers from the Eight Symposium Platonicum*, edited by John Dillon and Luc Brisson, 3–16. Sankt Augustin: Academia Verlag.

Friedländer, Paul. 1969. *Plato*. Vol. 3. Translated by H. Meyerhoff. Princeton: Princeton University Press.

Gadamer, Hans-Georg. 1991. *Plato's Dialectical Ethics: Phenomenological Interpretations Relating to the* Philebus. New Haven: Yale University Press.

Garner, John. 2017. *The Emerging Good in Plato's* Philebus. Evanston: Northwestern University Press.

Gauthier, Rene Antoine, and Jean Yves Jolif. 2002. *L'ethique à Nicomaque*. Traduction et commentaire. Leuven: Peeters.

Gill, Mary Louise. 2010. "The Divine Method in Plato's *Philebus*." In *Plato's Philebus: Selected Papers from the Eight Symposium Platonicum*, edited by John Dillon and Luc Brisson, 36–46. Sankt Augustin: Academia Verlag.

Gonzalez, Francisco. 1991. "Aristotle on Pleasure and Perfection." *Phronesis* 36: 141–59.

———. 2010. "Plato's Dialectical Ethics: or Taking Gadamer at his Word." In *Hermeneutic Philosophy and Plato: Gadamer's Response to the* Philebus, edited by Christopher Gill and Francois Renaud. Sankt Augustin: Academia Verlag.

Gosling, J. C. B. 1959. "False Pleasures: *Philebus* 35c–41b." *Phronesis* 4: 44–53.

———. 1975. *Plato: Philebus*. Oxford: Clarendon Press.

———, and C. C. W. Taylor. 1982. *The Greeks on Pleasure*, Oxford: Clarendon Press.

Guthrie, W. K. C. 1978. *History of Ancient Greek Philosophy*. Vol. 5. Cambridge: Cambridge University Press.

Hackforth, Reginald. 1945. *Plato's Examination of Pleasure*. Cambridge: Cambridge University Press.

Hahn, Robert. 1978. "On Plato's *Philebus* 15b1–8." *Phronesis* 23: 158–72.

Hampton, Cynthia. 1987. "Pleasure, Truth, and Being in Plato's *Philebus*: A Reply to Professor Frede." *Phronesis* 32: 253–62.

———. 1989. "Plato's Later Analysis of Pleasure." In *Essays in Ancient Greek Philosophy III*, edited by J. P. Anton and A. Preus, 41–49. New York: State University of New York Press.

———. 1990. *Pleasure, Knowledge, and Being: An Analysis of Plato's* Philebus. Albany: State University of New York Press.

Harte, Verity. 2002. *Plato on Parts and Wholes: The Metaphysics of Structure*. Oxford: Clarendon.

———. 2004. "The *Philebus* on Pleasure: The Good, the Bad and the False." *Proceedings of the Aristotelian Society* 104: 111–28.

———. 2014. "The Life of Protarchus' Choosing: Plato's *Philebus* 20b–22c." In *Strategies of Argument: Essays in Ancient Ethics, Epistemology, and Logic*, edited by Mi-Kyoung Lee, 3–20. Oxford: Oxford University Press.

———. 2016. "The *Nicomachean Ethics* on Pleasure." In *The Cambridge Companion to Aristotle's Nicomachean Ethics*, edited by Ronald Polansky, 288–318. Cambridge: Cambridge University Press.

Harvey, George. 2006. "Politics, Slavery, and Home Economics: Defining an Expert in Plato's *Statesman*." *Apeiron* 39 (2): 91–120.

———. 2009. "*Techne* and the Good in Plato's *Statesman* and *Philebus*." *Journal of the History of Philosophy* 47: 1–33.

———. 2012. "The Supremacy of Dialectic in Plato's *Philebus*." *Ancient Philosophy* 32: 279–301.

Ionescu, Cristina. 2007. "The Unity of the *Philebus*: Metaphysical Assumptions of the Good Human Life." *Ancient Philosophy* 27: 55–75.

———. 2008a. "Hybrid Varieties of Pleasure and the Complex Case of the Pleasures of Learning in Plato's *Philebus*." *Dialogue* 47: 439–61.

———. 2008b. "Plato's Understanding of Pleasure in the *Philebus*: Absolute Standards of Repletion and the Mean." *The Journal of Philosophical Research* 33: 1–18.

———. 2015. "The Place of Pleasure and Knowledge in the Fourfold Articulation of Reality in the *Philebus*." *Proceedings of the Boston Area Colloquium in Ancient Philosophy* 30: 1–32.

Irwin, T. 1995. *Plato's Ethics*. New York: Oxford University Press.

Isenberg, M. W. 1940. "The Unity of Plato's *Philebus*." *Classical Philology* 35: 154–79.

Kahn, Charles. 2004. "Plato on the Good." In *Was ist das für den Menschen Gute?*, edited by Jan Szaif, 1–17. Berlin: De Gruyter.

———. 2010. "Dialectic, Cosmology, and Ontology in the *Philebus*." In *Plato's Philebus: Selected Papers from the Eighth Symposium Platonicum*, edited by J. Dillon and L. Brisson, 56–79. Sankt Augustin: Academia Verlag.

Lang, P. M. 2010. "The Ranking of the Goods at *Philebus* 66a–67b." *Phronesis* 55: 153–69.

Letwin, Oliver. 1981. "Interpreting the *Philebus*." *Phronesis* 26: 187–206.

McCabe, Mary Margaret. 2010. "Banana Skins and Custard Pies: Plato on Comedy and Self-Knowledge." In *Plato's Philebus: Selected Papers from the Eight Symposium Platonicum*, edited by John Dillon and Luc Brisson, 194–203. Sankt Augustin: Academia Verlag.

McCoy, Marina. 2015. "Commentary on Ionescu." *The Proceedings of the Boston Area Colloquium in Ancient Philosophy*, XXX: 33–37.

Menn. Stephen. 1998. "Collecting the Letters." *Phronesis* 43: 292–305.

Miller, Mitchell. 1990. "The God-Given Way: Reflections on Method and the Good in the Later Plato." *Proceedings of the Boston Area Colloquium in Ancient Philosophy* VI: 323–59.

———. 2008. "The Pleasures of the Comic and of Socratic Inquiry: Aporetic Reflections on *Philebus* 48a–50b." *Arethusa* 41: 263–89.

———. 2010. "A More 'Exact Grasp' of the Soul? Tripartition in the *Republic* and Dialectic in the *Philebus*." In *Truth: Studies of a Robust Presence*, edited by K. Pritzl, 40–101. Washington, DC: The Catholic University of America Press.

Mooradin, Norman. 1996. "Converting Protarchus: Relativism and False Pleasures of Anticipation," *Ancient Philosophy* 16: 93–112.

Moravcsik, J. M. 1979. "Forms, Nature, and the Good in the *Philebus*." *Phronesis* 24: 81–104.

Moes, Mark. 2000. *Plato's Dialogue Form*. New York: Peter Lang.

Moss, Jessica. 2012. "Pictures and Passions in the *Timaeus* and the *Philebus*." In *Plato and the Divided Self*, edited by Tad Brennan, Rachel Barney, and Charles Brittain, 259–80. Cambridge: Cambridge University Press.

Mouroutsou, Georgia. 2016. "Placing Pure Pleasures Beyond the Chain of Hunger." In *Proceedings of the Ninth Symposium Platonicum Pragense*, edited by Jakub Jirsa, Filip Karfík, and Štepan Špinka, 130–51. Praha: Oikoymenh.

Muniz, Fernando. 2014. "Propositional Pleasures in Plato's *Philebus*." *Journal of Ancient Philosophy* 8: 49–75.

Nails, Debra. 2002. *The People of Plato: A Prosopography of Plato and Other Socratics*, Indianapolis: Hackett.

Oghihara, Satoshi. 2012. "False Pleasures: *Philebus* 36c–40e." In *Presocratics and Plato, Festschrift at Delphi in Honor of Charles Kahn*, edited by Richard Patterson, Vassilis Karasmanis, and Arnold Hermann, 291–309. Las Vegas: Parmenides.

Owen, G. E. L. 1971. "Aristotelian Pleasures." *Proceedings of the Aristotelian Society* 72: 135–52.

Penner, T. M. I. 1970. "False Anticipatory Pleasures: *Philebus* 36a3–41a6." *Phronesis* 15: 166–78.

Reidy, David A. 1998. "False Pleasures in Plato's *Philebus*." *Journal of Value Inquiry* 32: 343–56.

Reshotko, Naomi. 2010. "Restoring Coherence to the Gods' Gift to Men: *Philebus* 16c9–18b7 and 23e3–27b8." In *Plato's Philebus: Selected Papers from the Eight Symposium Platonicum*, edited by John Dillon and Luc Brisson, 92–97. Sankt Augustin: Academia Verlag.

Russell, Daniel. 2007. *Plato on Pleasure and the Good Life*. Oxford: Clarendon Press.

Ryle. Gilbert. 1966. *Plato's Progress*, Cambridge: Cambridge University Press.

Sanday. Eric. 2016. "Truth and Pleasure in the *Philebus*." In *Proceedings of the Ninth Symposium Platonicum Pragense*, edited by Jakub Jirsa, Filip Karfík, and Štepan Špinka, 347–70. Praha: Oikoymenh.
Sayre, Kenneth. 1987. "The *Philebus* and the Good: the Unity of the Dialogue in which the Good Is Unity." *Proceedings of the Boston Area Colloquium in Ancient Philosophy* 2: 45–78.
———. 2006. *Metaphysics and Method in Plato's Statesman*. Cambridge: Cambridge University Press.
Scolnicov, Samuel. 1974. "*Philebus* 15b1–8." *Scripta Classica Israelica* 1: 3–13.
———. 2010. "The Wonder of One and Many." In *Plato's Philebus: Selected Papers from the Eight Symposium Platonicum*, edited by John Dillon and Luc Brisson, 326–35. Sankt Augustin: Academia Verlag.
Silverman, Allan. 2002. *The Dialectic of Essence: A Study of Plato's Metaphysics*. Princeton: Princeton University Press.
Stokes, Michael. 1990. "Some Pleasures of Plato, *Republic* IX." *Polis* 9: 2–51.
Striker, Gisela. 1970. "*Peras* und *Apeiron*: das Problem der Formen in Platons *Philebos*." Göttingen: Vandenhoeck u. Ruprecht.
Tallon, Andrew. 1972. "The Criterion of Purity in Plato's *Philebus*." *New Scholasticism* 46: 439–45.
Taylor, A. E. 1972. *Plato: Philebus and Epinomis*. London: Dawsons of Pall Mall.
Taylor, C. C. W. 2003. "Pleasure: Aristotle's Response to Plato." In *Plato and Aristotle's Ethics*, edited by R. Heinamann, 1–20. Aldershot: Ashgate.
Thein, Karell. 2012. "Imagination, Self-Awareness, and Modal Thought in the *Philebus* 39–40." *Oxford Studies in Ancient Philosophy* 42: 109–49.
Tuozzo, Thomas M. 1996. "The General Account of Pleasure in Plato's *Philebus*." *Journal of the History of Philosophy* 34: 495–513.
Van Riel, Gerd. 2000. "Aristotle's Definition of Pleasure: A Refutation of the Platonic Account." *Ancient Philosophy* 20: 119–38.
Vogt, Katja Maria. 2010. "Why Pleasure Gains the Fifth Rank: Against the Anti-Hedonist Interpretation of the *Philebus*." In *Plato's Philebus: Selected Papers from the Eight Symposium Platonicum*, edited by John Dillon and Luc Brisson, 250–55. Sankt Augustin: Academia Verlag.
———. 2017. "Imagining Good Future States: Hope and Truth in Plato's *Philebus*." In *On the Psyche: Studies in Literature, Health, and Psychology*, edited by John Wilkins, 34–49. Oxford: Oxford University Press.
Warren, James. 2010. "Plato on the Pains and Pleasures of Knowing." *Oxford Studies in Ancient Philosophy* 39: 1–32.
———. 2014. *The Pleasures of Reason in Plato, Aristotle, and the Hellenistic Hedonists*. Cambridge: Cambridge University Press.
———. 2015. "The Bloom of Youth." *Apeiron* 48 (3): 327–45.
Waterfield, Robin. 1980. "The Place of the *Philebus* in Plato's Dialogues." *Phronesis* 25: 270–305.

———. 1982. "Introductory Essay." In *Plato: Philebus*. London: Penguin Books.

White, Kevin. 2013. "Pleasure, a Supervenient End." In *Aquinas and the Nicomachean Ethics*, edited by Tobias Hoffmann, Jörn Müller, and Matthias Perkams, 220–38. Cambridge: Cambridge University Press.

Whiting, Jennifer. 2014. "Fool's Pleasures in Plato's *Philebus*." In *Strategies of Argument Essays in Ancient Ethics, Epistemology and Logic*, edited by Mi-Kyoung Lee, 21–59. Oxford: Oxford University Press.

Wood, James Lewis. 2007. "Comedy, Malice, and Philosophy in Plato's *Philebus*." *Ancient Philosophy* 27: 77–94.

Index

Aporia, 96–99. *See also* One-Many
Aristotle, 121–145
Arithmetic, 25–26
Art(s), 5–9; educational, 25–26, 132; productive, 25–26, 102, 132. *See also* knowledge

Beauty, 3–4, 8–9, 15, 27, 78, 85, 104. *See also* Good (the)
Becoming (*genesis*), 26, 73, 82–83, 87, 118, 123–124, 155–156
Being (*ousia*), 26, 53–54, 73, 141, 155–156
body, 19, 22–24, 37, 40–41, 58–59, 62–64

Cause of the mixture, 12, 13, 32–33, 37–38
Collection and division, method of, xiv–xviii, xx–xxi, 5–8, 14; divine method, 16, 27, 96, 151, 156, 158n9
Comedy, 19, 24, 59–62, 64–66
Cosmological argument, 113, 155. See also *Noûs*

Desire, 22, 40–43, 104, 130
Dialectic, 9, 25–27, 55, 78, 84; and the *aporiai* of participation in the *Parmenides*, 147, 151, 156; and the hierarchy of types of knowledge, 132; and pleasures of learning, 90, 93–96, 100–103, 105
Discovery, 97–98, 108
Disruption: of natural balance, 111; of the normative standard, 142
Divided Line, 26, 156
Due measure, xvii, 6, 86–89, 115–117. *See also* mean (the)

Education, 67
Emptying, 19, 128
Epistēmē, xvi, 36, 131–132, 156, 173n12. *See also* knowledge

Fourfold articulation of reality, xiv, 11–17, 23–24, 29–30, 71, 91–92, 149
Forms, xxi, 2–3, 9; and the *aporiai* of participation in the *Parmenides*, 73, 86, 145–156, 161; and the Good, 27; and the One-Many puzzles in the *Philebus*, 28–30; in relation to Limit and the other articulations of reality, 12, 14, 15. *See also* Beauty, Truth, Good (the)

Geometry: and educational arts, xvi; and pure pleasures, 61

Good, the, and due measure, xvii, xviii, xix, 84–86, 91–92; and Forms, 3, 8–9, 15, 21, 73, 78–79; as rationality, 29

Good life, 14, 32; and due measure, 88–89, 115–116; its ingredients, 17, 27–28, 55–56, 63–64, 86, 114–116; of a philosopher, 105; and normative state of well-being, 129–130; as pertaining to the class of Mixtures, 137; and pleasure for Aristotle, 122

Happiness, and due measure, 88; Aristotle's conception of, 122–125; and pleasure, 143

Harmony, Form of, 8; degrees of, 13; and normative state of well-being, 129; and replenishments, 19; pertaining to members of the Mixture, 89; resulting from imposing Limit to the Unlimited, 12; of the soul, 71

Hedonist, xiii, xx, 34, 38, 46, 55, 76

Hierarchy, of pleasure, xxii, 74, 89; of knowledge, 26, 74, 78, 89

Ignorance, responsible for false pleasures, 38, 48–51; self-ignorance responsible for false pleasures, 60, 66–67, 94–99, 109, 117

Imagination, and the painter and scribe analogy, 48

Imprecise, types of knowledge or art, 8–9, 16, 52–53, 55, 93

Indefinite, nature of the members of the Unlimited, 6, 11–15, 32, 72, 73, 135, 149. *See also* Unlimited, the

Indetermination, related to the Unlimited and its members, 11–12, 32, 148, 152

Knowledge, 1–2, 15–16, 139, 143; and *aporia*, 96–99; as cause of mixture, 31–32, 36–37; as constitutive to pleasure, 43–45; in dialogue with pleasure, 55–56; types of, 25–28; and pleasures of learning, 52–54; and pure pleasure, 51–52; and purity, 70–71; in relation to pleasure, 37–58; and the separation of Being and becoming, 154–156. *See also* dialectic, collection and division, and pleasures of learning

Kairos, 85, 88–89, 94–95, 113, 115. *See also* due measure

Laws, xviii, 89

Learning, xxiv, 24, 52–56, 62, 71–72, 93–119

Letters, and the method of collection and division, 6–9

Limit, and the Fourfold articulation of reality, xiv–xx, 11–15; and the *aporiai* of participation, 148–151; and (due) measure, 91–92; and Forms, 12–13; and the hierarchy of the ontological articulations of reality, 73; in relation to pure and mixed pleasures, 24–25, 28, 32, 35–36, 48, 55–56, 135–136; and the value of pleasures, 141

Mathematics, 7–9, 25–26, 115–116

Mean, the, 85–86, 88–92. *See also* due measure

Measure, 11–14, 27, 84–86

Memory, in relation to pleasure, 19; *a priori*, enabling *a priori* recollection, 40–43, 49, 130

Meno, 16, 97, 112

Metaphysical background, xix–xx, 15–16, 48

Mixture, as part of the fourfold structure of reality, 12, 13, 15; as class to which true pleasures belong, 32–33, 35, 37–38, 48, 73–74, 84–85, 91, 133, 135, 152
Monad, xxi, 2–4, 15
More and less, 11, 32–34, 134–136
Music, and the method of collection and division, 6–9, 21, 29; and due measure in our pleasures thereof, 84

Natural balance, 20, 36, 47–48, 133–134
Natural state/condition, 80–82, 84, 133–134
Neutral state/condition, 22–23, 46, 58, 77, 79, 80–81, 134
Noũs, 12–13, 24, 36, 85–86, 129

One-Many, 2–4, 9, 28, 96–97
Ontological model, 91. *See also* the Fourfold

Pain, 18, 22–23, 34, 36, 48–54, 77–84, 111–112
Phaedrus, xviii, 16, 73, 83, 104
Philosopher, 54, 105–106, 117–118
Pleasure, mixed (or impure), xv–xvi, 23–24, 35–37, 50–51, 58–60, 63–68, 102–106; of anticipation, 22, 45–47, 77–83; Aristotle's account of, 122–128; of the body, 2–4, 9, 28, 96–97; cognitive structure of, 32, 37–43; degree of, 48; false, 11, 21–23, 25, 43–50, 68–72, 99–102, 106–113; of learning, 24, 52–54, 93–119; object of, 107–108; pure, xvi, 9, 20, 23–24, 51–52, 60–62, 68–72, 95–99, 137–143; as something supervening upon activity, 123, 126, 141–142; of the soul, 19, 23–24, 59, 62–64, 131; true, 24, 27–28, 35–37, 63–68; as unimpeded activity of our faculties, 81, 123–125
Precise, precision, arts, types of knowledge, xvi–xvii, 8–9, 25–27, 52–53, 61, 70, 101–103, 111
Proportion, 28, 33, 78, 84, 169

Ratio, 19–21, 48, 149, 154
Recollection, 16, 42–43, 130
Replenishment/filling, metaphysical, xv, 20–21, 129–130; perceived 17–20, 36, 58, 71, 91; physiological, xv, 18, 131
Republic, xviii, 3, 15, 23, 26, 29, 53, 65, 69, 72, 73 79, 83, 85, 88, 104, 109, 112, 118
Restoration, 17–20, 46–47, 75–76, 103. *See also* replenishment
Ridiculous, 50–51, 66–67, 117

Self-irony, 50–51, 66–67. *See also* comedy
Sensation, pleasure reducible to, xiv, xxiii, 32, 38, 46, 55, 131
Soul, depicted by analogy to a book containing a scribe and a painter 9; cosmic soul in relation to our own soul, 37; disposition thereof and state of *aporia*, 94–98; pleasures of 19, 22–24, 62, 64; and recollection, 40–41, 58–59, 72, 82, 88; tripartition of, 112–113
Statesman, xviii, 4, 85, 86, 88, 103
Symposium, xxi, 3, 65, 73, 104

Timaeus, xviii, 3, 65
Timely, the (*to kairon*), 85, 88–89, 94–95, 113, 115. *See also* due measure

Truth, as reflection of the Good, xviii, xxi, 3, 9, 27, 84; and the *aporia* of the separation of sensible things from Forms, 154; our innate desire or love for, 42, 49, 130; and pleasures of learning, 53; true pleasures, 58, 62–74, 78, 84

Unlimited, the, as part of the fourfold structure of reality, xix, 11–13, 27, 29; and the *aporiai* of participation of sensible things in the Forms, 148–155, 160–161; as class to which pleasures belong, 32–36, 73, 89, 135–136

Unlimited, in quantity, indefinitely many, 5, 6, 8, 14–15, 148

Virtue, and pleasure, 55, 64, 78, 84, 99, 122, 136; true vs. civic, 142–143

Wisdom, and the cosmological argument, 36–37, 155; as ingredient of a good life, 86, 110; and the malicious person's pleasures, ridicule, 50, 60, 66; as member in the class of Causes of mixtures, 71

www.ingramcontent.com/pod-product-compliance
Lightning Source LLC
Chambersburg PA
CBHW030652230426
43665CB00011B/1060